Broadening Horizons

Broadening Horizons
Multidisciplinary Approaches to Landscape Study

Edited by

Bart Ooghe
Geert Verhoeven

CAMBRIDGE SCHOLARS PUBLISHING

Broadening Horizons: Multidisciplinary Approaches to Landscape Study
Edited by Bart Ooghe & Geert Verhoeven

This book first published 2007 by

Cambridge Scholars Publishing

15 Angerton Gardens, Newcastle, NE5 2JA, UK

British Library Cataloguing in Publication Data
A catalogue record for this book is available from the British Library

TABLE OF CONTENTS

LIST OF ILLUSTRATIONS

LIST OF TABLES

PREFACE

The process which gave rise to this book began in the spring of 2006, in the wake of the first 'Broadening Horizons' conference on multidisciplinary landscape study (Ghent, Belgium). At the time, we - a group of 'mere' doctoral students - were already happy enough to have pulled off the organisation of an international conference; the idea of having it flow over into a publication was probably the farthest from our mind as we were enjoying our well-earned closing dinner. But after the dust of those hectic final weeks had settled and the ideas put forward in the presentations had sunk in, we began to play with the idea nonetheless.

And so a year later, we are pleased to present this volume on behalf of all who contributed before, during and after the conference. We expressly opted to make the leap from a 'conference proceedings' to a stand-alone volume of selected essays, as we felt the latter would better lend itself to the distribution of the interdisciplinary and supra-regional scope that we deem an absolute necessity of landscape research. The selected texts as a result take diverse angles at tackling the 'landscape problem', covering ground from the Central Mediterranean to the Middle-East and from semi-automated remote sensing to cuneiform historical geography. By including contributions from beginning and more established researchers alike, we aimed to produce a volume of potential interest to both the student and the specialist. Aside from offering concrete examples of applied methodology, we hoped the book might through this intentionally broad gaze also help further interdisciplinary awareness.

Thanks go out firstly to the authors who contributed to this volume; we also regret that, given the preset publication size, not all papers which we received could be included. A special acknowledgement must be made to Prof. Tony Wilkinson, whose contribution to the conference and key-note lecture proved more stimulating than we could ever have hoped for and who has kindly agreed to write the introduction to this book. Finally, we thank our colleagues here at the university: Sarah Deprez, Joke Dewulf, Tanja Goethals and Wouter Gheyle; for their shared enthusiasm, hours of overtime and combined expertise which made Broadening Horizons possible.

Bart Ooghe and Geert Verhoeven

INTRODUCTION

TONY J. WILKINSON

The landscape is all around us, but because of its ubiquity and complexity it is necessary to harness a wide range of approaches and techniques if it is to be described and understood. Hence the sub-title of this volume underscores the multidisciplinary nature of landscape study. Although the landscape might be characterized as simply the physical landscape that has been progressively transformed by human agencies, it is more complex than this, because in its turn the landscape also frames and is indeed part of the human experience. That said, humans do not follow linear trajectories through time: they experience and worship, they trade and perish, they fight and farm, with the result that it is no easy task to frame a landscape study in a way that is satisfactory to all. As a result of such problems I sometimes yearn for a return to an archaeology that treats typologies of urns, socketed axes and spear heads.

On the positive side, many of the everyday human activities referred to above do leave a recognizable physical signature on the landscape in the form of archaeological features or geoarchaeological traces. A number of years ago Colin Renfrew remarked that every problem in archaeology starts off as a problem in geoarchaeology. This statement remains very true to this day, whether one is looking at the sequence of an excavated site, the distribution, sourcing and technology of artefacts, or the development of regional patterns of settlement. In fact landscape archaeology, which forms the subject of this volume, should necessarily include a component of geoarchaeology. The combination of geoarchaeology and landscape archaeology therefore provides an academic field of considerable scope and rigour, an approach that is followed by many of the papers in this volume. This of course is not novel, indeed fundamental pioneer studies were made by Karl Butzer (1971) and Claudio Vita-Finzi (1969) a generation ago, and earlier in the 20th century Ellsworth Huntingdon (1907) and Aurel Stein (1921) included a wide range of landscape and geological studies in their investigations of Central Asian archaeology. Nevertheless, the articles in this volume demonstrate that the field continues to evolve, develop and innovate, and an exciting feature of it is that several papers

offer new techniques or approaches that have been developed only within the
past few years.

'Broadening Horizons' showcases a range of landscape studies drawn from
the Mediterranean and Near East backed up by field studies stretching
geographically from southern Mesopotamia to the Central Mediterranean. The
sub-title 'multidisciplinary approaches to landscape studies' might raise a note
of concern, because in recent years 'landscape archaeology' (this was the most
represented discipline in the original conference – *editorial note*) has become so
broad that it has sometimes lost sight of its disciplinary core. However, by
focussing on the recognizable signatures of human activity in the landscape, as
well as elaborating relations between human movements, networks or industrial
activities, this volume takes an approach that often successfully combines
geoarchaeological techniques with the insights developed by the broader
perspectives of the landscape archaeologist.

Although the techniques and subject matter of the contained papers are
rather different – ranging from OSL dating of riverine sediments, remote
sensing, the creative interrogation of cuneiform texts, soil analysis, and
archaeological site survey – the volume avoids the trap of being so broad in its
coverage that it loses thematic coherence. For example, several studies attempt
to unravel some of the geoarchaeological data that lurks at the core of most
landscape analysis. This approach is to be commended because when the term
geoarchaeology was originally coined,[1] this sub-field of archaeology seemed to
be quite remote from archaeology as a study of ancient society. Although we are
now witnessing a narrowing of the gap between the two fields, it is necessary to
be constantly vigilant to bring together both the physical and cultural analysis of
landscapes.

In my keynote paper to the conference I argued that many features normally
considered to be part of the cultural landscapes (roads, artefact scatters, fields
and so on) in fact register in the landscape as a geoarchaeological signature, and
that it is therefore imperative to examine landscapes from a geoarchaeological
perspective. By way of illustration: fields contribute to the sediment load of
rivers, or form extensive sediment traps that contribute either positively or
negatively to what Walling (1996) has described as the 'sediment delivery
problem'; roads conduct overland flow to become incipient channels that extend
drainage density;[2] and archaeological sites become the resting place of materials

---

[1] Davidson and Shackley, *Geoarchaeology*.
[2] Wilkinson, *Archaeological Landscapes of the Near East*.

such as food residues derived from their surrounding territories. One can even observe entire landscapes in which human action has wrought a geoarchaeological signature, in the form of highly 'eroded' quarry scapes as described by Heldal and colleagues in this volume. Several of the papers pursue what I would describe as 'landscape geoarchaeology', and many examine a range of human signatures and attempt to interpret them through the lens of the landscape via the techniques of geoarchaeology. As Lucke and colleagues describe, the use of geoarchaeology (and indeed pedology and geomorphology) as a way of exploring the dynamics of landscapes, enables one to side-step some of the one-way arguments that prevailed earlier in the 20th century, when humans were simplistically seen as contributing to wholesale landscape degradation. By describing the full complexity of the landscape, its soils and associated features, they provide a more nuanced and perhaps realistic analysis of processes of landscape transformation.

Topics covered in this volume include the recognition of tells and medieval sites by the use of remote sensing and field methods (Menze et al.; Saggiore), the examination of site territories and coastal communication networks (Fulminante, Storme et al., and Ivrou), the reconstruction of river systems using cuneiform texts (De Graef), the dating of their alluvial products (Deckers and Vandenberghe), 'quarryscapes' (Heldal et al.) and the long-term degradation of the land (Lucke et al.). All of these subjects fall within the general remit of landscape archaeology, and most also include a component of geoarchaeology either explicitly or implicitly.

Sadly, one of the named authors, Andrew Sherratt, did not live to see the fruits of this conference. For Andrew the landscape, frequently viewed through the medium of maps, was one of the fundamental components of archaeological analysis and in recent years his remarkably prolific 'Arch Atlas' web site has demonstrated just how the physical environment, trade and settlement could be brought together within one multi-facted web site. The pioneering paper by Menze, Muhl and Sherratt, which supplements earlier preliminary publications, demonstrates successfully how new technologies can be harnessed to actively map and record the landscape. This innovative method, developed as a collaborative venture, provides a fitting tribute to the memory of Andrew Sherratt.

References

ArchAtlas: URL: www.archatlas.dept.shef.ac.uk/web/archatlas-images/ArchAtlasFrontpage.jpg

Butzer, K. *Environment and Archeology; An Ecological Approach to Prehistory.* Chicago: Aldine-Atherton, 1971.

Davidson, D. and M. Shackley. *Geoarchaeology. Earth Science and the Past.* London: Duckworth, 1976.

Huntingdon, Ellsworth. *The Pulse of Asia: A Journey in Central Asia Illustrating the Geographic Basis of History.* Boston: Houghton, Mifflin and company, 1907.

Stein, M. *SerIndia* (5 volumes). Oxford: Clarendon Press, 1921.

Vita-Finzi, Claudio. *The Mediterranean Valleys.* Cambridge: Cambridge University Press, 1969.

Walling, D. 'Erosion and sediment yield in a changing environment.' In *Global Continental Changes: the Context of Palaeohydrology*, edited by J. Branson, A.G. Brown, and K.J. Gregory, 43-56. Geological Society of London Special Publication 115, 1996.

Wilkinson, T. *Archaeological Landscapes of the Near East.* Tucson: University of Arizona Press, 2003.

Chapter One

Virtual Survey on North Mesopotamian Tell Sites by Means of Satellite Remote Sensing

Björn H. Menze, Simone Mühl and Andrew G. Sherratt (†)

The role of virtual survey

The study of "tells" is a fundamental category of archaeological research to which several authors within this volume have made notable contributions. At present, most of our knowledge of the distribution of tells derives from ground survey. This paper is a progress-report on a project aimed at examining whether we can begin to detect them more or less at will, from the kinds of information which are becoming available to us from space, from data sources such as multi-spectral imagery, digital elevation models on a global scale, or high resolution scenes with wide spatial and temporal coverage. Since in many areas tells are disappearing rapidly under agricultural improvement schemes or the growth of modern settlements, and since the data collected from space are constantly improving in their resolution, it makes sense to elaborate methods for what we may reasonably call "virtual survey": From the settlement mounds we know, we can derive mathematical descriptions within the satellite remote sensed data, and then systematically search the Earth's surface for phenomena with similar properties. With luck, most of what turns up should indeed be prehistoric settlement mounds (rather than, for instance, piles of road-stone awaiting distribution). While only "ground-truthing" through a site visit can confirm this, we will present an approach to such a systematic evaluation of remotely sensed data in the following, in particular by relying on data of the SRTM digital elevation model. It is not a substitute for traditional methods, but may become a valuable supplement to them.

Tells are a specific form of settlement-choice,[1] occurring over a well-defined area, from eastern Hungary to northern India, in places where mudbricks were used for building. Tell-formation is also characteristic of specific social and historical circumstances, since it is a phenomenon of a particular period and closely related to the advent of urban settlement systems. In cases in which sites lasted over millennia – and especially in which they achieved urban status – their size can be very impressive. Therefore it is not surprising that such sites have been the object of intensive investigation for decades.

Unfortunately, even the locations of large and important tell sites occur in the archaeological literature with unknown reliability (accuracy) and precision. Indeed, it is not uncommon to find significantly different co-ordinates being given for the same site in different sources. Even when the suggested co-ordinates do not plot in the sea (as some of the entries in archaeological gazetteers have been known to do), we are seldom sure whether they are intended to give merely a generalised indication of position, or a precise location. Just providing accurate co-ordinates for some very well-known mounds is one useful contribution of the present work. However, these major sites are only prominent representatives of a whole distribution of settlement mounds, still visible in wide areas in the Near East.

The major desire to interrogate the landscape for potential tells is that we have no clear idea how representative our current distribution maps really are. Naturally, they represent the cumulative result of several kinds of survey, with differing intensity. But have these been deployed in such a way as to sample the total pattern in a representative way, or are they just arbitrary and involuntarily self-confirming visits to the same places over and over again? (This is a characteristic problem of distribution maps, summarised in the aphorism that "archaeological distribution maps are maps of the distribution of archaeologists"). Do archaeological distributions really stop at international borders, as they uncannily seem to do on certain maps? While we cannot answer this question for finds of archaeological material (for instance particular categories of artefacts), we nevertheless can begin to do so for physical phenomena such as hills of a certain size and shape. Thus, providing comprehensive overviews of both their *spatial and physical distributions*, together with an accurate estimate of the "cut-off point" beyond which the smaller ones cease to be recognisable by current methods, is the primary incentive for the present work.

---

[1] Rosenstock, Tells in Südwestasien und Südosteuropa.

So, how could this be achieved? In the following we will briefly review the remote sensing of tells (section 2) and will describe the (semi-) automatic tell detection strategy which allows the virtual survey, and present first quantitative results on the distributions of tells in northern Mesopotamia (section 3). Finally, we will evaluate both the results qualitatively in a detailed case study and illustrate how the virtual survey on the SRTM model can be extended easily by other means of remote sensing (section 4).

Remote sensing of settlement mounds

From a simple physical point of view, tells are features of 5 to 50 m in height, 50 to 500 m in diameter, and usually of conical shape. Also, they primarily consist of loam and mud-based materials. Both features might be used in the identification of tell sites.

High resolution satellite imagery allows the resolution of objects even on a scale of meters or less (e.g. SPOT 10 m, ICONOS 1 m). They provide information similar to standard aerial images and can often be interpreted without ground control. Providing views onto scenes of the 1960s, before much of the modern transformations took place,[2] declassified CORONA imagery is used to study ancient sites in the Near Eastern landscapes.[3] Tells can be *directly* identified in the images or can be identified *indirectly* from the structure of hollow ways. Multi-spectral imagery, e.g. LANDSAT or Aster data, are a standard tool in the classification of ground cover and soil types.[4] In the detection of settlement mounds they are potentially helpful to identify the often un-vegetated and eroding tell sites.[5]

Investigation of tells from a three dimensional perspective is provided by digital elevation models (DEM). At a resolution of 3-8 m, the stereo views of CORONA imagery also allow to generate highly resolved elevation models[6], but only with considerable effort and within limited regions. The potential usefulness of data from the Shuttle Radar Topography Mission (SRTM) in the search for tells was identified shortly after the data were released.[7] With uniform coverage at a global basis and a high spatial resolution, it provides for the first time an opportunity to observe topographic phenomena at the scale of tell

---

[2] Intensified agricultural activities, but also increasing industry and transport lead also to the destruction of ancient sites and landscape features shaped in antiquity.
[3] Kennedy, Declassified Satellite Photographs and Archaeology in the Middle East.
[4] Fowler, Satellite Remote Sensing and Archaeology.
[5] Altaweel, The Use of ASTER Satellite Imagery in Archaeological Contexts.
[6] Gheyle et al., Evaluating CORONA.
[7] Sherratt, Spotting Tells from Space.

settlements: representing well-defined anomalies in the flat lowland landscapes in which they are typically situated, these artificial mounds can be easily 'spotted' in this DEM. This elevation model also provides insights to landscape evolution in alluvial environments, which was recently discussed by C. Hritz and T.J. Wilkinson.[8]

A wide, supra-regional survey sets certain constraints on the data which is being used. First, the availability of the data is a relevant issue. While high resolution and complete coverage is so far only available from commercial suppliers, also the use of 'low cost' data products, such as CORONA or Aster, amounts to considerable sums, when surveying wide regions is desired. Second, a high degree of automation in the routine work is required, to relieve the operator in the processing of voluminous data and to obtain a high objectivity and reproducibility in the analysis. It is also a basic necessity in an complete analysis of complex information, i.e. high-dimensional multi-spectral imagery. While a detailed *spatial* analysis of monochrome scenes still lies beyond the means of current image processing, methods for a machine-based evaluation of this (multi-) *spectral* information are readily available.

Consequently, in this stage of our survey we restrict ourselves to Landsat ETM+ and SRTM data. The favoured reliance of CORONA and Aster data will be restricted to a regional case study, due to their limited availability, but also due to labour-intensive manual effort required in the preparation of the CORONA images when registering the scenes, and heterogeneous data quality of raw Aster data. Unfortunately, by itself, the spectral signature of known tells has so far proven too unspecific to serve as a diagnostic characteristic in an automated detection. Thus, our search for tell sites is primarily based on the processing of the DEM data, only with the *ancillary* use of the satellite imagery and other geo-referenced information.[9] The algorithm for the evaluation of local *elevation pattern,* tailored to the search of small conical mounds,[10] will be described in what follows.

---

[8] Hritz and Wilkinson, Recognition of ancient irrigation channels in Mesopotamia using digital terrain data.

[9] I.e. detailed military topographic charts where eye-catching features in the huge Mesopotamian plains are carefully mapped for orientation and tactical purposes offers a fertile source of additional material to be considered.

[10] Menze, Ur, and Sherratt, Detection of Ancient Settlement Mounds.

Automated tell detection

The SRTM data used in Menze et al.[11] is derived from a test area in the north of Mesopotamia (Figs. 1 and 2).[12] The upper Khabur catchment has a long settlement history, and witnessed the major expansion of nucleated settlements in the third millennium BC, a region which is still a focus of current research.[13] The basin is covered by six SRTM one-degree tiles (36° N to 38° N; 38° E to 41° E) at three arc-second resolution (90 m, Fig. 2, *top*). As part of ongoing archaeological investigation of this region, 133 sites with an indication of settlement activity had been identified within the tile 36° N, 38° E. The tell sites had been identified from CORONA images and several seasons of fieldwork associated with excavation projects.[14] These tells range from one to 60 ha in area and from less than 5 m to more than 50 m in height.

In order to keep this validated data as an independent test set in the comparison between archaeological ground survey and computer based DEM survey, a second data set was acquired for the training of the classification algorithm. For this purpose the remaining SRTM tiles of the Khabur were visually searched for presumed settlement mounds. By means of Landsat ETM+ images and topographic maps it proved possible to identify a further set of 184 settlement mounds.[15]

Within the DEM data, these mounds usually appear as small contrasting spots. Although the geographic region under study is a relatively flat plain, natural variation of the land surface exists on different scales, ranging from slowly varying slopes to steep canyon walls (Fig. 2, *top*). This variation is superimposed on the characteristic point-like pattern of the tells. Following techniques developed for face recognition ('eigenface' subspace filters), a classifier was trained from the second set of the 184 tells which discriminates between the typical spot pattern of a mound in the DEM and the variation in its

---

[11] Menze, Ur and Sherratt, Detection of Ancient Settlement Mounds, 321-327.
[12] When implementing a machine-based search algorithm, a reliable ground truth is highly relevant both in the design of the algorithm ("training") and the critical assessment of its performance ("test").
[13] Ur, Urbanism and Society in the Third Millennium Upper Khabur Basin.
[14] Ur, Settlement and Landscape in Northern Mesopotamia; Wilkinson, Archaeological Landscapes of the Near East.
[15] Soviet topographic maps, 1:100000, U.C. Berkeley map collection.

background.[16] Applied to new data, the classification algorithm is able to provide ranked lists of positions with decreasing *settlement mound probability.*

On the SRTM test tile[17], it is possible to detect 85 out of the 133 test sites at a threshold, which results in 327 false positives for the 600*1200 pixels of the test region (northern half of the test tile); most of the undetected sites were lower than 5 to 6 m in the DEM. False positives were mostly either due to natural elevations resembling tells in height and size, which occur frequently in the undulating slopes of Jabal Abd al-Aziz and Jabal Sinjar, or they were due to artefacts caused by the presence of water surfaces. Obviously the first of these error sources sets natural limits to the presented application.

Virtual survey

Overall, the algorithm is able to guide an investigator to elevations which are most probably tells, under objective criteria, high sensitivity and specificity. Nevertheless, other sources of (digital) information are available and necessary either to increase the confidence in positions proposed by the classifier, or to rule out obvious false positives. Topographic maps and Landsat imagery are primary sources of this information. Topographic maps reveal typical place-names (i.e. 'Tell', 'Tall', 'Tepe', 'Höyük') or in some regions even indicate a settlement mound with an appropriate symbol. Landsat, but also commercial satellite imagery such as Corona, Ikonos, Quickbird and Spot give a direct view onto sites and serve as the first component for their visual inspection,[18] e.g. in the exclusion of natural elevations in mountainous areas or simply to identify recent 'tell-like' elevations (such as the piles of road-stones mentioned above). At a resolution which is more than five times higher than the one of the SRTM, and in conjunction with information from maps or based on the prior knowledge of the human operator, it also enables the detection of tell sites which are either too small to be seen in the DEM or which are missed by the algorithm, as they for example do not have the typical elevation pattern as a tell in the Khabur.

Technically the proposed 'virtual survey' is organized as follows: The classifier marks positions which are above a predefined 'tell mound probability' within an SRTM patch (Fig. 8). By means of comparison with maps and satellite imagery, which cover the same area, a human expert is able to mark any of these positions which appear to him as probable tell sites. A subsequent tool allows to

---

[16] Menze, Ur and Sherratt, Detection of Ancient Settlement Mounds; Menze, Virtual Survey.

[17] Menze, Ur and Sherratt, Detection of Ancient Settlement Mounds.

[18] Wilkinson, Archaeological Survey of the Tell Beydar Region.

study these sites in detail and to register any available information: names and further evidence from the map, position in the DEM (and thus the height), extensions in the satellite imagery. A final comparison against names and positions from the nearest known tell sites, as obtained from external data sets,[19] links the results of the virtual survey against real ground truth.

Survey results – northern Mesopotamia

So far, 60 one-degree SRTM tiles in the region between 33° E and 48° E and 34° N and 39° N have been surveyed (Fig. 1), comprising the territory of south-eastern Turkey, parts of northern Syria and Iraq, but also parts of Lebanon and Iran. In all, 2148 probable tell-sites were recorded.

To obtain the height of a mound, a plane was fit repeatedly to selected reference points in its surrounding. The elevation was assessed as the maximal difference between the surface of the mound and the plane. Elevations in the SRTM are quantities averaged over nearly one hectare; therefore the base-to-top height of the mounds might be somewhat higher in reality. The accuracy of this procedure was in the range of metres, depending on the size of the mound and the topography of its environment.[20] The observed heights range from less than one metre to more than 50 (Fig. 3). Small (or low) sites predominate in the distribution of the recorded mounds.[21] Although some of the mounds reach considerable heights – even at DEM resolution – the majority of the sites lies well below 15 m. The distribution peaks little above the detection limit of c. 5 m (SRTM data accuracy)[22], few mounds reach heights of over 40 m.

The spatial distribution of the recorded sites shows a high degree of regularity, a feature which can be observed both in the western and in the eastern region. A high number of the mounds lie on a hexagonal grid as expected under 'ideal' conditions. Alternatively, they line up along rivers or wadis. Such observations had been recognised for other regions earlier,[23] but can now be studied in more quantitative terms. When resolving the height analysis to spatial subregions (Fig. 2), two tendencies can be observed: first,

---

[19] E.g. Hours, Atlas des sites du Proche Orient; Ur, Settlement and Landscape in Northern Mesopotamia, Rosenstock, Tells in Südwestasien und Südosteuropa; Lehmann, Bibliographie der archäologischen Fundstellen und Surveys in Syrien und Libanon.

[20] Menze, Ur and Sherratt, Detection of Ancient Settlement Mounds.

[21] The distribution of the recorded heights can be approximated by a gamma distribution with shape parameter 2.70 (+/- 0.08) and rate 0.29 (+/- 0.01).

[22] Menze, Ur and Sherratt, Detection of Ancient Settlement Mounds.

[23] E.g. Adams, Nissen, The Uruk Countryside, 19, Fig. 8.

mounds at the 'outward margin' of the fertile crescent, in the direct vicinity to the Antilebanon and the Tauros mountains, tend to be higher than mounds at the inward regions with less precipitation (Figs. 1 and 2). Second, a decrease in the number of minor sites can be observed from east to west (Fig. 3). While a test for significant differences reveals that the height distribution of sites above 10 m is identical in all three areas indicated in Fig. 1, the number of smaller mounds decreases significantly from east to west.[24]

It is observed that rank-size-distributions of settlement systems ('Zipf's law') fulfill characteristic rules.[25] When testing whether this relation also applies to the distribution of tell-settlement heights, it is observed that a strict linear relationship might hold on the upper tail of the distribution, but a linearity cannot be assumed on the full distribution of mound heights (Fig. 4). Summing the heights of all recorded 'tell-like' mounds on a spatial grid, one might be tempted to interpret the resulting map as a proxy to tell-specific settlement activity (Fig. 5). However, turning a distribution of *characteristic mounds* into a map of verified *settlement mounds* remains the objective of further work. A detailed analysis of further satellite imagery is one way to obtain a more reliable assessment of the sites.

Case study

The plain of Makhmur

In the following case study we concentrated on the area east of Ashur, the first capital of the Assyrian state, cult centre and seat of the highest god of the Assyrian pantheon, Ashur. The plain of Makhmur is located in the triangle framed by the upper Zab in the north, the Qara Chauq mountains in the west, the lower Zab in the south and the river Tigris in the west, belonging to the heartland of the Assyrian state (Figs. 1 and 6).

The region provides the interesting opportunity to show the relation between settlements, climate and dependence on the accessibility of water resources. The north-eastern part of this plain lies within the 200-250 mm precipitation belt, which forms the fluid border between the Fertile Crescent, where dry farming is possible,[26] and the Syro-Arabian steppe, where the western part strongly

---

[24] Wilcoxon rank test at 0.01% level.

[25] Gabaix and Ioannides, The Evolution of City Size Distributions; Nitsch, Zipf zipped; also see references therein.

[26] It is to keep in mind that these values underlie strong annual fluctuations (cf. Wirth, Agrargeographie des Irak, 19-20). Efficiency of dry farming in relation to socio-

depends on irrigation with water from the river Tigris. Huge irrigation projects dating back to the Middle-Assyrian, Neo-Assyrian, Parthian/Sasanian, but also Early Islamic periods can still be traced on the ground and are clearly visible on satellite images (Fig. 6).[27]

Amazingly little is known about this area. Although anciently important routes directly linking major centres like Ashur, Arba-'ilu (modern Arbil) or Arrapkha (modern Kirkuk) crossed the plain, only single sites had been investigated, most of them situated close to the Tigris.[28] Important work in the inland has been conducted by M.E.L. Mallowan and M. El-Amin who opened soundings at Kaula Kandal, Old Makhmur (Tall Ibrahim Bayis) and Tall Akrah showing the importance of this region,[29] but also by W. Bachmann who mapped and described sites he visited during his work at Ashur and Kar-Tukulti-Ninurta, posthumously published by R. Dittmann.[30] A screening of the western part with remote sensing methods has been conducted by M. Altaweel.[31] Due to this rather limited number of ground surveys, a "ground truth" in its classical meaning is hard to archive. Fortunately, another possibility is offered by the remains of ancient routes and ways itself which are traceable by means of air photography, satellite imagery, respectively satellite photography, and to some degree on the ground.[32]

Hollow ways or more descriptive linear swales are depressions in soft ground through prolonged usage for intersite and interregional traffic.

---

economic, political and environmental developments had been pointed out by Wilkinson (Linear hollows in the Jazira, Upper Mesopotamia, 549).

[27] E.g. Altaweel, Land of Ashur, 108-120, 129-32; Wilkinson et al, Landscape and Settlement in the Neo-Assyrian Empire, 27-32.

[28] Like Tall Kushaf, Kar-Tukulti-Ninurta, Ashur or Tall al-Naml. The river and the area close to it is still a major route from north to south. Archaeologists and travellers of the 19th and early 20th century mainly focused on the huge capitals of the Neo-Assyrian Empire which flank the Tigris. The main route to Arbil and then to Kirkuk and Baghdad started in Mosul where Ninive could be visited along the way. So there was no incentive to cross the Makhmur plain, which was partly deserted and pasture of nomadic tribes, and hard to cross (cf. Andrae, Das wiedererstandene Assur, 275; Wirth, Agrargeographie des Irak, map F).

[29] El-Amin and Mallowan, Soundings in the Makhmur Plain: Part I, 145-153; Soundings in the Makhmur Plain: Part II, 55-68.

[30] Dittmann, Ruinenbeschreibungen der Machmur-Ebene aus dem Nachlaß von Walter Bachmann, 87-102, Fig. 1.

[31] Altaweel, The Land of Ashur.

[32] Ur, CORONA Satellite Photography and Ancient Road Networks, 104-106; Oates, Studies in the Ancient History of Northern Iraq, pl. 1a.

Furthermore they also had been used for reaching the fields in the surroundings of a site, the closest sphere of activities.[33] From the air these features are distinguishable from the soil by darker colour than the surrounding area. This is due to infillings of soil wash and continuous agricultural activity. Differences in vegetation,[34] resulting from a drainage effect can also be recognised at wadis which are filled by plough wash (Fig. 9). While on CORONA photographs they appear as lines distinguishable from the surrounding terrain by their dark colour,[35] additional multi-spectral ASTER images can complete the picture as they visualize hollows which are just apparent in the near infrared spectrum.[36] Ideally, these hollows allow to identify former settlement sites indirectly.

Especially radial hollows concentrating around central tell sites are interesting for verifying a tell-like mound of the DEM. Critical voices could argue that not every site or tell site shows linear hollows in its proximity. This might be due to 'short term' occupation, lower population density and little agricultural activities (in comparison with the larger Bronze Age centres), soil erosion through recently intensified agriculture possible by making use of fuel pumps for intensified field irrigation, and of modern harvesting machines. However, this will primarily affect very small tell settlements and low mounded sites, not visible in the DEM, and the presence of linear hollows in the vicininty of tell-like elevations still remains a positive indicator of a settlement mound.

Mounds in the DEM

Compared to the upper Jazira, which is known for its high number of tell settlements, the concentration of sites visible in the DEM is relatively low. Most of them can either be found in the centre or in the southern part of the plain (Fig. 8). Some examples of those sites shall be discussed in the following.

Out of these, the biggest settlement mound (in the means of the height of its debris in relation to its probable outline)[37] spotted by the classifier is Tall Akrah

---

[33] Wilkinson and Tucker, Settlement Development in the North Jazira, Iraq; Wilkinson, Linear hollows in the Jazira, Upper Mesopotamia; for a brief introduction of the investigation and interpretation of hollow ways in the Near East see Ur, CORONA Satellite Photography and Ancient Road Networks, 102-104.

[34] For example obvious differences of heights of the natural cover or grain (see Oates Studies in the Ancient History of Northern Iraq, pl. 1a).

[35] Ur, CORONA Satellite Photography and Ancient Road Networks, 106.

[36] Altaweel, The Use of ASTER Satellite Imagery in Archaeological Contexts, 153-157.

[37] Altaweel, Land of Ashur, 164.

which is supposed to be the Old-Assyrian *Ekallatum*[38] (Fig. 7, no. 1). On CORONA images, the radial hollow lines centred around Akrah (white arrows), are clearly visible, as well as a bigger hollow (black arrows) leading from the eastern bank of the Tigris opposite to Ashur straight to a col through the southern Qara Chauq in the east.[39] The circular shape of this site and its sharp slope within a plain terrain, features typical for tells in the upper Jazira, offers ideal conditions for the automated screening. Tall Aswad (Fig. 10 and Fig 6, no. 2): 16.5 km south east of Tall Akrah, is also characterised by its round shape and a hard slope. Just a few traces of radial hollows coming from north and from west (Fig. 10, no. 2) are visible on CORONA image. Tulul al-Nawwar (Fig. 11, Fig. 6, no. 3) is a site consisting of two elevated spots. Four radially hollow lines are traceable. One coming from the south-east might links this site with another one which could have been occupied during a time span when al-Nawwar was also inhabited. Complex sites like MKH0050 (Fig. 6, no. 4) consisting of a group of mounds which are positioned close to each other, appearing as an unified elevated structure in the SRTM model. Nevertheless, this "unified" mound, as well as all mounds described above, were reliably detected in the DEM by the "tell spotting algorithm" and could easily be identified as tells when checking the proposed sites with maps and LANDSAT data.

A high number of false positive hits are present in the northern part of the Makhmur plain, in vicinity to Qara Chauq. Here the lower quality of the data, but also the natural topography which is dominated by distorting wadis (Fig. 8) yields a variation of the DEM which results in a high number of erroneously proposed sites, prohibiting a reliable analysis of results from the automated screening, although tell sites are known in this part of the Makhmur.[40]

---

[38] Dittmann, Ruinenbeschreibungen der Machmur-Ebene aus dem Nachlaß von Walter Bachmann, 100-102.

[39] This longer distance road would strengthen the identification of Tall Akrah with *Ekallatum* which is known to have lain close to a royal road *hūr šarri* (Schoeder, Keilschrifttexte aus Assur verschiedenen Inhalts, VAT 9658 (+) VAT 9626: 9; Kataja and Whiting, SAA XII 1:9); to 'royal roads' see Kessler, 'Royal Roads' and other Questions of the Neo-Assyrian Communication System, 129-136; Altaweel, The Roads of Ashur and Niniveh, 222, 224-225.

[40] For example Tell Kushaf at the estuary of the Upper Zab to the Tigris or Tell Ibrahim Bayis at the Husain al-Ghazi pass leading through the Qara Choq (Sarre and Herzfeld, Archäologische Reise im Euphrat- und Tigris-Gebiet, 210-212; El-Amin and Mallowan, Soundings in the Makhmur Plain 2, 55-60).

Discussion

The proposed survey on the SRTM model allows one to spot a high number of sites on a supra-regional scale. According to supplemental information of Landsat imagery and topographic maps, the recorded sites are likely to represent artificial mounds of characteristic tell-like shape. Mapping the mounds together with relevant physical parameters, such as height in the present step, spatial extension in a next, represents the major contribution of the proposed "virtual survey".

The survey has, so far, been applied to the plains of northern Mesopotamia. Limits arise both from the natural topography and the data quality. With a horizontal resolution of 90 m and a (relative) vertical accuracy of about five metres, it was only possible to reliably detect sites above these limits. While in the northern planes also a considerable number of mounds could be identified which did not surpass a height of 5 m in the DEM, but stood clearly from the surrounding area, the quality of the data deteriorated towards the south yielding a "rough" SRTM surface model, resulting in a high number of false positive hits (Fig. 8). The presence of geologic features resembling settlement mounds in height and size (in the DEM) also limited the usefulness of the SRTM in some regions. As a result, our survey is so far limited to north Mesopotamian plains and adjacent landscapes, where the link between tell-like elevation and real settlement mound might be allowed with the highest probability.

Overall, decisions about the presence of a *tell-like* elevation remain subjective to some degree. Thus, a more systematic evaluation of other sources of information is indicated to ease this decision and to increase the quality of the maps of the recorded mounds (e.g. Figs. 1 and 2). Besides the demonstrated usefulness of a detailed but time-consuming interpretation of CORONA imagery, it is the analysis of spectral data which, differently from mono-colour images, provides patterns which potentially are also interpretable in an automated, computer-assisted fashion. Although spectral imagery has proven to be an unreliable source in a rather global search over wide areas so far, it might yield valuable information on the local evaluation of a site in a further extension of the "virtual survey".

A final ground truth can only be obtained by real ground control. Linking the recorded co-ordinates with known sites and published information remains the ultimate step to verifying the mounds and to obtaining a temporal dimension for distribution maps as in figures 1, 2 and 5. However, the present results already allow the opportunity for further analysis, such as a study of the the spatial point pattern of the identified mounds or their correlation with other (geo-) physical parameters such as distance to river systems, precipitation, soil characteristics, to name just a few. The supra-regional data set resulting from the survey on the SRTM model might also serve as basis for either predictive[41] or generative[42] modelling approaches.

Conclusions

It has been demonstrated how the globally available SRTM elevation model can be used for archaeological remote sensing of wide areas. This considerably extends the current application of satellite imagery in restricted survey regions.

In general, we envisage a program of archaeological "virtual survey" for settlement mounds over a large part of the Near East, making use of a combination of automated and quantitative methods which are indispensable in a systematic screening of large amounts of complex data. The present work offers a methodology which increases our ability to screen for relevant sites, and to detect and evaluate rapidly and objectively any tell-sized mound within the SRTM elevation model. Further extensions of the survey to other parts of the Fertile Crescent not so far systematically subjected to ground-survey will incorporate new forms of analysis of multi-spectral data where necessary to overcome limitations associated with the particular topography and data quality of specific regions.

This ability to "virtually survey" tell sites over a huge geographical area provides unprecedented opportunities to uncover an enormous amount of information about the early history of human habitation in tell-building areas on a uniformly detailed scale. When calibrated chronologically it has the potential to tell us much about the formation and evolution of settlement patterns and the growth and reconfiguration of urban systems in a crucial part of the Old World.

Acknowledgments

BM and SM gratefully acknowledge fianancial support by the MFG Steinbuch award. We thank Paul Yule, Susan Sherratt and Peter Miglus for valuable comments.

---

[41] e.g. Brand, Groenewoudt and Kvamme. An Experiment in Archaeological Site Location; or: Mehrer and Wescott, GIS and Archaeological Site Location Modeling
[42] Manrubia and Z Manrubia and Zanette, Intermittency model for urban development, and references therein.

References

Adams, Robert McC. "Settlement and Irrigation patterns in Ancient Akkad.' In *The City and the Area of Kish*, edited by MacGuire Gibson, 182-208. Miami, Coconut Grove: Field Research Projects, 1972.

Adams, Robert McC., Hans-Jürgen Nissen. *The Uruk Countryside. The Natural Settings of Urban Societies*. Chicago-London: The University of Chicago Press, 1972.

Altaweel, Mark R. 'The Roads of Ashur and Niniveh.' *Akkadica* 124 (2003): 221-228.

—. 'The Land of Ashur: A Study of Landscape and Settlement in the Assyrian Heartland.' Unpublished PhD dissertation, University of Chicago, 2004.

—. 'The Use of ASTER Satellite Imagery in Archaeological Contexts.' *Archaeological Prospection* 12 (2005): 151-166.

Andrae, Walter. *Das wiedererstandene Assur*. Munich: C.H. Beck, 1938 (1977, 2nd edition edited by Bartel Hrouda).

Baek, Jangsun, and Minsoo Kim. 'Face recognition using partial least squares components.' *Pattern Recognition* 34, no. 1 (2004): 1303–1306.

Bagg, Ariel M. *Assyrische Wasserbauten. Landwirtschaftliche Wasserbauten im Kernland Assyriens zwischen der 2. Hälfte des 2. und der ersten Hälfte des 1. Jahrtausends v. Chr. (Bagdader Forschungen 24)*. Mainz am Rhein: Phillip von Zabern, 2000.

Brandt, Roel, Bert J. Groenewoudt and Kenneth L. Kvamme. 'An Experiment in Archaeological Site Location: Modeling in the Netherlands using GIS Techniques.' *World Archaeology* 24 (1992): 268-282.

Dittmann, Reinhard. ,Ruinenbeschreibungen der Machmur-Ebene aus dem Nachlaß von Walter Bachmann.' In *Beiträge zur Kulturgeschichte Vorderasiens: Festschrift für Rainer Michael Boehmer*, edited by Uwe Finkbeiner, Reinhard Dittmann and Harald Hauptmann, 87-102. Mainz am Rhein: Phillipp von Zabern, 1995.

El-Amin, Mahmud and Max E.L. Mallowan. 'Soundings in the Makhmur Plain.' *Sumer* 5, no. 2 (1949): 145-153.

El-Amin, Mahmud and Max E.L. Mallowan. 'Soundings in the Makhmur Plain: Part 2.' *Sumer* 6, no. 1 (1950): 55-68.

Fowler, Martin J. F. 'Satellite Remote Sensing and Archaeology: a Comparative Study of Satellite Imagery of the Environs of Figsbury Ring, Wiltshire.' *Archaeological Prospection* 9 (2002): 55-69.

Gabaix, Xavier and Yannis M. Ioannides, 'The Evolution of City Size Distributions.' In *Handbook of Urban and Regional Economics, Volume IV: Cities and Geography*, edited by J. Vernon Henderson and Jacques Francois Thisse, Amsterdam: North-Holland Publishing Company, 2003.

Gheyle, Wouter, Raf Trommelmans, Jean Bourgeois, Rudi Goossens, Ignace Bourgeois, Alain De Wulf and Tom Willems. 'Evaluating CORONA: A Case Study in the Altai Republic (South Siberia).' *Antiquity* 78, no. 300 (2004): 391-403.

Hritz, Carrie and Tony J. Wilkinson 'Recognition of ancient irrigation channels in Mesopotamia using digital terrain data.' *Antiquity* 80 (1996): 415-425.

Hours, Francis et al. *Atlas des sites du Proche Orient (14000-5700BP)*. Lyon: Maison de l'Orient méditerranéen, 1994.

Kataja, Laura and Robert M. Whiting, *Grants, Decrees and Gifts of the Neo-Assyrian Period (SAA XII)*. Helsinki: Helsinki University Press.

Kessler, Karlheinz. *"Royal Roads" and other Questions of the Neo-Assyrian Communication System.'* In *Assyria 1995. Proceedings of the 10th Anniversary Symposium of the Neo-Assyrian Text Corpus Project Helsinki, September 7-11, 1995*, edited by Simo Parpola and Robert M. Whiting, 129-136. Helsinki: Neo-Assyrian Text Corpus Project, 1997.

Lehmann, Gunnar. *Bibliographie der archäologischen Fundstellen und Surveys in Syrien und Libanon*. Rahden/Westfalen: Marie Leidorf 2002.

Manrubia, Susanna C. and Damian H. Zanette. 'Intermittency model for urban development' *Physical Review* E 58 (1998): 285-302.

Mehrer, Mark W. and Konnie L. Wescott (eds.). *'GIS and Archaeological Site Location Modeling'* Boca Raton: CRC-Taylor & Francis, 2006.

Menze, Björn. 'Virtual Survey: a Semi-Automated Tellspotting Algorithm.' In *ArchAtlas*, November 2005. 1st Edition, URL: www.archatlas.org/Menze/MenzeTellspotting.php (last date accessed: August, 28th, 2006): 2005.

Menze, Björn H., B. Michael Kelm and Fred A. Hamprecht. 'From Eigenspots to Fisherspots - Latent Subspaces in the Nonlinear Detection of Spot Patterns in a Highly Varying Background.' to appear in the Proceedings of the Gfkl Conference, Heidelberg: Springer Publisher, 2007.

Menze, Björn H., Jason A. Ur and Andrew G. Sherratt. 'Detection of Ancient Settlement Mounds: Archaeological Survey Based on the SRTM Terrain Model.' *Photogrammetric Engineering & Remote Sensing* 72, no. 3, (2006): 321-327.

Nitsch, Volker. 'Zipf Zipped.' *Journal of Urban Economics* 57, no. 1, (2005): 86-100.

Rosenstock, Eva. *Tells in Südwestasien und Südosteuropa. Untersuchungen zu Verbreitung, Entstehung und Definition eines Siedlungsphänomens*. Unpublished Ph.D. dissertation, University of Tübingen, 2005.

Sarre, Friedrich and Ernst Herzfeld. *Archäologische Reise im Euphrat- und Tigris-Gebiet 1*. Berlin: Dietrich Reimer (Ernst Vohsen): 1911.

Scollar, I., A. Tabbagh, A. Hesse and I. Herzog. *Archaeological Prospecting and Remote Sensing.* Cambridge: Cambridge University Press, 1990.

Schroeder, Otto. *Keilschrifttexte aus Assur verschiedenen Inhalts (Wissenschaftliche Veröffentlichungen der Deutschen Orient-Gesellschaft 35)*, Leibzig: Hinrichs, 1820.

Sherratt, Andrew G. 'Spotting Tells from Space.' *Antiquity* 78 (2004), URL: antiquity.ac.uk/projgall/sherratt/ (last date accessed: February, 16th, 2006).

Ur, Jason A. 'Settlement and Landscape in Northern Mesopotamia: The Tell Hamoukar Survey 2000–2001.' *Akkadica* 123 (2002): 57-88.

—. 'CORONA Satellite Photography and Ancient Road Networks: A Northern Mesopotamian Case Study.' *Antiquity* 77 (2003): 102-115.

—. *Urbanism and Society in the Third Millennium Upper Khabur Basin.* PhD. dissertation, University of Chicago, URL: oilib.uchicago.edu/ dissertations/urj.pdf (last date accessed: February, 23rd, 2006): 2004.

Van Lierre, M.J. and J. Lauffray. 'Nouvelle prospection archéologique dans la haute jezireh syrienne.' *Les Annales Archéologiques de Syrie* 4-5 (1954-1955): 129-148.

Weiss, Harvey "The Origins of Tell Leilan and the Conquest of Space in Third Millennium Mesopotamia.' In *The Origins of Cities in Dry-Farming Syria and Mesopotamia in the Third Millennium B.C*, edited by Harvey Weiss, 71-108. Guilford: Four Quarters Publishing Co, 1986.

Wilkinson, Tony J. 'Linear hollows in the Jazira, Upper Mesopotamia.' *Antiquity* 67 (1993): 548-562.

Wilkinson, Tony J. and David J. Tucker. *Settlement Development in the North Jazira, Iraq: A Study of the Archaeological Landscape.* Warminster: Aris & Phillips, 1995.

Wilkinson, Tony J. 'Archaeological Survey of the Tell Beydar Region, Syria, 1997: A Preliminary Report.' In *Tell Beydar: environmental and technical studies* edited by Karel van Lerberghe, G. Voet, 1-37. Turnhout: Brepols, 2000.

—. *Archaeological Landscapes of the Near East.* Tucson: University of Arizona Press, 2003.

Wilkinson, Tony J., Eleanor B. Wilkinson, Jason A. Ur and Mark R. Altaweel. 'Landscape and Settlement in the Neo-Assyrian Empire.' *Bulletin of the American Schools of Oriental Research* 340 (2005).

Wirth, Eugen. *Agrargeographie des Irak (Hamburger Geographische Studien 13).* Hamburg: Institut für Geographie und Wirtschaftsgeographie der Universität Hamburg, 1962.

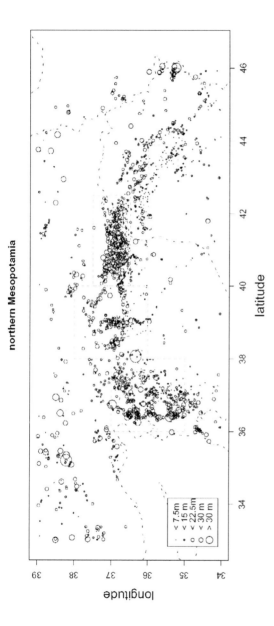

Fig. 1-1: Detected sites in northern Mesopotamia, heights of the mounds indicated by circles. Coastlines and borders of modern territories of Turkey, Syria, the Lebanon, the Iraq and Iran are indicated. The three survey test regions (Fig. 2) and the region of the case study (Makhmur plain) are indicated by dashed gray boxes.

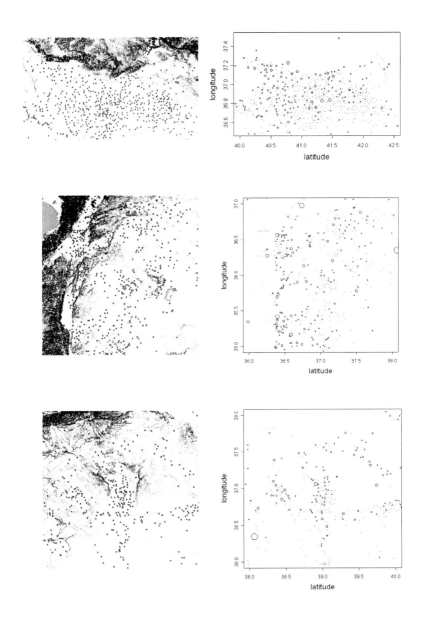

Fig. 1-2 (opposite page): Detected mounds in the eastern, central and western test regions (from top to bottom: Khabur, Galih, Antilebanon). Borders of modern territories, coastline and rivers are indicated. Symbols as in Fig. 1. Parts of the western Khabur plain also served as test bed in the design of the classifier.

Northern Mesopotamia, normalized

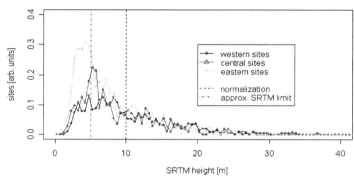

Fig. 1-3: Size distribution of the recorded mounds. While the distribution of mounds higher than ~10 m do not differ in the three test areas (disregarding a normalization constant), the eastern region (Khabur) is characterized by a high number of small mounds, which still are above the approximate SRTM detection limit of 5 m.

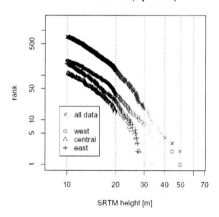

rank size rule (Zipf's law)

Fig. 1-4: Relationship between the height of a mound and its rank (log-log) within the whole distribution of sites ("Zipf's law"); for all sites in northern Mesopotamia and in the three defined test regions of Fig. 1.

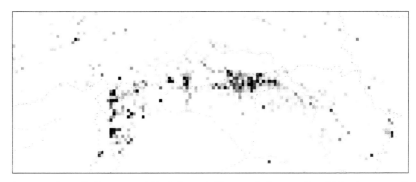

Fig. 1-5: Cumulation over all heights of all recorded mounds within the area of
the indicated pixels. Black pixels indicate a high number of mounds *and / or* the
presence of high mounds.

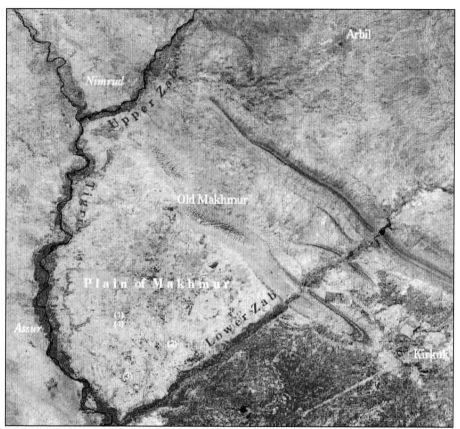

Fig. 1-6: The Makhmur Plain; 1. Tall Akrah, 2. Tall Aswad, 3. Tulul al-Nawwar, 4. MKH0050.

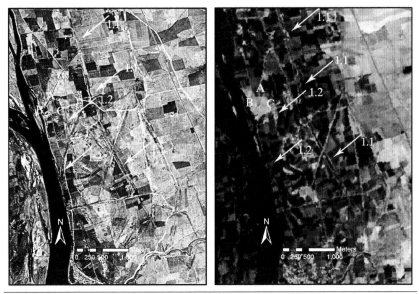

Fig. 1-7: Western part of the Makhmur plain. 1.1: Main branch of the Middle-Assyrian pattu meshari (Bagg, Assyrische Wasserbauten, 41-43.); 1.2: Off-take of the pattu meshari flowing though the northern part of Kar-Tukulti-Ninurta and draining to the Tigris in the south; letters are indicating architectural features (left: CORONA 16.8.1968; right: ASTER 05.3.2002).

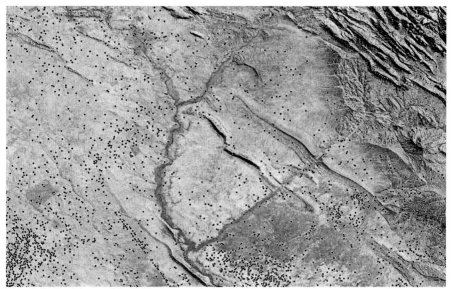

Fig. 1-8: Positions of 'tell like' mounds in the Makhmur plain, as proposed by the classifier. Clearly visible are regions where the natural topography prohibits a search for settlement mounds in the DEM.

Fig. 1-9: Radial hollow ways visible on CORONA photographs (16.8.1968) and multispectral ASTER (05.3.2002) with an archaeological site in the upper middle part.

Fig. 1-10: Tall Aswad visible on CORONA (06.12.1969). White arrows indicate traces of radial hollow ways.

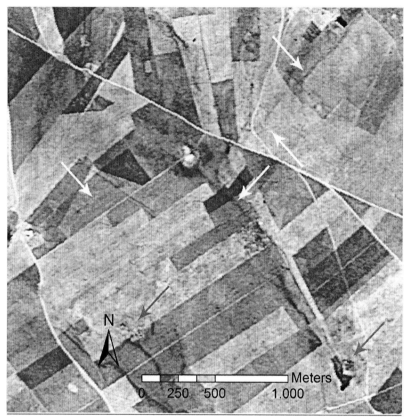

Fig. 1-61: Radial hollows with Tulul al-Nawwar in the centre (CORONA 16.8.1968).

CHAPTER TWO

LANDSCAPE TRANSFORMATION IN THE DECAPOLIS REGION (NORTHERN JORDAN) – A CRITICAL RE-EXAMINATION OF A PARADIGM

BERNHARD LUCKE, MICHAEL SCHMIDT, RUPERT BÄUMLER AND ZIAS AL-SAAD

Introduction

Man-made erosion as reason of desertification and land degradation in the Mediterranean is a paradigm deeply rooted in popular and scientific narratives. It is without doubt one of the favourite explanations for the abandonment of ancient sites,[1] and phases of colluvia deposition are usually interpreted as phases of unsustainable land use.[2]

Although Vita-Finzi challenged this paradigm as early as 1969,[3] it was widely accepted and huge projects were launched to combat desertification by preventing erosion. However, it soon became evident that things were more complex than expected. For example, construction of field stone walls in the Zarqa river basin, Jordan, did not achieve the desired success.[4] Sedimentation of the Zarqa river dam was reduced only insignificantly – and while significance may remain a matter of definition, one heavy rainstorm in 1991 brought as much sediment into the dam as ten years of average precipitation before. And that happened despite newly constructed soil conservation installations.[5]

---

[1] Dregne, Desertification of Arid Lands, Hillel, Out of the Earth.
[2] Pope and van Andel, Late Quaternary alleviation and soil formation in the southern Argolid, Fuchs et al., The history of Holocene soil erosion in the Phlious Basin, NE Peloponnese, Greece, based on optical dating.
[3] Bintliff, Erosion in the Mediterranean Lands.
[4] ZRB project, Zarqa River Basin Project: Final Report.
[5] al-Sheriadeh and al-Hamdan, Erosion Risk Assessment and Sediment Yield Production of the King Talal Watershed, Jordan, 240.

In the light of this, it is not surprising that other projects to combat desertification in the Mediterranean also found other results than initially expected. Examples are the MEDALUS[6] and ARCHAEOMEDES[7] projects, which essentially conclude that ecology and climate are the most important factors determining success or failure of agriculture. If soil erosion had relevance for the settlement history, it was only locally and cannot be understood in a generalising way without considering the societal framework and local environment.[8]

While it is increasingly acknowledged that the situation is too complex to allow for one-fits-all solutions of combating desertification, the question arises how future land use strategies should look like. This paper intends to present some ideas how cross-disciplinary research of the environmental history could be utilised to educe sustainable land management plans.

The investigation area:
northern Jordan (region of the ancient Decapolis)

The Decapolis region in northern Jordan is situated close to the Arabian Desert (Fig. 1), determining strong variations of rainfall and agricultural capacity. Its settlement history is fairly well known,[9] and high-resolution past climate data are available from the Dead Sea[10] and speleothems in Israel.[11] The region served as typical example for the negative effects of deforestation, unsustainable browsing and erosion due to agriculture.[12] But as the ups and downs of the settlement history are coincident with the climate record, it has also been suggested that climate change determined historical developments.[13]

The investigation area includes an alluvial plain (the Jordan valley), a mediterranean highland and the transition area to the Arabian Desert, allowing comparison of regions characterised by different precipitation and sedimentation regimes. The geological structure consists of only two basic

---

[6] Grove and Rackham, The Nature of Mediterranean Europe, Mazzoleni et al., Recent dynamics of the Mediterranean vegetation and landscape.

[7] van der Leeuw and the Archaeomedes Research Team, Climate, hydrology, land use, and environmental degradation in the lower Rhone valley during the Roman Period.

[8] Butzer, Environmental history in the Mediterranean world.

[9] Hoffmann and Kerner, Gadara-Gerasa und die Dekapolis.

[10] Migowski, Untersuchungen laminierter holozäner Sedimente aus dem toten Meer.

[11] Bar-Matthews et al., Middle to Late Holocene (6500 yr Period) Paleoclimate in the Eastern Mediterranean Region from Stable Isotopic Composition of Speleothems from Soreq Cave.

[12] Beaumont, Man-induced erosion in northern Jordan.

[13] Issar and Zohar, Climate Change – Environment and Civilisation in the Middle East.

source rocks: basalt and limestone. The limestone occurs in form of several calcareous sediments of varying hardness, which are laid down evenly and capped by basalt sheet flows at various locations.[14] Dominant soils in the area are Red Mediterranean Soils, while Yellow Mediterranean Soils and Rendzinas are found in the wadis. The greatest part of the agricultural area is situated on a level high plateau, covered by red soils and increasingly dissected by deeply incised wadis as precipitation and height differences rise towards the Jordan valley.

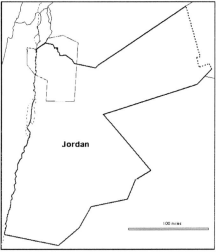

Fig. 2-1: Approximate location of the Decapolis region in northern Jordan.

Methods

Two types of investigation were combined: analysis of air photos and current agricultural data, and soil studies. Series of air photos, maps and CORONA satellite imagery, covering the time from 1918-2000, were examined for relict structures, land use changes, and persistence of field systems. The coverage of the 1918 air photos is very patchy, and a complete time series 1918-2000 could only be established for the Madaba plains, south of the Decapolis region. But the visible patterns are identical in Madaba and the Decapolis region, and are therefore compared in this paper. Today's agriculture

---

[14] Bender, Geology of Jordan.

was investigated using data from the Ministry of Agriculture of Jordan and interviewing farmers.

Soil research was based on a comparative study of soils. By comparing soil genesis with regard to source rock, relief, climate and land use, it is possible to identify the most relevant factors of soil development. The Decapolis region is very well-suited for such an analysis, as only two basic source rocks and a climatic gradient from west to east are present. Rainfalls decrease and become more irregular when approaching the Arabian desert in the east. Rainfall intensity is also mirrored in the relief, which is more heavily dissected towards the west (where height differences increase when approaching the Jordan valley rift).

Additionally, the database of the National Soil Map and Land Use Project of Jordan was evaluated and compared with our samples.[15] Profiles were opened up to bedrock to clarify the development process of soils and to get the in situ parent material. In situ developed soils were compared with fossil soils and relict air-dried mudbrick preserved in ruins. To assess the influence of cultivation, culture material was collected with the soil samples which gave clues for the intensity and periods of historic land use.   ·

Paleosols are preserved at numerous locations, for example under Wadi colluvia, in the Jordan valley, or in the eastern steppe/desert. Also, ruins covered and preserved ancient land surfaces. The ruins deliver not only a time frame for dating soils, but also give indications for soil forming processes (out of debris) in historical periods.

Results

Air photo analysis

Land use patterns showed a remarkable stability. Evaluation of air photos dating back to 1918 revealed abandoned long fields, with some parcels divided into small rectangular plots (Fig. 2). While it is not possible to date the abandonment of these fields, the same pattern is still in use at the site of Jerash (Figs. 3 and 4). Long fields cross the plateaux and valleys, reportedly cultivated with wheat,[16] while irrigated vegetables are grown on the small rectangular plots. Close to the town of Madaba, these small plots are missing as is the water that could be used for irrigation (Fig. 5). Long fields dominate agriculture around the town, a picture that remains unchanged in 1992 (Fig. 6). It can be

---

[15] Schmidt et al., The Decapolis region (northern Jordan) as historical example of desertification?

[16] Dalman, Arbeit und Sitte in Palästina.

concluded that land use systems are adapted to the terrain and little change took place since 1918 – a picture confirmed for other parts of our investigation area.[17] However, at least two phases of land use have to be distinguished: slightly sloping areas show short slope-parallel rectangular fields under long slope-crossing fields (Fig. 7). The latter ones are seemingly younger, but up to now no dating is available.

Fig. 2-2: Abandoned fields south of Madaba in 1918. As all presented air photos dating back to 1918, this picture was taken by fighter squadron 304 during WWI. Copyright: Bavarian War Archive, Munich, no. 1191 (with permission).

---

[17] Lucke et al., Soils and Land Use in the Decapolis region (Northern Jordan).

Fig. 2-3 (opposite page, top): Jerash in 1918. The ruins have partially been turned into gardens and vegetables are grown in small plots close to the creek. Outside the town, wheat is grown on long fields. Copyright: Bavarian War Archive, Munich, no. 1123 (with permission).

Fig. 2-4 (opposite page, bottom): Close-up to the gardens in the ruins of Jerash, 1918. Copyright: Bavarian War Archive, Munich, no. 1131 (with permission).

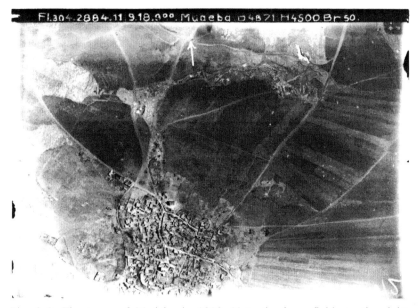

Fig. 2-5: The town of Madaba in 1918. Note the long fields to the right. Copyright: Bavarian War Archive, Munich, no. 1185 (with permission).

Fig. 2-6: The town of Madaba and part of its vicinity in 1992. Although urban areas have strongly expanded, the general character of the remaining eastern long field systems has not changed. Copyright: Royal Geographic Centre of Jordan, Amman (with permission).

Fig. 2-7: Gently sloping hills close to Irbid. The low sun during dusk reveals remains of slope-parallel fields overlain by slope-crossing long fields, which would otherwise be invisible. Photo by B. Lucke, 2005.

Interpretation of field patterns

The above discussed historic air photos show that if water was available for irrigation (as e.g. with cisterns or as close to the creek in Jerash, Fig. 4), small rectangular plots appear that were planted with vegetables. These areas received a lot of manure and were an important part of a farmer's income.[18] Apart from that, the best soils were planted with olives, while the average soils and greatest part of the agricultural area carried wheat fields.[19] This land use system is strongly adapted to the terrain and seems to be characterised by persistence and stability. Persistence and stability have also been reported from nearby areas. According to Dar (1986), land use patterns in the highlands of Samaria date back to the Iron Age. Dar describes a fossil landscape that experienced little change since Jewish farmers were displaced by the Romans, proven by land use installations and material culture. With regard to soil cover, it should be mentioned that rock outcrops in Samaria served as water collection and transportation devices and were utilised for viticulture.[20] This picture can be confirmed for Jordan. Most rocky areas in Jordan are covered with caliche crusts, which were a preferred building material and show signs of ancient quarrying. While the age of the caliche has not been determined yet, local caliche was identified as source material for Roman and Byzantine columns, for example in Umm Queis.[21] This indicates that rock outcrops were not less prominent during the Iron Age and Roman period than today, but an important part of the land use system.

Traditional Arab agriculture did not strongly alter field systems in Jordan since 1918. This contrasts sharply with the development in Israel (excluding the territories occupied after 1967, as e.g. Samaria). In Israel a modern, industrialised agriculture eradicated the ancient land use pattern as well as Arab settlements whose inhabitants had been displaced during the 1948 war.[22] It should be mentioned that Arab settlements usually occupied places that were already settled in earlier periods, thus providing easily accessible building material, as well as cisterns and vaults that could be re-used (if the sites were not continuously settled). As ancient settlements were usually located at places advantageous for agriculture (close to good soils, but not covering them),[23] it

---

[18] Dalman, Arbeit und Sitte in Palästina, II, 6.

[19] Barham, Geographische Probleme des Regenfeldbaus in Jordanien, 148.

[20] Dar, Landscape and Pattern.

[21] Pers. communication with Nizar Abu-Jaber, Yarmouk University, Jordan. See www.quarryscapes.no.

[22] Kedar, The changing land, Richter, Israel und seine Nachbarräume.

[23] Geraty and Herr, Madaba Plains Project, 37.

would have made sense to re-use the remains of land use installations in the vicinity as long as no heavy modern machinery was available. And although the Muslim inheritance law proposes splitting of the property between the heirs, Wåhlin (1993) demonstrated that the Arab tribes attempt to keep their territories unified and fields as units, even if they belong to several owners. It can thus be concluded that not traditional agriculture, but rather the introduction of modern machinery led to landscape change.

In order to assess the preservation state of the historic land use pattern, a selected area between the villages of Hubras and Hartha (north of Irbid, close to the ancient site of Abila) was analysed in depth, validating the results of air photo interpretation with ground observations. In this area, a Roman street had been confirmed from air photos (Figs. 8 and 9), but on the ground, if anything only an increase or decrease of stone cover is visible (Fig. 10). Without the evidence from the air photos, nothing would today indicate the presence of a Roman street. However, farmers stated in interviews that their grandparents had still seen the street's pavement intact, which was destroyed and ploughed over when tractors were introduced.[24] Also, small buildings and mausolea were reportedly destroyed and today only heaps of stone, or varying stone cover on the fields, are left. In light of this, it seems possible that the field patterns in the Decapolis region follow a basic structure dating back to the Iron Age. This structure might have looked as described by Dar (1986) for Samaria, or as still visible in Syria, in the area of the "Dead cities".[25] It seems that the remains of ancient fields experienced more damage during the last fifty years than during thousands of years before, which was connected with the introduction of industrial, mechanised agriculture.

Regarding the agricultural potential, the problems of present land use in Jordan seem quite similar to those of historic land use.[26] Crops are highly dependent on rainfall patterns. Therefore, farmers usually decide after the first rains which crops to sow.[27] If there are no well-distributed rains at the beginning of the rainy season, a hard drought crust is likely to form in the summer heat, impeding germination of most crop seeds. Additionally, harvest is endangered if there are no late rains with regard to the growing season. Inversely, excessive rains are also reported to be of disadvantage, since the soils

---

[24] Michael Fuller was able to observe a few parts of the street still intact in 1982, see users.stlcc.edu/mfuller/abila/AbilaSurveys.html.
[25] Strube, Die toten Städte.
[26] Lucke et al., Soils and Land Use in the Decapolis region (Northern Jordan).
[27] Lanzendörfer, Agricultural Mechanisation in Jordan, 11.

get elastic and hence make the field work difficult.[28] Agriculture on the plateaus is fully dependent on rainfall, as there are no other water sources than cisterns, and irrigation is very difficult even today. While dependency on winter rains prevents salinization, shallow soils rich in calcium carbonate are vulnerable to drought.

Fig. 2-8: Roman street between Hubras and Hartha in 1979. Copyright: Royal Geographic Centre of Jordan, Amman (with permission).

---

[28] Lucke et al., Soils and Land Use in the Decapolis region (Northern Jordan).

Fig. 2-9: The same Roman street in 2000. Although still well visible, the street line has become broader and more diffuse. Copyright: Royal Geographic Centre of Jordan, Amman (with permission).

Fig. 2-10: A high stone content on the field is all that is left from the street today. Photo by B. Lucke, 2006.

Soils

Red Mediterranean Soils – state of research

Red Mediterranean Soils are usually assumed to be very old, as limestone produces little residue and hematite formation (responsible for the red colour) takes place only after long and intensive weathering.[29] According to

---

[29] Reifenberg, The soils of Palestine, Bronger and Sedov, Vetusols and Paleosols.

paleomagnetic measurements of Bronger and Bruhn-Lubin (1997), Red Mediterranean Soils in Morocco are approximately 100000 years old. However, hematite might also be of geogenic origin and pre-Pleistocene age as constituent of the source rock.[30] Also, the high age of hematite formation has been questioned: if the weathering products contain a high amount of $FeCO_3$, combined with strong variations of soil moisture and a mean annual temperature of > 7 °C, hematite might form during much shorter time periods.[31] Such conditions are present in Jordan. Another unsolved question is the role of Aeolian deposition. It has been suggested that the sharp boundary between the karstic rock and soil, as well as the little amount of limestone residue, point to dust as the main parent material of soils.[32] Also quartz in basalt soils has been taken as evidence of dust input, since the basalts did not contain quartz. According to Yaalon and Ganor (1973), this dust input is too slight and steady to be observed in the profile, and has its sources in the Sahara from where it is brought with the winter rains.

Finally, the boundary between karstic rock and soil might in fact not be sharp.[33] Many diagenetic replacements in sedimentary rocks occur along thin solution films between the authigenic and host phases. Authigenic terra rossa clay might replace limestone pseudomorphically and isovolumetrically, meaning that soil formation takes place in a 1:1 replacement of rock with soil.[34]

Soils in the Decapolis region

Our research on the limestone plateau revealed strong variations of soil depth, although the highland looks like a vast, level and homogeneous plain. Depth variation numbered between 30 cm to 3 m in small areas,[35] which was surprising as the evaluation of air photos gave no clues for varying soil depth. The vegetation is seemingly not affected – in contrast, trees seem to grow better in rocky areas as their roots find water in the rock's fissures.[36] Depth differences

---

[30] Bronger, Kalksteinverwitterungslehme als Klimazeugen?

[31] Cornell and Schwertmann, The Iron Oxides, 445.

[32] Yaalon and Ganor, The Influence of Dust on Soils during the Quaternary, Yaalon, Soils in the Mediterranean Region.

[33] See a talk of Enrique Merino:
gsa.confex.com/gsa/2005AM/finalprogram/abstract_90146.htm.

[34] Maliva and Siever, Diagenetic replacement controlled by force of crystallization.

[35] Schmidt et al., The Decapolis region (Northern Jordan) as historical example of desertification?, 77.

[36] Grove and Rackham, The Nature of Mediterranean Europe: an Ecological History, 193.

could be related to different weathering behaviour of the source rocks. The limestone's hardness varies strongly due to water and salt movement processes within the rock, although the different calcareous sediments seem to be chemically identical.[37]

As the observed depth differences are quite huge and the area is characterised by Karst features,[38] it seems possible that ploughing over centuries levelled a once undulating landscape, moving the former topsoil into what is today the B-horizon of deep profiles.[39] In addition, soil colour and stone content vary and seem to follow field borders.[40] At a location studied more in detail, the brighter plot was characterised by enrichment of nutrients, higher calcium content and stronger weathering of bedrock. Differences due to the parent rock or relief could be excluded and both sampled plots revealed many ancient sherds, mostly from the Late Roman and Byzantine-Umayyad period.[41] The most likely explanation for the colour difference is $CaCO_3$-content, as there is a clear correlation of redness rating and $CaCO_3$-content in the investigation area. But it is an open question why $CaCO_3$-contents vary locally, and why this seemingly follows field borders. At the examined site close to Abila, Ayyubid-Mamluk sherds were reported from the brighter area by Fuller (1985), indicating that prolonged medieval land use might be responsible for nutrient enrichment and deposition of calcareous material.

A different picture was obtained for the basalt caps. Here, the soil was homogeneous and very deep, and carried a lot of material culture. It seems that manure intensity was highest on the best soils as proposed by Dar (1986) – the examined basalt soils were assessed to be the best ones for agriculture in Jordan.[42] It thus seems evident that source rock plays a dominant role for soil properties: the homogeneous depth of the basalt soils seems related to a lack of karst features due to the underlying basalt cap. However it was not a small surprise to discover a caliche crust on the basalt bedrock. Earlier soil surveys, e.g. in the framework of the National Soil Map and Land Use Project of Jordan (NSM&LUP) did not undertake a sampling of the bedrock, as it was assumed

---

[37] Pers. comm. with Sven-Oliver Lorenz, University of Würzburg, May 2006.

[38] al-Farajat, Karstification in (B4) Unit Northwest of Irbid and It's Role in Enhancing Human Impacts on the Local Groundwater Resources.

[39] Schmidt et al., The Decapolis region (Northern Jordan) as historical example of desertification?, 83.

[40] Lucke et al., The Abandonment of the Decapolis Region in Northern Jordan, 71.

[41] Lucke et al., The Abandonment of the Decapolis Region in Northern Jordan, 72.

[42] Schmidt et al., The Decapolis region (Northern Jordan) as historical example of desertification?, 81.

that 1,50 m deep profiles tied in with the rooting depth of most crops.[43] As it seems, chalk dust was blown into the pores of the basalt during its deposition and led to a $CaCO_3$-content of approximately 10% in both rock and soil. This points on the one hand to the likelihood of dust deposition from local sources. Chalk exposed at deep wadi slopes is partially so soft that it can be ploughed, and dust released from streets before the arrival of asphalt was reported as a very unpleasant feature of Palestinian towns.[44] On the other hand, if calcareous dust was already deposited when the basalt was laid down, measuring quartz does not say much anymore.

Debris in the ruins and remains of mudbrick tiles indicate that aeolian deposition was limited during historical times – as it seems, no more than 20 cm of soil cover can be attributed to aeolian deposition during the past 1000 years.[45] But what is sure is that some aeolian activity took place, because the bulk density and structure of soil just on top of the ruins strongly suggests dust origin. Whether local or distant sources were involved cannot be determined at the moment.

Other indicators also point to little soil change during historical periods. Relict mudbrick tiles, as far as examined, seem to be identical with present plateau soils, indicating that no major change of soil properties took place since the Bronze Age.[46] This is consistent with colluvia, for example in Wadi Ziqlab. Here relict land surfaces, dating back to the Kebaran and Neolithic periods, were identified by Field and Banning (1998). Sedimentation took place in the form of landslides, allowing to distinguish different soil units and to date them according to archaeological material on covered relict surfaces.[47] The pattern revealed in Wadi Ziqlab is very similar to that of the Zarqa river basin project:[48] extreme events were responsible for the greatest part of the erosion. And the by far greatest part of colluvia had been deposited during prehistoric periods, a picture that has been confirmed from other wadis.[49] In this context, it seems that erosion in the Decapolis region was governed by climate – a picture that would fit remarkably well to the suggestions of Vita-Finzi (1969). It seems however

---

[43] NSM&LUP, National Soil Map and Land Use Project.

[44] Dalman, Arbeit und Sitte in Palästina, I (2).

[45] Schmidt et al., The Decapolis region (Northern Jordan) as historical example of desertification?, 79.

[46] Lucke et al., The Abandonment of the Decapolis Region in Northern Jordan, 76.

[47] Field and Banning, Hillslope processes and archaeology in Wadi Ziqlab, Jordan, 600.

[48] ZRB project, Zarqa River Basin Project: Final Report.

[49] Cordova, Geomorphological Evidence of Intense Prehistoric Soil Erosion in the Highlands of Central Jordan.

not yet clarified whether increase or decrease of precipitation leads to erosion, respectively how the occurrence of extreme rainfall events is linked with the general precipitation regime.[50] In any case, it seems safe to conclude that the rainfall conditions present today are rather optimal and that earlier epochs had to face much stronger earth movements despite lacking modern mechanised agriculture.[51] Soil investigations confirm the picture outlined by air photo interpretation: historic wooden ploughs and oxen did not cause significant erosion and landscape change.

Discussion and conclusion

Both land use systems and soils in the Decapolis region point to stability and little change during historical times. It seems possible that the present field systems are partially inherited from very ancient ones and reflected in slight differences of soil development. In future research, we intend to systematically combine the study of air photos with mapping of material culture, historic sources and soil studies, which might make it possible to reconstruct ancient land use patterns and phases of land use change in detail.

While soil development seems to be governed by source rock and relief, prolonged land use might have levelled a once undulating landscape. In contrast, greater earth movements seem to be connected with climate and not land use. This means that present soil conservation measures and land use strategies, based on average precipitation, will fail if global warming leads to an increase of extreme events in the region. Thomas and Middleton (1994) discussed already the weakness and contradictions connected with the term "desertification": what in fact happens might simply be climate change, even if its impacts are locally accelerated by human activity.

As agriculture and erosion control are closely connected with freshwater supply, it would be worth considering land use strategies that are based on coping with very extreme rainfall events. In this context, traditional Arab agriculture seems to be less backward than previously assumed: as most traditional land use systems, it is characterised by diversification.[52] Diversification may produce lower yields, lead to an increase of pasture and neglect of field stone walls in times of reduced economic benefits, but provides

---

[50] Vita-Finzi, Medieval Mud and the Maunder Minimum.
[51] Grove and Rackham, The Nature of Mediterranean Europe, 311.
[52] Lanzendörfer, Agricultural Mechanisation in Jordan.

landscape stability and a maximum chance of survival as crop failure does not immediately cause famine.

Studying the past could help to better evaluate such strategies and to determine the possible impact of possibly increasing extreme events. Considering ancient land use and the abandonment of sites, it seems very likely that climate change played a most important role. If the climatic changes as reflected in Soreq cave[53] and Dead Sea records[54] were an increase of extreme events interrupting prolonged droughts, it is well possible that they caused very severe crop damage, swept fields away, destroyed water systems, silted up cisterns, and damaged livestock. Hand in hand with earthquakes[55] and wars, they might have been the most important cause for abandonment of ancient sites. Given the negative water balance of countries in the region, climate change might even today become a very severe challenge.

Acknowledgements

This research was supported by German Research Foundation (DFG) and Hugo-Gressman-Foundation, which we gratefully acknowledge. We thank the Bavarian War Archive, Munich, for providing air photos from Bavarian fighter squadron 304, and the Royal Geographic Center of Jordan, Amman, for making sets of pictures available which cover the time span from 1953-2000.

References

al-Farajat, M. *Karstification in (B4) Unit Northwest of Irbid and It's Role in Enhancing Human Impacts on the Local Groundwater Resources*. MA thesis, University of Jordan, 1997.
al-Sheriadeh, M. and A. al-Hamdan. 'Erosion Risk Assessment and Sediment Yield Production of the King Talal Watershed, Jordan.' *Environmental Geology* 37, no. 3 (1999): 234-242.
Barham, Nasim. *Geographische Probleme des Regenfeldbaus in Jordanien*. Dissertation, University of Hannover, 1979.

---

[53] Bar-Matthews et al., Middle to Late Holocene (6500 yr Period) Paleoclimate in the Eastern Mediterranean Region from Stable Isotopic Composition of Speleothems from Soreq Cave, Israel.
[54] Migowski, Untersuchungen laminierter holozäner Sedimente aus dem toten Meer.
[55] Which might be a neglected but very important reason of erosion/landslides, pers. comm. with Konstantin Pustovoytov, University of Hohenheim, June 2006.

Bar-Matthews, Mira, Avner Ayalon, Aharon Kaufmann. 'Middle to Late Holocene (6500 yr Period) Paleoclimate in the Eastern Mediterranean Region from Stable Isotopic Composition of Speleothems from Soreq Cave, Israel.' In *Water, Environment and Society in Times of Climatic Change*, edited by Arie Issar and Neville Brown, 203-215, Dordrecht: Kluwer Academic Publishers, 1998.

Beaumont, P. 'Man-induced erosion in northern Jordan.' *Studies in the History and Archaeology of Jordan* 2 (1985): 291-296.

Bender, Friedrich. *Geology of Jordan*. Gebrüder Bornträger, Berlin 1974.

Bintliff, John. 'Erosion in the Mediterranean Lands: A reconsideration of pattern, process and methodology.' In *Past and Present soil Erosion: Archaeological and Geographical Perspectives*, edited by M. Bell. and J. Boardman, J., 125-131. Oxford: Oxbow Monograph 22, 1992.

Bronger, Arnt. 'Kalksteinverwitterungslehme als Klimazeugen?' *Z. Geomorph. N. F. Supplement* 24 (1976): 138-146.

Bronger, Arnt and N. Bruhn-Lobin. 'Paleopedology of Terrae rossae – Rhodoxeralfs from Quaternary calcarenites in NW Morocco.' *Catena* 28 (1997): 279-295.

Bronger, Arnt and Sergej Sedov. 'Vetusols and Paleosols: Natural versus Man-Induced Environmental Change in the Atlantic Coastal Region of Morocco.' *Quaternary International* 106-107 (2003): 33-60.

Butzer, Karl W. 'Environmental history in the Mediterranean world: cross-disciplinary investigation of cause-and-effect for degradation and soil erosion.' *Journal of Archaeological Science* 32 (2005): 1773-1800.

Cordova, Carlos. 'Geomorphological Evidence of Intense Prehistoric Soil Erosion in the Highlands of Central Jordan.' *Physical Geography* 21, no. 6 (2000): 538-567.

Cornell, R. and Uwe Schwertmann. *The Iron Oxides*. Weinheim: Wiley VCH, 2003.

Dalman, Gustav. *Arbeit und Sitte in Palästina*, Band I-VII. Gütersloh: Bertelsmann, 1928-1941.

Dar, Shimon. *Landscape and Pattern*. Oxford: BAR International Series 308, 1986.

Dregne, Harold. *Desertification of Arid Lands. Advances in Desert and Arid Land Technology and Development, Vol. 3*. London: Harwood, 1983.

Field, John and Edward Banning. 'Hillslope processes and archaeology in Wadi Ziqlab, Jordan.' *Geoarchaeology* 13, no. 6 (1998): 595-616.

Fuchs, Markus, Andreas Lang, G.A. Wagner. 'The history of Holocene soil erosion in the Phlious Basin, NE Peloponnese, Greece, based on optical dating.' *The Holocene* 14, no. 3 (2004): 334-345.

Fuller, Neathery. Analysis of ethnoarchaeological studies. *Near East Archaeological Society Bulletin* 25 (1985): 73-90.

Geraty, L. and L. Herr, eds. *Madaba Plains Project: The 1984 season at Tell el-Umeiri and Vicinity and Subsequent Studies.* Berrien Springs: Michigan, Andrews University Press and the Institute of Archeology, 1989.

Grove, A.T. and Oliver Rackham. *The Nature of Mediterranean Europe: an Ecological History.* New Haven: Yale University Press, 2003.

Hillel, Daniel. *Out of the Earth. Civilization and the life of the soil.* New York: The Free Press, 1991.

Hoffmann, Adolf and Susanne Kerner, eds. *Gadara-Gerasa und die Dekapolis.* Mainz: Phillip von Zabern Verlag, 2002.

Issar, Arie and Matti Zohar. *Climate Change – Environment and Civilisation in the Middle East.* Heidelberg: Springer Verlag, 2004.

Kedar, Benjamin. *The changing land. Between the Jordan and the sea.* Jerusalem: Yad Izhak Ben-Zvi Press, 1999.

Lanzendörfer, Mattias. *Agricultural Mechanisation in Jordan. A study of its Processes in a Socioeconomic Context.* PhD thesis, Sozioökonomische Schriften zur ruralen Entwicklung 62, University of Göttingen, 1985.

Leeuw, Sander van der, and The ARCHAEOMEDES research team. 'Climate, hydrology, land use, and environmental degradation in the lower Rhone valley during the Roman Period.' *C. R. Geoscience* 337 (2005): 9-27.

Lucke, Bernhard, Michael Schmidt, Ziad al-Saad, Oliver Bens and Reinhard F. Hüttl. 'The Abandonment of the Decapolis Region in Northern Jordan – Forced by Environmental Change?' *Quaternary International* 135 (2005), Special issue: Geochronology and Environmental Reconstruction: a Tribute to Glenn A. Goodfriend, 65-81.

Lucke, Bernhard, Ziad al-Saad, Michael Schmidt, Rupert Bäumler, Sven-Oliver Lorenz, Peter Udluft, Karl-Uwe Heussner and Bethany Walker. 'Soils and Land Use in the Decapolis region (Northern Jordan). Implications for landscape development and the impact of climate change.' *Zeitschrift des Deutschen Palästina-Vereins*, accepted (1st issue 2007).

Maliva, Robert and Raymond Siever. 'Diagenetic replacement controlled by force of crystallization.' *Geology* 16 (1988): 688-691.

Mazzoleni, Stefano, Gaetano Pasquale, Mark Mulligan, Paolo di Martino and Francisco Rego. *Recent dynamics of the Mediterranean vegetation and landscape.* Chichester: Wiley, 2004.

Migowski, Claudia. ,Untersuchungen laminierter holozäner Sedimente aus dem toten Meer: Rekonstruktion von Paläoklima und –seismizität.' Scientific Technical Report STR02/06, GeoForschungszentrum Potsdam, 2004.

NSM&LUP. Hashemite Kingdom of Jordan, Ministry of Agriculture, Hunting Technical Services Ltd., Soil Survey and Land Resources Centre, Cranfield

University, UK. *National Soil Map and Land Use Project*. Amman: Ministry of Agriculture, 1993.

Pope, K.O. and T.H. van Andel. 'Late Quaternary alleviation and soil formation in the southern Argolid: its history, its causes, and archaeological implications.' *Journal of Archaeological Sciences* 11 (1984): 281-306.

Reifenberg, A. *The soils of Palestine*. London: T. Murby, 1947.

Richter, W. *Israel und seine Nachbarräume. Ländliche Siedlungen und Landnutzung seit dem 19. Jahrhundert*. Erdwissenschaftliche Forschung 14, Wiesbaden: Steiner Verlag, 1979.

Schmidt, Michael, Bernhard Lucke, Rupert Bäumler, Ziad al-Saad, Bakr al-Qudah and Austin Hutcheon. ‚The Decapolis region (Northern Jordan) as historical example of desertification? Evidence from soil development and distribution.' *Quaternary International* 151, Special Issue I, Dark nature: responses of humans and ecosystems to rapid environmental changes (2006): 74-86.

Strube, Christine. *Die toten Städte*. Mainz: Phillip von Zabern, 2000.

Thomas, D. and N. Middleton. *Desertification – Exploding the Myth*. Chichester: Wiley, 1994.

Vita-Finzi, Claudio. *The Mediterranean Valleys. Geological Changes in Historical Times*. Cambridge: Cambridge University Press, 1969.

—. 'Medieval Mud and the Maunder Minimum.' In *Solar Output and Climate During the Holocene*, edited by B. Frenzel, 95-104. Stuttgart: Gustav Fischer Verlag, 1995.

Wåhlin, Lars. *Villages North of es-Salt, Jordan: A Historical Geographical Survey*. Kulturgeografiskt Seminarium 4/93, 1993.

Yaalon, Dan and E. Ganor. 'The Influence of Dust on Soils during the Quaternary.' *Soil Science* 116, no. 3 (1973): 146-155.

Yaalon, Dan. 'Soils in the Mediterranean Region: What makes them different?' *Catena* 28 (1997): 157-169.

ZRB project. Hashemite Kingdom of Jordan, Ministry of Agriculture, Department of Projects, Federal Republic of Germany, German Agency for Technical Cooperation, Agrar- und Hydrotechnik Essen GmbH. *Zarqa River Basin Project: Final Report*. Amman, 1991.

CHAPTER THREE

CONFRONTING LUMINESCENCE WITH RADIOCARBON DATES FOR FLUVIAL DEPOSITS IN THE UPPER KHABUR BASIN OF NORTHEASTERN SYRIA

KATLEEN DECKERS
AND DIMITRI VANDENBERGHE

Introduction

In the United Kingdom[1] and the United States[2] many well-dated fluvial deposits exist, which make it possible to evaluate the relative impact of people and climate on the landscape and to reconstruct archaeological sites in their environmental contexts. In the Near East, fluvial deposits are generally less well-dated[3] and preliminary chronologies are mostly established by typological analysis of off-site artefacts contained within the sediments. However, artefacts in fluvial contexts are often severely abraded, which renders them typologically undatable. Deckers et al.[4] recently developed a rapid and inexpensive thermoluminescence (TL)-screening method for obtaining age estimates for these sherds. Although the method is useful for developing preliminary fluvial chronologies and for framing archaeological research questions, it indicates an approximate maximum date for sediment deposition. Hence, the older the sherds occurring in the sediments are, the larger the potential gap between the age of

---

[1] Macklin, HoloceneRriver Alluviation in Britain.
[2] Abrogast and Johnson, Climatic Implications of the Late Quaternary Alluvial Record of a Small Drainage Basin in the Central Great Plains; Waters and Haynes, Late Quaternary Arroyo Formation and Climate Change in the American Southwest.
[3] Lewin et al., Mediterranean Quaternary River Environments – Some Future Research Needs, 283-284.
[4] Deckers et al., Thermoluminescence Screening of Non-Diagnostic Sherds from Stream Sediments to Obtain a Preliminary Alluvial Chronology: An Example from Cyprus.

the sherd and the date of sediment deposition. The sediment deposition chronology can be refined by optically stimulated luminescence (OSL) dating of the sediments,[5] as well as through radiocarbon dating of intercalated organic material.

It is clear that each of the three chronological tools (TL-screening, optical dating, and radiocarbon dating) have potential for establishing and improving fluvial chronologies in the Near East. We report our first results from a pilot study, which had as main objective to investigate the possibilities and limitations of these techniques into greater detail, more specifically as to their application to fluvial sediments from the upper Khabur basin in northeastern Syria.

Geographical setting and sampling

The upper Khabur basin of northeastern Syria is one of the better geomorphologically studied regions of the Near East.[6] Indeed, especially within this area which is situated on the border of the dry farming limit (i.e. the region where no irrigation is necessary for agriculture), water availability played an important role for former societies. However, the chronological insight into the regional landscape evolution still needs a lot of refinement to enable correlation of the well-known settlement history with the river evolution. The upper Khabur basin consists of a plain drained by several small north-south flowing streams that have their source in the Taurus foothills of Turkey (Fig. 1). The streams of relevance to the present study are the Jarrah, the Jaghjagh, and the Khanzir. The Jarrah and the Khanzir are intermittent streams, while presently, in the absence of damming and irrigation, the Jaghjagh would be a perennial stream.[7] The streams have their mouths in the presently east-west flowing Wadi-el-Radd, which has its confluence with the Khabur at Hassakeh. The Khabur is a main tributary of the Euphrates. However, Nützel suggested that the Wadi-el-Radd might have been drained towards the Tigris in antiquity.[8] This is an important issue that certainly needs further research, though is beyond the scope of this paper.

---

[5] Aitken, Thermoluminescence Dating.

[6] E.g. Courty, Le Cadre Paléogéographie des Occupations Humaines dans le Bassin du Haut-Khabur (Syrie du Nord-Est); Rösner, Zur quartären Landschaftsentwicklung in den Trockengebieten Syriens; Wilkinson, Remote Sensing and Geographical Information Systems; ibid., Physical and Cultural landscapes of the Hamoukar area; Besonen and Cremaschi, Geomorphological Field Survey Report; French, Geoarchaeology in Action.

[7] Kerbe, Climat, Hydrologie et Aménagements Hydro-Agricoles de Syrie.

[8] Eine Antike Flußverbindung zwischen dem Oberen Khabur-Gebiet und dem Tigris.

During the summer of 2002 about 70 fluvial exposures were studied in the field and about 500 sediment samples and 72 sherds were exported for laboratory analysis. In the course of 2003, the TL-screening approach was applied to a series of sherds from these fluvial sections. Based on these preliminary results, three areas were selected for further geomorphological and chronological study during the summer of 2003. More specifically, those locations were chosen where sediments pre-dating ca. AD 1500 are exposed, hence sequences that contain older sherds and/or stronger developed soils. The chronology of sequences with recent off-site sherds is better known than those with old sherds. Therefore, our objective was to gain a better insight into the age of the older sediments.

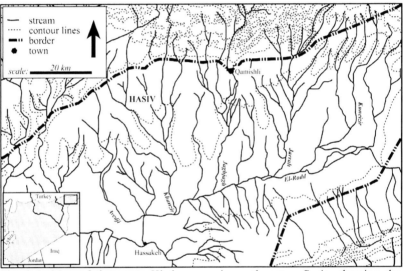

Fig. 3-1: Map of the upper Khabur area in northeastern Syria, showing the location of the three investigated sites (HASIV, HAM and FAR).

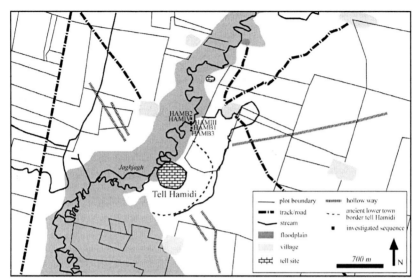

Fig. 3-2: Detailed map showing the location of sections (HAMIII-IV) and boreholes (HAMB1-3) near Tell Hamidi along the Wadi Jaghjagh. The map is based on a rectified Corona satellite image D025-012, 11 Dec67 1102-1AFT.

Fig. 3-3 (opposite page): Stratigraphy of the sediments as observed in the sections and boreholes from the HAM site. The location of the OSL and ^{14}C samples is indicated, together with the corresponding dating results (where available).

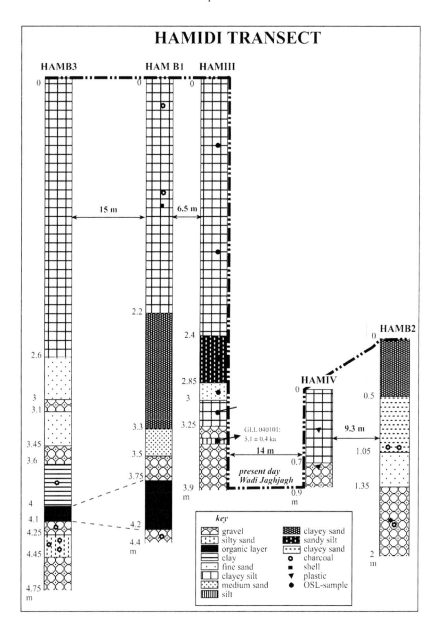

The first study area is located alongside the Jaghjagh, about 650 m north of Tell Hamidi (Fig. 1: "HAM"; Fig. 2). Tell Hamidi is a well-known excavated archaeological settlement mound (tell) with the lower town located along the Wadi Jaghjagh.[9] The excavated occupation levels span from the second millennium BC to recent times. The two sections investigated in the present work are called HAMIII and HAMIV; they are situated just outside the town wall and are naturally incised by the Wadi Jaghjagh (Figs. 2 and 3). It became rapidly clear that section HAMIV was recent as evidenced by a piece of plastic within it (Fig. 3).

Borehole HAMB2 was retrieved on the same side of the Jaghjagh at a distance of ca. 9.3 m from HAMIV. It probably consists of recent deposits as well, but further investigations are necessary to confirm this. Section HAMIII, conversely, was thought to be older because soil formation took place within the uppermost deposits. The base of section HAMIII consists of graded small gravels, while the upper 2.4 m consists of clay silt. Six samples for OSL dating were retrieved from the sediments exposed in section HAMIII (Fig. 3), of which three have been analysed so far (samples GLL 040101, GLL 040102, and GLL 040106). Additional geomorphological investigations were carried out by means of boreholes.

Borehole HAMB1 and HAMB3 were retrieved on the same side of the Jaghjagh as HAMIII, at a distance of 6.5 and 21.5 m, respectively, from the section. Within these boreholes an in-situ waterlogged organic-rich layer was found at a depth of ca. 4 m below the plain (Fig. 3). The layer overlies fluvial gravel, and probably corresponds to a level just below the exposed section HAMIII. One organic fragment from this layer was submitted for radiocarbon dating (sample KIA24908). Similar to the exposed HAMIII section, only the lower portion of boreholes HAMB1 and HAMB3 contain small-sized gravel units, while ca. the upper 2.5 m consist of clayey silt.

---

[9] Wäfler, The Excavations at Tell Hamidi; id., Tall al-Hamidiya 4. Vorbericht 1988-2001.

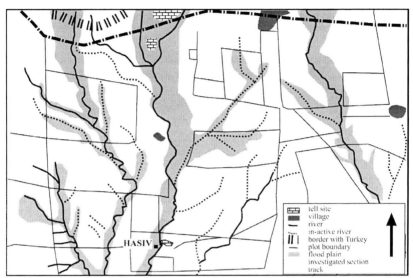

Fig. 3-4: Detailed map showing the location of the HASIV site, near Tell Has along the Wadi Khanzir. The map is based on a rectified Corona satellite image D025-055, 5 Nov 68, 1105-1FWD.

A second spot of interest is situated in nearby Tell Has, at a distance of 6 m from the present day Wadi Khanzir (Fig. 1: "HASIV", Fig. 4). The investigated section HASIV (Fig. 5) is located within a bulldozed water pit. At a depth of 3.8-3.6 m under the present plain, poorly sorted coarse fluvial gravel was found, overlain by alternating beds of fine-grained fluvial deposits and thin cultural ash-like layers. Between 2.7 and 0.9 m below the present plain, occupation layers have been found. The upper 0.9 m consists of fine-grained fluvial sediments. Several sherd-like artefacts were retrieved from the occupation layers. Two OSL samples were collected as well, of which one has been analysed so far (GLL 040108, collected in the gravel unit). A charcoal fleck from the fine-grained layer above this gravel was sampled for radiocarbon dating (sample KIA24913).

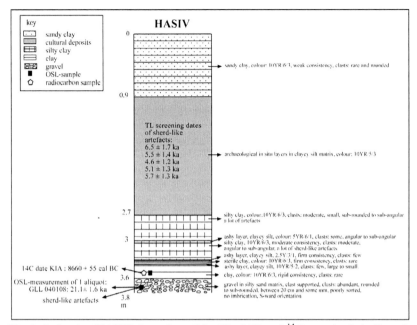

Fig. 3-5: Section HASIV. Location of the TL, OSL and ^{14}C samples is indicated, together with the corresponding dating results (where available). The optical age estimate (sample GLL 040108) is indicated for the sake of completion.

A third study area was in the neighbourhood of Farsouk Kabir (Fig. 1: "FAR"; Fig. 6) along the Wadi Jarrah. The investigated section FAR is located ca. 230 m southeast of the archaeological site Tell Farsouk Kabir, where artefacts were dated to the sixth to second millennium BC.[10] The section mainly consists of clay material (Fig. 7). Between 3.55 and 3.70 m a reddish colour occurs, corresponding to higher organic matter content. It is not totally clear at the moment whether or not it represents redeposited soil sediments or an in situ A-horizon. The boundary with the underlying sediments appears to be rather abrupt, suggesting that it is a redeposited A-horizon. Further study, including micromorphological investigations, could enhance this interpretation. A sediment sample from this redeposited soil was submitted for radiocarbon dating (sample KIA24912), while several OSL samples were collected throughout the exposed section, of which four were dated (GLL 040103, GLL 040104, GLL 040105, and GLL 040107; Fig. 7).

---

[10] Meijer, A Survey in Northeastern Syria.

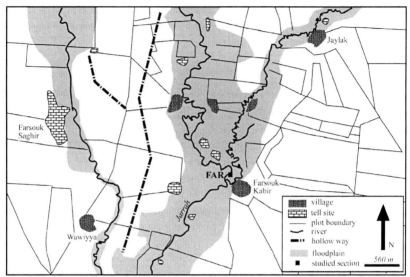

Fig. 3-6: Detailed map showing the location of section FAR near Farsouk Kabir along the Wadi Jarrah. The map is based on a rectified Corona satellite image D025-012, 11 Dec67 1102-1AFT.

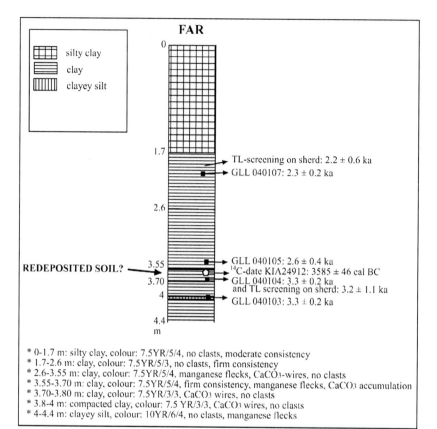

Fig. 3-7: Section FAR with location and results (where available) of the TL, OSL and ^{14}C samples indicated

Dating methodology and results

TL-screening of sherds

The surface of each sherd was removed and the inner material was gently crushed using pestle and mortar. Polymineral coarse-grains (90-150 μm) were subsequently extracted through dry sieving. These coarse-grained undifferentiated mineral mixtures were then treated with HCl to remove carbonates, washed, and finally deposited onto stainless-steel discs. For each sample the following measurement and analysis steps were carried out:

1) The natural TL was measured from four aliquots (sub-samples).
2) Two of the aliquots were then irradiated with a laboratory beta dose of 5 Gy, two with a dose of 10 Gy.
3) The artificial 5 and 10 Gy TL glow curves were measured.
4) The ratio of the natural to the artificial TL was plotted versus measurement temperature, and the region was identified where the data formed a plateau.
5) Assuming a natural dose-rate of 3 mGy/year,[11] the approximate age of each aliquot can be estimated by multiplying the plateau-ratio from step 4) by the ratio $\dfrac{laboratory\ beta\ dose\ (5\ or\ 10\ Gy)}{3 \times 10^{-3}\ Gy\ /\ year}$.
6) The average value of the four results yields the approximate age of the sherd.

The measurements were performed using a Risø TL-DA-12 reader. The glow curves were recorded to 500°C at 5°Cs⁻¹, followed by automatic re-heat and background subtraction. The luminescence was detected through a heat absorbing HA-3 and a Corning 7-59 filter combination. The reader is referred to Deckers et al.[12] for a detailed account of this screening-approach. Of more relevance here is that the method is limited in precision and accuracy. This is owing to the restricted number of TL-measurements, the large uncertainties associated with the dose-rate term (it is assumed rather than measured for each coarse-grained polymineral sample), the lack of any supralinearity assessment, and the possible interference of anomalous fading and/or sensitivity changes. Therefore, the results should not be considered as accurate calendar dates, but rather as approximations.

---

[11] Deckers et al., Thermoluminescence Screening of Non-Diagnostic Sherds from Stream Sediments to Obtain a Preliminary Alluvial Chronology: An Example from Cyprus.
[12] *Ibid.*

For each sherd from the HASIV section the age results were quite reproducible, with standard errors in the range of 4.4 to 7.3%. The standard errors on the results obtained for the FAR-sherds, alternatively, ranged from 15 to 22.5%. To allow for the above-mentioned limitations in the screening technique, an additional 25% uncertainty was adopted to calculate the overall error on the ages. The screening results are summarized in Figs. 5 and 7 for the HASIV and FAR sections, respectively.

Radiocarbon dating of organic material

Prof. P. Grootes of the Leibniz laboratory in Kiel performed the radiocarbon dating. The organic samples KIA24908, KIA24913, and KIA24912 were first microscopically checked for impurities. Subsequently, the samples were treated with 1% HCl, 1% NaOH (at 60 °C), and 1% HCl. The material was then combusted to CO_2 at 900°C in a quartz ampoule filled with CuO and silverwool. The CO_2 of all samples was subsequently reduced to graphite using H_2 at 600°C through an iron catalyst. Finally, the iron-graphite mix was pressed into a sample container for AMS measurements.

The ^{14}C-concentrations of the samples were obtained by comparing the simultaneously acquired ^{14}C, ^{13}C, and ^{12}C contents with those of the CO_2-standard (Oxalic Acid standard II), and by subtracting the zero effect as measured in samples of fossil coals. The conventional ^{14}C-age was calculated after Stuiver and Polach[13] with correction for isotopic fractionation through simultaneously measured AMS ^{13}C/^{12}C-proportions. The total uncertainty on the ^{14}C-result incorporates the uncertainties arising from statistics, the stability of the AMS-equipment, and the subtracted zero effect. For the first two the largest of the internal (derived from statistics) and external (observed variety) uncertainty was adopted. The calibration was performed using the online calibration program "CALPAL".[14]

The dating results for the three samples are summarized in Table I of the Appendix. The amount of carbon that could be extracted from sample KIA24908 was larger than is necessary for precision dating. The amount of organic carbon extracted from samples KIA 24913 and 24912, in contrast, was rather small (0.08% and 0.2% C, respectively). Therefore, the ages measured for these samples are sensitive to very small quantities of fluvial transported C in

---

[13] Stuiver and Polach, Discussion Reporting of ^{14}C Data.
[14] Wegener et al., Calpal – Cologne Radiocarbon Calibration and Palaeoclimate Research Package.

the sediment and might be too high. The $\delta^{13}C$-values lie within the normal reach for organic samples. It is perhaps worth pointing out that these $\delta^{13}C$-values also represent the effects of the graphitisation and of isotopic fractioning in the AMS-equipment. Therefore, the values are not directly comparable with $\delta^{13}C$-values that have been measured in a CO_2-mass spectrometer.

OSL-dating of sediments

Coarse (63-90 μm or 90-125 μm) quartz grains were extracted from the inner material of the sampling tubes using conventional sample preparation procedures (HCl, H_2O_2, sieving, HF). The analyses were carried out on quartz grains dispersed on the inner 7 mm of 9.7 mm stainless steel discs. No coarse quartz grains could be extracted from samples GLL 040103, GLL 040104, GLL 040105, and GLL 040107. For these samples, the 4-11 μm polymineral fraction was separated through sedimentation.[15] The polymineral fine fraction was subsequently etched for 7 min using 40% HF to obtain silt-sized quartz. For analyses, 1 ml aliquots of a 2 mg ml^{-1} silt/acetone suspension were precipitated on 10 mm diameter aluminium discs. The purity of all quartz extracts was confirmed by the absence of a significant infrared stimulated luminescence (IRSL) response at room temperature to a large (~50 Gy) regenerative β-dose. The luminescence measurements were made with a Risø TL/OSL-DA-12 reader equipped with high-power blue diodes emitting at 470 ± 30 nm and an infrared laser diode emitting at 830 nm. The luminescence was detected through a 7.5 mm thick Hoya U-340 filter. Irradiations were carried out with a $^{90}Sr/^{90}Y$ β-source mounted on the reader. Details on the measurement apparatus can be found in Bøtter-Jensen et al. and the references therein.[16] The equivalent dose (D_e) was determined using the single-aliquot regenerative-dose protocol (SAR) as described by Murray and Wintle.[17] Optical stimulation was for 40 s at 125°C. For each sample, a preheat of 10 s at 220°C and a test dose cut heat of 160°C was used. After measuring the response to the test dose, a high temperature optical stimulation of 40 s at 280°C was inserted to minimize the effect of recuperation. The suitability of the SAR measurement conditions was confirmed through dose recovery tests.[18] Low-level high-resolution gamma-ray

[15] Frechen et al., Improvements in Sample Preparation for the Fine Grain Technique.

[16] Bøtter-Jensen et al., Developments in Radiation, Stimulation and Observation Facilities in Luminescence Measurements.

[17] Luminescence Dating of Quartz using an Improved Single-Aliquot Regenerative-Dose Protocol; The Single Aliquot Regenerative Dose Protocol.

[18] Murray and Wintle, The Single Aliquot Regenerative Dose Protocol.

spectrometry was used for the determination of the natural dose rate.[19] Concentrations were converted into annual doses using the conversion factors of Adamiec and Aitken.[20] For the coarse-grained samples (GLL 040101, GLL 040102, GLL 040106, and GLL 040108) the external beta dose-rate was corrected for the effect of attenuation and etching using the data tabulated by Mejdahl.[21] An internal dose rate of 0.035 Gy ka^{-1} was assumed. For the fine-grained samples (GLL 040103, GLL 040104, GLL 040105, and GLL 040107), an alpha efficiency factor of 0.04 ± 0.01 was used.[22] The contribution from Rb was calculated assuming a K:Rb ratio of 200:1.[23] The alpha, beta, and gamma contributions were corrected for the effect of moisture. Measurements of present day water contents in sediments from the immediate surroundings of the samples indicate saturation from about 3 m deep. Hence, it was assumed that the samples were near saturation over the entire burial period. The contribution of cosmic radiation was calculated following Prescott and Hutton.[24]

All analytical results and the calculated optical ages are summarized in Table II of the Appendix. For samples GLL 040102 and GLL 040103, where the ^{238}U and/or ^{232}Th daughter isotopes give consistent results, the unweighted average was used for calculating the corresponding dose rates. All other samples exhibit disequilibria in the ^{238}U decay chain. For these samples, the present-day dose rate was assumed to have prevailed throughout the entire period of burial (based on the findings by Olley et al.[25]). Uncertainties on the luminescence ages were calculated following the error assessment system as outlined in Aitken.[26] All sources of systematic uncertainty were as quantified by Vandenberghe et al.[27]

---

[19] See Hossain, A Critical Comparison and Evaluation of Methods for the Annual Radiation Dose Determination in the Luminescence Dating of Sediments; Vandenberghe, Investigation of the Optically Stimulated Luminescence Dating Method for Application to Young Geological Sediments, for details.

[20] Adamiec and Aitken, An Introduction to Optical Dating.

[21] Mejdahl, Thermoluminescence Dating.

[22] Rees-Jones and Tite, Optical Dating Results for British Archaeological Sediments.

[23] Aitken, Thermoluminescence Dating.

[24] Prescott and Hutton, Cosmic Ray Contributions to Dose Rates for Luminescence and ESR Dating: Large Depths and Long-Term Time Variations.

[25] Olley et al., The Effects of Disequilibria in the Uranium and Thorium Decay Chains on Burial Dose Rates in Fluvial Sediments.

[26] Aitken, Thermoluminescence Dating.

[27] Vandenberghe et al., Exploring the Method of Optical Dating and Comparison of Optical and ^{14}C ages of Late Weichselian Coversands in the Southern Netherlands; Vandenberghe, Investigation of the Optically Stimulated Luminescence Dating Method.

Only a very small amount (~50-60 mg) of pure 90-125 μm quartz could be extracted from samples GLL 040101, GLL 040102, and GLL 040106. This limited the number of analyses that could be carried out for these samples. About 3 mg of pure quartz could be extracted from sample GLL 040108; i.e. sufficient for only one single D_e determination. The lack of sufficient datable material prevented us from obtaining a reliable optical age for this sample. For the sake of completeness, however, we also included the results of these analyses in Table II.

With the exception of sample GLL 040105, both the coarse and silt-sized quartz extracted from the samples exhibited satisfactory luminescence characteristics in terms of brightness, OSL decay, recycling ratios (consistent with unity), recuperation (less than a few % of the corrected natural OSL), and dose recovery (see Table II of the Appendix). The silt-sized quartz extracted from sample GLL 040105 was dim. Only ca. 20-40 counts were registered in the first 0.3 s of stimulation. As a consequence, the reproducibility of the D_e determinations was poor. It can be noted that, on average, a good dose recovery could be achieved for this sample, albeit with a relatively large uncertainty (Table II). Samples GLL 040101 and GLL 040102 contained gravel and pebbles. Such non-uniformities in the sediments might cause heterogeneity in the environmental beta dose rate, and introduce additional scatter in the results.

Finally, it should be noted that the depositional context for all samples is alluvial. Owing to the possibility of incomplete resetting of the OSL clock in such an environment, the optical ages should, therefore, be considered as maximum ages.

Discussion

The organic rich layer 4 m below the plain near Tell Hamidi was radiocarbon dated at 3449 ± 49 cal BC (Fig. 3). As mentioned before, this layer probably corresponds to the bottom of section HAMIII, for which several SAR OSL dates have been obtained. Therefore, the OSL-dates should be younger than the radiocarbon date. The date achieved for the silty unit at ca. 3.5 m below the plain is 5.1 ± 0.4 ka and corresponds well with the radiocarbon date. The dated clayey silt at 3.15 m below the plain has been OSL-dated at 4.5 ± 0.3 ka. The sandy silt at ca. 2.6 m below the present plain, however, provided a slightly older date of 5.5 ± 0.4 ka and appears to be less consistent. But within analytical uncertainties, the date should be considered consistent with the other dates. The overall uncertainties of the optical ages range in between 6 to 10%, illustrating the typical time-resolution available through optical dating. As noticed above, the OSL ages should, by way of precaution, be considered as maximal ages. However, the consistency with the radiocarbon age does suggest that the optical ages do not significantly overestimate the true age of sediment deposition, and that the OSL clock in these samples was adequately zeroed in the past.

Thus, the lower halves of HAMB3, HAMB1, and HAMIII represent mid-fourth to ca. mid-third millennium BC deposits. Typical cross-stratified coarse sands with occasional clay rip-up clasts visible in the larger exposure at HAMIII suggest that, between ca. 3500 and 2500 BC, the Jaghjagh consisted of a meandering channel with a migrating bed. The evidence indicates a relatively steady stream-flow. Recent anthracological research at the nearby archaeological site Tell Mozan indicated that open oak park woodland was present within this area between ca. 2500 and 2000 BC,[28] unlike the present treeless landscape of today. A denser tree cover, by increasing rainfall interception and inhibiting runoff, may have resulted in steadier perennial flow and raised groundwater tables. Further evidence from northwestern Iraq confirms that raised water tables occurred between 6000 and 3000 BC.[29] Sometime after ca. 2500 BC, perhaps towards the end of the third millennium BC, fine grained clay silt sediments were deposited at the location HAM, which might indicate that the stream bed had changed its location and/or that stream velocities decreased. The abstraction of water for irrigation might have played a role in diminution of stream flow within this rather modest-sized river. Human activity also might have contributed significantly to aggradation of the floodplain. The plain was intensively inhabited during the middle of the third millennium BC,[30] and the delivery of fine sediments in the shape of plough wash could have been greater than the flow could remove. Another possible cause for the deposition of fine-grained sediments at HAM after 2500 BC relates to drier climatic conditions at the end of the third millennium BC. This might have caused a reduced stream-flow,[31] with a possible impact on human societies in this area. It has been intensively debated why settlement evidence is so scarce within this area towards the end of the third millennium BC.[32] In order

---

[28] Deckers and Riehl, The Development of Economy and Environment from the Bronze Age to the Early Iron Age in Northern Syria and the Levant.

[29] Wilkinson and Tucker, Settlement Development in the North Jazira, Iraq.

[30] Lyonnet, La Prospection Archéologique de la Partie Occidentale du Haut-Khabur (Syrie du Nord-Est).

[31] Courty, Le Cadre Paléogéographie des Occupations Humaines dans le Bassin du Haut-Khabur (Syrie du Nord-Est); Bar-Matthews and Kaufman, Middle to Late Holocene (6500 yr. Period) Paleoclimate in the Eastern Mediterranean Region from Stable Isotopic Composition of Speleothems from Soreq Cave, Israel; and Wick et al., Evidence of Lateglacial and Holocene Climatic Change and Human Impact in Eastern Anatolia.

[32] e.g. Dalfes et al., Third Millennium BC Climate Change and Old World Collapse; Peltenburg, From Nucleation to Dispersal.

to gain better insight into the fluvial history and causes for the fining upwards, the upper 2.5 m of the HAMIII section should be absolutely dated.

At section HASIV along the Wadi Khanzir, the poorly sorted gravel deposit situated at a depth of 3.8-3.6 m under the present plain was tentatively dated at 21.1 ± 1.6 ka (Fig. 5; Table II). This age estimate was obtained using only a single aliquot of quartz grains; its reliability is questionable, as one simply cannot decide whether or not the result is an outlier. Additionally, it is most likely that the sample was transported over only a very short distance during a flash flood event. Hence, the sample probably experienced insufficient exposure to daylight for the OSL clock to be completely reset. Therefore, we refrain ourselves from deducing any interpretations from the result obtained for sample GLL 040108. However, several redeposited sherd-like artefacts were found within the poorly sorted gravel. As the earliest pottery in Mesopotamia normally dates to the Ceramic Neolithic (from ca. 6000 BC onwards), this does indeed suggest that the Pleistocene OSL-date is inconsistent. The sherd-like artefacts, however, are not as strong as normal sherds and have a strange brittle and dark organic-rich inner content with a baked outer layer. Whether they do represent sherds or not, this kind of technological advancement in pyrotechnology is usually ascribed to the Holocene. Above the gravel unit, a charcoal fleck from a clay overbank deposit was radiocarbon dated at 8648 ± 58 cal BC. As previously mentioned, this age is possibly an overestimate owing to contamination with older carbon. Moreover, it is unsure whether or not this fleck is in situ or represents redeposited organic material. From about a depth of 3 until 0.9 m within the HASIV section, in situ occupation levels were found, again containing sherd-like artefacts. TL-screening of these sherds yielded age estimates in the range of approximately 4.5 to 2.6 ka BC. Some care is required with the evaluation and interpretation of these TL-estimates because the composition of the dark brittle content on the inner side of the sherd-like artefacts is unknown. Consequently, it is also not clear how it may affect the accuracy of the TL age estimates.

Neither OSL nor radiocarbon yield reliable age results for section HASIV. However, TL-screening of the sherds from the overlying occupation layers indicate that flash flood sediments at the base of section HASIV should have been deposited before ~4.5 ka BC. It is clear that the chronology for this site still needs a lot of improvement before any relation between landscape evolution and settlement can be established. Additional samples are being investigated at the time of writing.

For the FAR section at Farsouk Kabir, a sediment sample taken at a depth of ca. 4 m below the present plain yielded an OSL age of 3.2 ± 0.2 ka (Fig. 7). An OSL-sample and a TL-screened sherd taken from a slightly higher level yielded similar dates. Between 3.55 and 3.70 m the organic matter of a possible redeposited A-horizon was radiocarbon dated at 3584 ± 68 cal. BC. Radiocarbon dates on A-horizons represent maximal ages for the sediment that buries the A-horizon.[33] It also should deliver a date younger than the sediment in which it developed. However, the ^{14}C age is significantly older than the luminescence ages. This could imply that the organic-rich layer represents a redeposited soil, which is supported by the apparent abrupt boundary with the units below. The possibility that the ^{14}C age is an overestimate due to contamination with older fluvially transported carbon prevents us from drawing a more solid conclusion. Moreover, it is well-known that soils are one of the most difficult materials to date using the radiocarbon method. An OSL-sample above the organic rich layer provided a date of 2.6 ± 0.4 ka. Therefore, a period of ca. 700 years of soil formation could have taken place. Between 2.6 ± 0.4 ka and 2.3 ka ± 0.2 ka the plain slowly aggraded. A sherd TL-screened to approximately 2.2 ka seems to be consistent with this, considering the minimum 30% uncertainty on this date. Incipient soil formation on the present day surface confirms that at least some time has passed since the uppermost sediments have been deposited. More precisely, an A-horizon developed and carbonate accumulation took place to a depth of ca. 50 cm. Soil formation studies within this area suggest that this degree of soil formation might correlate to about 2000 years of soil formation.[34]

Our finds at Farsouk Kabir might support the findings of Wilkinson for the southern Wadi Jaghjagh near Tell Brak (Fig. 1).[35] He found that at around 1300-1000 BC a distinct clay-rich upper fill accumulated, and the river developed a deeper and more meandering course. There was still water within the Wadi Jaghjagh and Jarrah, but probably less vigorously than during the Bronze Age. Although this reduced streamflow may result from climatic drying during the first millennium BC (as indicated by isotopic research from stalactites from Soreq Cave in Israel)[36], it may alternatively result from the development of large-scale irrigation systems. Of special interest is the possible redeposited soil

---

[33] Alexandrovskiy and Chichagova, The [14]C Age of Humic Substances in Paleosols.

[34] Wilkinson, Soil Development and Early Land Use in the Jazira Region, Upper Mesopotamia.

[35] Remote Sensing and Geographical Information Systems.

[36] Bar-Matthews and Kaufman, Middle to Late Holocene (6500 yr. Period) Paleoclimate in the Eastern Mediterranean Region from Stable Isotopic Composition of Speleothems from Soreq Cave, Israel.

from section FAR. At this stage of archaeological research, however, it is impossible to investigate the impact of anthropogenic activity on the landscape for this time period because the settlement history is insufficiently known. Indeed, although it is often mentioned that the region was deserted during this period[37] this is contradicted by a recent survey in the Tell Brak area.[38]

Conclusions

TL-screening of sherds is a fast and inexpensive technique, but only has limited precision and accuracy. Comparison of the TL-screening results with those obtained through optical and radiocarbon dating, however, demonstrates the usefulness of the technique for gaining preliminary chronological insight. Where enough material could be extracted from the samples, optical dating allowed refining the preliminary chronology to a precision of typically 6-10%. The main advantages of the method are that the time of sediment deposition is dated, and that it is applicable to situations where organic material, suitable for dating, is lacking. The main potential disadvantage is incomplete resetting of the luminescence clock, which leads to age overestimations. However, in the two case studies where we could apply optical dating it offered stratigraphically consistent results, which were in agreement with archaeological and geomorphological expectations. For the HAM section, the OSL results were also consistent with the ^{14}C age. We therefore conclude that, in the investigated sediments, the OSL clock appears to have been adequately reset. Radiocarbon dating is the more established method and yields the most precise ages. The main limitations to its usefulness, however, concern the possibility of contamination with older carbon and the difficulty in relating the age of the organic sample to the actual date of sediment deposition. Ideal was the situation where in-situ organic material intercalated between fluvial deposits could be dated, as was the case in the HAM section.

The three case studies illustrate the site to site variability in usefulness and reliability of each method. We conclude that the combinatory application of the three techniques offers the most promising and most robust approach in research programs aiming to establish and improve the chronology of fluvial sequences in Syria. We are convinced that this conclusion holds for other areas of the Near East as well.

---

[37] e.g. Lyonnet, Settlement Pattern in the Upper Khabur (N.E. Syria) from the Achaemenids to the Abbasid Period: Methods and Preliminary Results from a Survey.
[38] Joan Oates, pers. comm., 2006.

The fluvial chronological evidence suggests that the presently dry Jaghjagh was a meandering stream with a relatively steady flow between the mid-fourth to mid-third century BC. Sometime after the mid-third millennium BC, possibly towards the end of the third millennium BC, stream velocities decreased in the investigated sequences. This might relate to climatic drying at the end of the third millennium BC. Further OSL-dating will make it possible to establish whether or not the sequences support other evidence of drier climatic conditions. This, in turn, might then contribute to the discussion on the impact of climatic drying on human societies. The investigated Khanzir sediments reflect more the flashy intermittent regime of this stream – like it still is today – with flash flood evidence pre-dating ca. the mid-fifth millennium BC. Further dating is necessary in order to correlate it with the settlement history. Near Farsouk Kabir along the Jarrah, organic rich soil sediments were probably deposited at ~1300 BC. However, we cannot rule out the alternative possibility that a phase of soil formation and/or river incision took place between ca. 1300 and 600 BC, which might correlate to climatic drying. Between about 600 and 300 BC clay sedimented at Farsouk Kabir. At this stage of our investigation it is impossible to relate this phase of landscape development to anthropogenic activity, since little is known about the settlement history and economy for this period.

Acknowledgements

Research and fieldwork was possible thanks to a DFG-post-doctoral fellowship in the Graduate College "Anatolia and its Neighbours" and a position in the project "Die Entwicklung von Wirtschaft und Umwelt zur Spätbronzezeit bis zur frühen Eisenzeit in Nordsyrien (ca. 1500-900 (600) BC)" under the direction of Simone Riehl (Strukturfonds of the University of Tübingen). The project is part of the Tell Mozan excavations under the direction of Peter Pfälzner, Georgio Buccellati and Marylin Kelly-Buccellati. Our sincere thanks also go to the Directorate General of Antiquities and Museums, Syria, who kindly permitted the survey and allowed export of sediment and sherd samples. Many thanks are also due to the Belgische Stichting Roeping to support this vocational project. P. Grootes from the Leibniz Laboratory in Kiel dated the radiocarbon samples. D. Vandenberghe wishes to thank N. Seelen and J. Temmerman for their assistance with the sample preparation for luminescence analysis, J.-P. Buylaert for stimulating discussions, and the Fund for Scientific research – Flanders (FWO – Vlaanderen) for partial financial support.

References

Abrogast, A.F. and W.C. Johnson. 'Climatic Implications of the Late Quaternary Alluvial Record of a Small Drainage Basin in the Central Great Plains.' *Quaternary Research* 41 (1994): 298-305.

Adamiec, G. and M.J. Aitken. 'Dose-Rate Conversion Factors: Update.' *Ancient TL* 16 (1998): 37-50.

Aitken, M.J. *Thermoluminescence Dating.* London: Academic Press, 1985.

—. *An Introduction to Optical Dating.* Oxford: Oxford University Press, 1998.

Alexandrovskiy, A. and O.A. Chichagova. 'The ^{14}C Age of Humic Substances in Paleosols.' *Radiocarbon* 40, no. 2 (1998): 991-97.

Bar-Matthews, M. and A. Kaufman. 'Middle to Late Holocene (6,500 yr. Period) Paleoclimate in the Eastern Mediterranean Region from Stable Isotopic Composition of Speleothems from Soreq Cave, Israel.' In *Water, Environment and Society in Times of Climatic Change*, edited by A.S. Issar and N. Brown, 203-14. Dordrecht: Kluwer Academic Publishers, 1998.

Besonen, M and M. Cremaschi, *Geomorphological Field Survey Report. Tell Leilan, June 2002.*
URL: research.yale.edu/leilan/geomorph/index.html, 2002.

Bøtter-Jensen, L., L.E. Andersen, G.A.T. Duller and A.S. Murray. 'Developments in Radiation, Stimulation and Observation Facilities in Luminescence Measurements.' *Radiation Measurements* 37 (2003): 535-41.

Courty, M.A. 'Le Cadre Paléogéographie des Occupations Humaines dans le Bassin du Haut-Khabur (Syrie du Nord-Est). Premier Résultats.' *Paléorient* 20, no. 1 (1994): 21-55.

Dalfes, H.N., G. Kukla and H. Weiss, eds. *Third Millennium BC Climate Change and Old World Collapse* (Global Environmental Change 49). Heidelberg: Springer, 1997.

Deckers, K. and S. Riehl. 'The Development of Economy and Environment from the Bronze Age to the Early Iron Age in Northern Syria and the Levant. A Case-Study from the Upper Khabur Region.' *Antiquity* 78, no. 302 (2004): project gallery.

Deckers, K., D.C.W. Sanderson and J.Q.C. Spencer. 'Thermoluminescence Screening of Non-Diagnostic Sherds from Stream Sediments to Obtain a Preliminary Alluvial Chronology: An Example from Cyprus.' *Geoarchaeology: An International Journal* 20, no. 1 (2005): 67-77.

Frechen, M., U. Schweitzer and A. Zander. 'Improvements in sample preparation for the fine grain technique.' *Ancient TL* 14 (1996): 15-7.

French, C. *Geoarchaeology in Action. Studies in Soil Micromorphology and Landscape Evolution.* New York: Routledge, 2003.

Hossain, S.M. *A Critical Comparison and Evaluation of Methods for the Annual Radiation Dose Determination in the Luminescence Dating of Sediments.* Ph.D. Thesis, Ghent University, Ghent, 2003.

Kerbe, J. *Climat, Hydrologie et Aménagements Hydro-agricoles de Syrie.* Talence: University of Bordeaux Press, 1987.

Lewin, J., M.G. Macklin and J.C. Woodward. 'Mediterranean Quaternary river environments – some future research needs.' In *Mediterranean Quaternary River Environments*, edited by J. Lewin, M.G. Macklin and J.C. Woodward, 283-84. Rotterdam: Elsevier, 1995.

Lyonnet, B. 'Settlement Pattern in the Upper Khabur (N.E. Syria) from the Achaemenids to the Abbasid Period: Methods and Preliminary Results from a Survey.' In *Continuity and Change in Northern Mesopotamia from the Hellenistic to the Early Islamic period*, edited by K. Bartl and R. Hauser, 149-354. Berlin: Reimer, 1996.

—. 'La Prospection Archéologique de la Partie Occidentale du Haut-Khabur (Syrie du Nord-Est): Méthodes, Résultats et Questions autour de l'Occupation aux IIIe et Iie Millénaires av. n. E.' In *Mari et les hourites*, edited by J.-M. Paris : ERC, 1998.

Macklin, M.G. ,Holocene River Alluviation in Britain.' *Zeitschrift für Geomorphologie. Supplement Bände* 88 (1993): 109-22.

Mejdahl, V. 'Thermoluminescence Dating: Beta-Dose Attenuation in Quartz Grains.' *Archaeometry* 21 (1979): 61-72.

Meijer, D.J.W. *A Survey in Northeastern Syria.* Istanbul: Nederlands Historisch-Archeologisch Instituut, 1986.

Murray, A.S and A.G. Wintle. 'Luminescence Dating of Quartz using an Improved Single-Aliquot Regenerative-Dose Protocol.' *Radiation Measurements* 32 (2000): 57-73.

Murray, A.S and A.G. Wintle. 'The Single Aliquot Regenerative Dose Protocol: Potential for Improvements in Reliability.' *Radiation Measurements* 37 (2003): 377-81.

Nützel, W. 'Eine Antike Flußverbindung zwischen dem Oberen Khabur-Gebiet und dem Tigris.' *Mitteilungen des Deutschen Orient Gesellschaft* 124 (1992): 87-95.

Olley, J.M., A. Murray and R.G. Roberts. 'The Effects of Disequilibria in the Uranium and Thorium Decay Chains on Burial Dose Rates in Fluvial Sediments.' *Quaternary Science Reviews (Quaternary Geochronology)* 15 (1996): 751-60.

Peltenburg, E. 'From Nucleation to Dispersal. Late Third millennium BC Settlement Pattern Transformations in the Near East and Aegean.' In *La Djéziré et l'Euphrate syriens des le Protohistoire à la fin du Ier millénaire av. J.-C. Tendences dans l'Interprétation des Données Nouvelles*, edited by O. Rouault and M. Wälfer, *Subartu* 7 (2000): 183-206.

Prescott, J.R. and J.T. Hutton. 'Cosmic Ray Contributions to Dose Rates for Luminescence and ESR Dating: Large Depths and Long-Term Time Variations.' *Radiation Measurements* 23 (1994): 497-500.

Rees-Jones, J. and M.S. Tite. 'Optical Dating Results for British Archaeological Sediments.' *Archaeometry* 36 (1997): 177-87.

Rösner, U. *Zur quartären Landschaftsentwicklung in den Trockengebieten Syriens*. Berlin: Gebrüder Borntraeger, 1995.

Stuiver, M. and H.A. Pollach. 'Discussion Reporting of ^{14}C Data.' *Radiocarbon* 19, no. 3 (1977): 355-63.

Vandenberghe, D. *Investigation of the Optically Stimulated Luminescence Dating Method for Application to Young Geological Sediments*. PhD. Thesis, University of Ghent, 2004.

Vandenberghe, D., C. Kasse, S.M. Hossain,, F. De Corte, P. Van den haute, M. Fuchs and A.S. Murray. 'Exploring the Method of Optical Dating and Comparison of Optical and ^{14}C ages of Late Weichselian Coversands in the Southern Netherlands.' *Journal of Quaternary Science* 19 (2004): 73-86.

Wäfler, M. 'The Excavations at Tell Hamidi.' In *Tall al-Hamidiya 2*, edited by S. Eichler and M. Wäfler, Orbis Biblicus et Orientalis 6, 219-28. Freiburg: Vandenhoeck & Ruprecht Göttingen, 1990.

—. *Tall al-Hamidiya 4. Vorbericht 1988-2001*. Orbis Biblicus et Orientalis 21. Freiburg: Vandenhoeck & Ruprecht Göttingen, 2001.

Waters, M.R. and C.V. Haynes. 'Late Quaternary Arroyo Formation and Climate Change in the American Southwest.' *Geology* 29 (2001): 399-402.

Wegener, B., O. Jöris and U. Danzeglocke. *Calpal – Cologne Radiocarbon Calibration and Palaeoclimate Research Package*. URL: www.calpal.de, 2005

Wick, L., G. Lemcke and M. Sturm. 'Evidence of Lateglacial and Holocene Climatic Change and Human Impact in Eastern Anatolia: High-Resolution Pollen, Charcoal, Isotopic and Geochemical Records from the Laminated Sediments of Lake Van, Turkey.' *The Holocene* 13, no. 5 (2003): 665-75.

Wilkinson, T.J. 'Soil Development and Early Land Use in the Jazira region, Upper Mesopotamia.' *World Archaeology* 22, no. 1 (1990): 87-103.

—. *Remote Sensing and Geographical Information Systems. 1999-2000 Annual report*. URL: www-oi.uchicago.edu/OI/AR/99-00/99-00_Jazira.html.

—. 'Physical and Cultural Landscapes of the Hamoukar Area.' *Akkadica* 123 (2002): 89-103.

Wilkinson, T.J. and D.J. Tucker. *Settlement Development in the North Jazira, Iraq. A study of the Archaeological Landscape*. Warminster: Aris Phillips, 1995.

Appendix

section	lab code	δ13C (‰)	conventional	calibrated
HAM	KIA 24908	-25.98 ± 0.06	4665 ± 25 BP	3449 ± 49 cal BC
HASIV	KIA 24913	-23.03 ± 0.09	9375 ± 45 BP	8660 ± 55 cal BC
FAR	KIA 24912	-23.75 ± 0.12	4790 ± 40 BP	3485 ± 46 cal BC

Table 3-I: Results from ^{14}C AMS dating. Summarized are the δ^{13}C-values, and the conventional and calibrated ^{14}C ages. Uncertainties are 1s.

sample	GLL code	^{238}U (Bq kg^{-1})	^{226}Ra (Bq kg^{-1})	^{210}Pb (Bq kg^{-1})	^{232}Th (Bq kg^{-1})	^{40}K (Bq kg^{-1})
HAMIII OSL4 [a]	040106	10 ± 1	29.2 ± 1.4	15 ± 1	15.4 ± 0.2	149 ± 3
HASIV OSL1 [c]	040108	12 ± 1	19.5 ± 1.4	14 ± 1	9.6 ± 0.2	92 ± 2
HAMIII OSL1	040101	7 ± 1	18.0 ± 1.0	11 ± 1	8.2 ± 0.2	60 ± 1
HAMIII OSL2	040102	14 ± 1	17.6 ± 0.3	14 ± 1	15.6 ± 0.3	152 ± 2
FAR OSL1	040103	33 ± 2	36.9 ± 0.5	32 ± 2	32.5 ± 0.4	379 ± 3
FAR OSL2	040104	24 ± 3	38.8 ± 0.7	30 ± 2	32.8 ± 0.5	393 ± 4
FAR OSL3	040105	26 ± 2	40.0 ± 2.3	30 ± 3	33.8 ± 0.4	395 ± 4
FAR OSL5 [b]	040107	20 ± 2	41.0 ± 2.7	25 ± 2	32.0 ± 0.4	361 ± 3

sample	$F*W$	Dose rate $(Gy\ ka^{-1})$	D_e (Gy)	Dose recovery	Age (ka)
HAMIII OSL4 [a]	0.27	0.96 ± 0.02	5.2 ± 0.2 (11)	1.05 ± 0.01 (3)	5.5 ± 0.4
HASIV OSL1 [c]	0.27	0.72 ± 0.02	15.2 ± 0.4 (1)	-	21.1 ± 1.6
HAMIII OSL1	0.27	0.58 ± 0.01	3.0 ± 0.1 (13)	1.04 ± 0.02 (3)	5.1 ± 0.4
HAMIII OSL2	0.27	1.00 ± 0.01	4.5 ± 0.1 (8)	1.00 ± 0.02 (3)	4.5 ± 0.3
FAR OSL1	0.27	2.45 ± 0.02	8.0 ± 0.2 (37)	1.02 ± 0.02 (9)	3.3 ± 0.2
FAR OSL2	0.27	2.35 ± 0.03	7.7 ± 0.1 (14)	1.02 ± 0.01 (2)	3.3 ± 0.2
FAR OSL3	0.27	2.40 ± 0.04	6.1 ± 0.9 (21)	0.99 ± 0.08 (3)	2.6 ± 0.4
FAR OSL5 [b]	0.24	2.27 ± 0.03	5.2 ± 0.3 (18)	1.02 ± 0.03 (3)	2.3 ± 0.2

Table 3-II (opposite page and above): Shown are the radionuclide concentrations used for dose rate evaluation, the estimates of past water content, the calculated dose rates, the D_e values, the results from the dose recovery experiments, the calculated ages, and the total uncertainties. The uncertainties mentioned with the D_e, dose recovery and dosimetry data are random; the uncertainties on the ages are the overall uncertainties, which include the systematic errors. All uncertainties represent 1s. The number of aliquots used for D_e determination and for the dose recovery tests is given between brackets.
[†]: small regenerated IRSL signals were observed for this sample, in the range of 5-10% of the corresponding regenerated OSL signals. This points at an incomplete elimination of feldspars from the quartz extract. To minimize the contribution from feldspars to the measured luminescence, this sample was analysed by stimulation with infrared light prior to each OSL measurement.

CHAPTER FOUR

LOOKING FOR LBA HARBOURS IN THE SOUTH-WEST AEGEAN AND CENTRAL MEDITERRANEAN: SOME PRELIMINARY REMARKS

VASILIKI IVROU

Introduction

It has become something of a commonplace to talk about the maritime orientation of the Late Bronze Age (LBA) Aegean and how the sea shaped and maybe forced particular attitudes on the culture of that area throughout most of its history. Maritime society is distinguished having a role in trade, communications, contacts and economic and political activities. Nonetheless it is acknowledged here that in order to approach thoroughly past practices in Aegean prehistory, an appreciation of the maritime landscape is essential.

This article will present the results of an initial study into these human-maritime interactions. For the purpose of this article, the area of the Mediterranean to be discussed comprises the SW Aegean and central and southern Italy. The region I am going to focus on is the South Peloponnese, Kythera and West Crete, which form something of a gateway between the East and Central Mediterranean (Fig. 1). The intention is to examine its coastline and the extent to which there are safe anchorages and harbourages that could have supported a maritime exchange network in the Late Bronze Age. The diversity of the landscape across this area with the multiple geotectonic features ranging from extensive alluviation (Helos plain) to uplift (West Crete) as well as the important archaeological sites found within this area (Pylos, Chania) provide us with good examples of the combination of different categories of data and the results that such an approach may produce. This data should form the baseline for further investigation and research on the coastal settlement pattern and the basis on which we should try to understand the thalassocentric character of the Mycenaean era.

For the purposes of this article we will follow the standard chronological terminology for the Mycenaean era defining 1450-1100 BC as the Later Bronze Age.

Fig. 4-1: Map of the area of study: southwestern Aegean and central and southern Italy.

Aims – scope – methodology

In the course of 2005, I conducted a survey of the coastline of West Crete, Kythera, the Messenia and Laconia looking at the coastal archaeological record of the LBA.[1] In presenting some of the results of this survey, I attempt on the one hand to compare them with one case study in Italy and on the other to place them in a wider context regarding the Mycenaean world. For my survey I used GPS, nautical charts and geographical maps, photographs and my own observations on features such as promontories, protected harbours, anchorages, landmarks and seamarks. In this way I gained an appreciation of the local

---

[1] Ivrou and Chalkioti, forthcoming.

maritime landscape, a key element when trying to approach past maritime activities. In pursuit of such insights, a spatial and chronological analysis of the known archaeological sites was prepared consisting of a gazetteer of coastal sites. This set out the sites' locations, setting and chronology.

Geomorphology and archaeology of southwestern Aegean

Many geologists have focused their research interests on the solution of practical and theoretical problems facing archaeologists in the initial recovery of data and subsequent analysis. However, the publication of such geological contributions has most often been limited to appendices in formal excavation reports of a particular project or as short technical reports, often in highly specialised journals. Consequently, a scholar in either of the two disciplines had no general reference work illustrating the wide range of application of geological techniques to archaeology of this particular region for the prehistoric era.[2]

The ultimate goal of many investigations has been to relate archaeological periods to climatic, geomorphic or man-affected changes. The coastal deltaic regions have been more carefully studied as they shed the most light on the nature of geomorphic and possible climatic changes over the past 5000 years. As is evident from these surveys, the distribution of coastal settlements forms a vivid part of the maritime landscape during the Bronze Age. The overall settlement pattern of the time is marked by a rather sudden increase on or near the coasts during the BA period.[3] These changes in settlement patterns enhanced changes in the landscape as well, which are more obvious if compared with later periods. After the Bronze Age, for example, the coasts of Crete were abandoned.[4] Among the factors that can determine the geomorphic configuration of a coast, the local geological setting is likely to dominate; one geological factor may overwhelm other processes. This is particularly so in the complex interplay of physical forces in coastal change over the short term of the Holocene. Since 14000 BP the sea level has risen towards its present position, rapidly at first, then slower ranging from 7.7 m in West Crete to 3 m in Antikythera.[5] The region under study here (Fig. 1) has suffered great changes

---

[2] Rapp et al, Excavations at Nichoria in southwest Greece, 5.

[3] Hope Simpson & Dickinson, Mycenaean Greece, 385.

[4] Moody and Rackham, The environmental and cultural prehistory of the Khania Region of West Crete. Neolithic through LMIII ,197.

[5] Kraft et al. Paleogeographical reconstructions of Aegean archaeological sites, Science 195: 943; Pirazzoli, Uplift of ancient Greek coastal sites: study, methods and results.

due to a number of geomorphological alterations,[6] caused by sea level changes, alluvial episodes and tectonic activities. For these reasons and due to the lack of systematic research along the coasts by archaeologists and geomorphologists, potential man-made harbours in this area have not been identified despite the fact that the archaeological record both on the Greek mainland and on the islands provides evidence for contacts and exchange between the two regions.

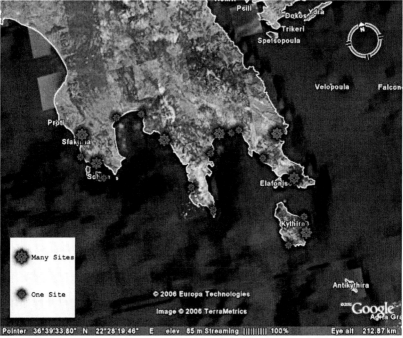

Fig. 4-2: LBA coastal sites Laconia, Messinia, Kythera and West Crete. Site map of the Helos plain and close up photo of Gythion harbour area and Kranae island.

---

[6] Flemming, Holocene eustatic changes and coastal tectonics in the Northeast Mediterranean: implications for models of crustal consumption; Kraft et al. Paleogeographical reconstructions of Aegean archaeological sites, Science 195: 943; Pirazzoli, Uplift of ancient Greek coastal sites: study, methods and results. 237-244; Moody and Rackham, The environmental and cultural prehistory of the Khania Region of West Crete. Neolihtic through LMIII.

The coastline in the southwestern Aegean appears to be quite densely occupied during the LBA (Fig. 2), as is evident mostly from the surface surveys that have been conducted in the area.[7] Favoured locations are small anchorages often near stream or river estuaries, promontories, and seashores protected by small islets sometimes connected with the shore by sandy spits (tomboloi). In studying this coastline, three units can be identified: Messinia/Laconia, Kythera/Antikythera, and West Crete. These units may be geographically closely related and bear broad similarities in their geological background, climatic features and cultural history, all of which have shaped the cultural landscape. They all have however a distinctive character generated by the interconnection of the above-mentioned parameters and the individualities of each particular region. They form a diverse landscape with indented coastlines and mountainous interior.

Nevertheless, with regard to known coastal settlements and bearing in mind the physical topography of the area, the following types of locations selected as "harbour" sites can be distinguished:[8]

- Estuaries of rivers or torrents crossing the coastal plain;
- Peninsulas or promontories that allowed dragging ships on the sandy beach;
- Peninsulas/promontories permitting anchorage on either side depending on the seasonal winds;
- Settlements established along shores with offshore islets.

Some case studies taken from each region are now presented to illustrate the potentials and difficulties that have arisen from my survey.

---

[7] Broodbank, Kythera survey: a preliminary report on the 1998 survey; Cavanagh et al. Continuity and Change in a Greek rural Landscape; the Lakonia Survey; Davis et al., The Pylos Regional Archaeological Project I: Overview and the Archaeological Survey; Hope Simpson and Dickinson, A Gazetteer of Aegean Civilization in the Bronze Age. Vol: I The Mainland and the Islands. Studies in Mediterranean Archaeology. LII; Moody, The environmental and cultural prehistory of the Khania Region of West Crete. Neolihtic through LMIII.

[8] following Chryssoulaki, The imaginary navy of Minoan Crete: Rocky coasts and probable harbours, see also for the Peloponnese: Kalogerakou, Τύποι οικισμών της Πρώιμης Εποχής του Χαλκού στην Πελοπόννησο.

Laconia

The **Helos plain** is an example of an estuary of river or torrents crossing the coastal plain. The settlements around that plain are numerous but mainly small; while they used to be coastal or near the coast, particularly during the Early and Middle Bronze Age, they are now further inland (Fig. 2). There appears to be a hierarchy of settlements into major and subordinate sites according to scale and size.[9] It is probable that the Laconian Gulf during the Bronze Age went further inland to Skala.[10] The present shoreline is relatively straight and sandy.

The most prominent of the settlements appears to be *Ayios Stephanos* which lies on the cross roads of the routes from the Sparta plain (via Krokeai) and from the Gythion coastal strip. Ayios Stephanos, probably a promontory jutting into the sea during the Bronze Age, is a conspicuous rocky limestone hill on the eastern end of a spur projecting into the Eurotas plain, now 20 km from the sea. The prehistoric settlement occupied an area about 160 m in diameter. It was inhabited firstly in EH II, after which there was a break in occupation; it was reoccupied some time in MH and was continuously inhabited from that time until the end of the LH IIIB.[11] *Lapis Lacedaemonius* from the nearby Psephi quarries was probably exported via Ayios Stephanos before the end of the MH.[12] The site may have served as the major port of central Laconia.[13] The size of the settlement and its excellent position commanding the western side of the Helos plain and the sea approaches to the main route inland via the Eurotas valley to the Sparta plain mark it as the most important of the many MH and LH settlements in the plain.[14]

Gythion is an example of currently partially submerged peninsulas that during the LBA could have been used as a sand spit or tombolo connecting the land to a rocky islet. The site, which lies on the NW shore of the Laconian Gulf, is an open anchorage that faces SE. In front of the anchorage, towards the SW there is the islet of Kranae, connected with the mainland today via a bridge, but formerly with a low land bridge (Fig. 2). This small islet together with the promontory of Mavrovouni on the SW, are good landmarks when approaching

---

[9] Hope-Simpson, Mycenaean Greece, 105.

[10] Kraft et al., Paleogeographical reconstructions of Aegean archaeological sites, Fig 11-12.

[11] Hope-Simpson & Dickinson, A Gazetteer of Aegean Civilization in the Bronze Age. Vol: I The Mainland and the Islands, 113.

[12] *Ibid.*, 105.

[13] *Ibid.*, 113.

[14] *Ibid.*, 99.

the harbour during daylight (Fig. 2). There are indications that Gythion was a major centre of the area in Mycenaean times.[15] However, no prehistoric remains have yet been discovered on the acropolis of ancient Gythion on the north edge of the modern town, but this may be due to the overlay of the Classical and later structures on the acropolis slopes. On the islet of Kranae itself, however, several Mycenaean (LH III) sherds, worn and of poor quality, have been identified on the western and central parts, over perhaps half of the surface of the island (which measures about 300 m E-W by 100 m N-S).[16]

Kythera

The landscape formation of Kythera requires specific attitudes towards the sea, as there are very few well-protected anchorage sites and no good harbour. The island has a mainly hilly appearance and therefore provides good landmarks. It is in very close proximity to the Peloponnesian coast and the island of Elafonissos. The west coast of the island is sparsely occupied, and that corresponds to the fact that no suitable anchorage has been found on this side of the island (Fig. 3).

Avlemonas is an example of a peninsula or promontory with adjacent sandy beach onto which ships could be dragged. It is a small anchorage lying in the Bay of Ayios Nikolaos facing SSE and protected by a promontory to the east. The beach on the west side is low and very rocky (Fig. 3a). The river of Skadeia drains into the bay and there has consequently been extensive silting. This area is considered the only well-protected harbour of the island during the Bronze Age.

Kapsali is a natural double harbour on the south of Kythera. Archaeological evidence for the Mycenaean era comes from a tholos tomb near Lioni (Fig. 3b). The harbour is very well protected and is used as the second harbour of the island even today. The site is located at the crossroads from Crete to the Mainland and from East to West Mediterranean. It may have been a potentially high traffic harbour in prehistory. The survey which I conducted on the promontories of the harbour of Kapsali (both inner and outer) brought to light pottery and buildings that need to be investigated further.

---

[15] Skoufopoulos-Stavrolakes, Ancient Gythion, the port of Sparta. History and survey of the submerged remnants.
[16] Hope-Simpson, Mycenaean Greece, 109.

Fig. 4-3: Map of Kythera and Photo (a - upper) of Avlemonas and (b - lower) from Kapsali where one can see the two harbours interior and exterior (as marked by the arrows) (photos by the author).

Fig. 4-4: Map of West Crete showing the area of Chania (1) and the area of Phalasarna (2) on the west coast.

West Crete

Crete, like the rest of the Aegean region, shows much evidence of earlier sea levels differing from the present level.[17] This variation records movements of the height of the land with respect to the shoreline of the western part of Crete and records one of the most important of these sea level changes in the region (Fig. 4).

Kydonia is another example of a peninsula that allowed dragging ships onto the sandy beach. The site overlooks the modern harbour of Chania, lying on the southeast shore of the open north-facing Gulf of Chania (Fig. 5). To the east it looks to the Akrotiri peninsula, while on the west it faces the islet of Thodorou. The waters are relatively shallow. The area is unprotected from the North winds, and the approach to the harbour is difficult when there are strong onshore winds.[18] The geological features are very difficult to trace because the area has been almost continuously occupied during the last 5000 years. Architecture of almost all periods from Final Neolithic till the present day can be found at the site. Most of what is exposed however belongs to the LM IB period, *ca.* 1450 BC. In the Splanzia quarter, SE of the Kastelli hill, part of a large Neopalatial building has been excavated. After various reconstructions, the building was finally destroyed at the end of LM IB. This is so far the most important building of the Minoan town of Kydonia whose function was either a civic or palatial sanctuary.[19] The commercial nature of this site is indicated by the LBA pottery that is known to have been exported from there.[20]

---

[17] Pirazzoli, Uplift of ancient Greek coastal sites: study, methods and results, 239.

[18] Heikell, Greek waters pilot. A yachtsman's guide to the coasts and islands of Greece, 443.

[19] Andreadakis-Vlazakis, Προϊστορικός οικισμός στα Νοπήγεια Κισσάμου, 1004-1008.

[20] Hallager, The Inscribed Stirrup Jars: Implications for Late Minoan IIIB Crete.

Fig. 4-5: View to the north facing anchorages of the site of Chania from Akrotiri to the east of the site (photo by the author).

Phalasarna: The Roman port of Phalasarna was constructed at the base of the Gramvousa peninsula, a large block of Jurassic limestone. The peninsula terminates to the south in a series of low hills, mostly composed of Miocene limestone and marl, part of an ancient graben. This area was uplifted in the fifth or sixth century AD by about seven meters, possibly during a single earthquake. Evidence for this uplift can be seen in the harbour, which is now dry and far above sea level in the floor of the ancient quarries to the south of the town. These quarries must have originally been close to sea level. There are also well-developed notches in the cliffs and raised wave-cut platforms around Cape Kastri. Another old sea level stand can be seen at an altitude of about 15 m.[21]

The site is a classic example of a promontory that overlooks two gulfs on the north side of the Roman port of Phalasarna (Figs. 6-7 see arrows). If we consider that Moody (1997) found traces of a prehistoric shrine on the mountain opposite the site, then we can reconsider the topography of the area for the Mycenaean era. Can we reasonably presume to the existence here of a pattern like that on Kythera at Avlemonas with the settlement and harbour near a fertile coastal plain? Further investigation should explore this hypothesis. Nonetheless the position of the site, next to the Roman port, makes it a very promising one for further investigations. Even if this is not a harbour, it could have been a stopover point.

---

[21] Higgins and Higgins, A geological companion to Greece and the Aegean, 199.

Fig. 4-6: Map of West Crete. The arrow marks the area of Phalasarna.

Fig. 4-7: (a - upper) Phalasarna general photo, (b - lower) close-up of the site showing the Roman port and Mycenaean station (photos by the author).

Central Italy

Passing from the SW Aegean to the Central Mediterranean we can focus on **Vivara** in the Bay of Naples (Fig. 8). This small island is one of the three islands of the Phlegrean Archipelago. The island is part of a volcanic crater and during prehistory was connected to Santa Margerita on Procida. The coastline is very depressed with embayments which continue below the sea level. The island's particular geographical position has made it an ideal point of control for entry into the Bay of Naples and a good outpost toward the Tyrrhenian Sea. The presence of Mycenaean pottery (imported from the Peloponnese) at more than one location on the island indicates that Mycenaeans were evidently using this base in the course of their trading activities in the West. There are three naturally protected harbours. Underwater researches have pointed out Mycenaean ladders cut in the rock that allowed access to the island from three points around it. The only striking difference between these ports and those in the Aegean is that these were naturally well fortified and ladders were used to access the island and its caves. This is a type of port that is not encountered in the southwestern Aegean because the site was not a Mycenaean base;[22] it was merely visited by Mycenaeans on numerous occasions.

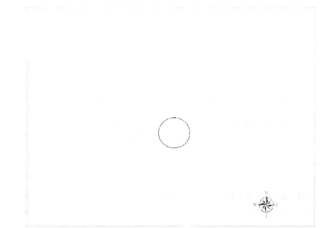

Fig. 4-8: Map of Italy, showing the area of Vivara in the Bay of Naples.

Conclusions

The coastal settlements presented above are part of a landscape study which aims to examine how different cultural systems interacted with broadly similar environments, resulting in human responses that show marked variations in time and space. There are many ways in which human communities can choose to exploit their landscapes depending upon a wide range of variables within natural and cultural environments. Besides changing settlement patterns through time there is differentiation in the utilization of maritime landscapes. Not all coastal sites have the same degree of maritime interaction. The coastal location by itself does not indicate that people drew the basis of their subsistence from the sea (see, for example, the case of Helos plain). Most of the fertile agricultural land in this area is confined to narrow coastal plains, which promotes the distribution

---

[22] Marazzi and Mocchegianni-Carpano, VIVARA: un'isola al centro della istoria, 92.

of settlements in such areas. There are coastal sites involved with the sea circumstantially as a complement to their subsistence strategies (fishing, for example), and others that have a closer and more intense relation to it or are part of sea networks in varying degrees (Chania).

Regarding the future of this preliminary research, there is first and foremost a need for a systematic coastal and underwater survey of submerged sites and harbours in the areas I have discussed. This will enable the reconstruction to be made of sea-level changes during the past two millennia in the southwestern Aegean and Central Mediterranean, with a particular focus on the geotectonic and alluvial depositions along the coast as well as the fertile integration of the archaeological data. When that information has been gathered it will be possible to tackle questions concerning the nature of LBA harbours and coastal interaction, the overall concept of harbour sites and what we regard as a LBA harbour. It will also be possible to anticipate the questions relating to how human communities decided to increase the intensity with which they exploited one particular type of environment - coastal - during the Mycenaean era. Only then will we be able to understand the maritime character of these sites and discuss issues of maritime cultural landscape and how it was conceptualized during the Mycenaean era.

Acknowledgements

I am mostly grateful to my supervisor Dr. R. E. Jones for his support and help during my research and for the fruitful discussions we have had.

References

Andreadakis-Vlazakis, M. (Ανδρεαδάκη-Βλαζάκη, M.). 'Προϊστορικός οικισμός στα Νοπήγεια Κισσάμου.' *Κρητική Εστία* 5 (1997): 11-45.

Broodbank, C. 'Kythera survey: a preliminary report on the 1998 survey.' *Ann. British School at Athens* 94 (1990): 191-214.

Cavanagh, W., J. Crouwel, R.W.W. Catling and G. Shipley. *Continuity and Change in a Greek rural Landscape; the Lakonia Survey.* British School at Athens Supplementary vol. 26, 2000.

Chryssoulaki, S. 'The imaginary navy of Minoan Crete: Rocky coasts and probable harbours.' In *Emporia in the Central and Eastern Mediterranean,* edited by R. Laffineur and E. Creco, *Aegaeum* 25, Proceedings of the 10th International Aegean Conference 14-18 April 2004, 77-90. Athens, 2005.

Davis J.L., S.E. Alcock, J. Bennet, Y. Lolos, C.W. Shelmerdine and E. Zangger. 'The Pylos Regional Archaeological Project I: Overview and the Archaeological Survey.' *Hesperia* 68, no. 3 (1997): 391-494.

Hallager, E. *The Master Impression. A Clay Sealing from the Greek-Swedish Excavations at Kastelli, Khania, Studies in Mediterranean Archaeology*, LXIX, Goteborg: Paul Astroms Forlag, 1985.

—. 'The Inscribed Stirrup Jars: Implications for Late Minoan IIIB Crete.' *Amercian Journal of Archaeology* 91 (1987): 171-190.

Heikell, R. *Greek waters pilot. A yachtsman's guide to the coasts and islands of Greece*. St Ives: Imray Laurie Norie and Wilson Ltd, 1992.

Higgins, R.A. and M.D. Higgins. *A geological companion to Greece and the Aegean*. New York: Cornell University Press, 1996.

Hope Simpson, R. *Mycenaean Greece*. Park Ridge: Noyes Press, 1981.

Hope Simpson, R. and O.T.P.K. Dickinson. *A Gazetteer of Aegean Civilization in the Bronze Age. Vol: I The Mainland and the Islands.* Studies in Mediterranean Archaeology LII, Göteborg: Paul Åströms Forlag, 1979.

Flemming, N.C. 'Holocene eustatic changes and coastal tectonics in the Northeast Mediterranean: implications for models of crustal consumption.' *Philosophical Transactions of the Royal society of London. Series A, Mathematical and Physical Sciences* 289, no. 1362 (1978): 405-458.

Ivrou, V. and C. Chalkioti, forthcoming. 'Maritime Cultural Landscapes: Views from the Bronze Age Aegean.' Proceedings of the *TROPIS IX, 9th International Symposium on Ship Construction in Antiquity,* (Ay. Napa – Cyprus 25-30 August 2005).

Kalogerakou, P.P. (Καλογεράκου, Π. Π.). 'Τύποι οικισμών της Πρώιμης Εποχής του Χαλκού στην Πελοπόννησο.' *Πελοποννησιακά: Πρακτικά Ε΄ Διεθνούς Συνεδρίου Πελοποννησιακών Σπουδών.* Άργος-Ναύπλιο 6-10 Σεπτεμβρίου 1995. Αθήνα, 125-141, 1996-1997.

Kraft J.C., S.E. Aschenbrenner and G.J. Rapp. 'Paleogeographical reconstructions of Aegean archaeological sites.' *Science* 195 (1977): 941-7.

Kraft, J.C., M. Kayan and S.E. Ashenbrenner. 'Geological studies of coastal change applied to archaeological sites.' In *Archaeological Geology*, edited by G. Rapp and J.A. Gifford, 57-84. New Haven and London, 1985.

Marazzi, M. and C. Mocchegianni-Carpano. *VIVARA: un'isola al centro della istoria*. Napoli, 2000.

Moody, J.A. 'The environmental and cultural prehistory of the Khania Region of West Crete. Neolihtic through LMIII.' PhD diss., University of Minnesota, 1987.

Moody, J.A. and O. Rackham. *The making of the Cretan Landscape*. Manchester and New York: Manchester University Press, 1996.

Pirazzoli, P. 'Uplift of ancient Greek coastal sites: study, methods and results.' In *Archaeoseismology. A joint publication by Institute for Geology and Mineral Exploration and British School at Athens.* Fitch Laboratory Occasional paper 7, edited by S. Stiros and R. Jones, 237-244. Exeter: Short Run Press, 1996.

Rapp, G. Jr. and S. Aschenbrenner, eds. *Excavations at Nichoria in southwest Greece. Volume 1: Site, Environs and Techniques.* Minneapolis: University of Minnesota Press, 1978.

Scoufopoulos-Stavrolakes, N. 'Ancient Gythion, the port of Sparta. History and survey of the submerged remnants.' In *Harbour archaeology,* edited by Raban, A., 23-37. Oxford: BAR International Series 257, 1985.

CHAPTER FIVE

UNRAVELLING ANCIENT STONE QUARRY LANDSCAPES IN THE EASTERN MEDITERRANEAN: THREE EGYPTIAN CASE STUDIES

TOM HELDAL, ELIZABETH G. BLOXAM AND PER STOREMYR

Introduction

The acquisition of stone for tools, monuments, construction and objects of art has been an important activity throughout the history of mankind, and traces of such exploitation are found literally all over the Mediterranean region. Campaigns to acquire stone in antiquity, from thousands of local, regional and distant quarries were partly statements of an elite to key places of primary production of prestigious stone, but also as a means for obtaining raw material for everyday construction and utilitarian products. The archaeological record at quarry sites comprises rare evidence of settlements, roads, harbours, extraction sites, tool marks, ceramics and inscriptions, which collectively constitute an "ancient quarry landscape". These landscapes can not only enhance our understanding of technological development and the lives of the non-elite in antiquity, but also provide rare insights into the political and ideological ambitions of an elite that drove resource exploitation to such heights.[1] In some instances, these landscapes have significantly contributed to physically and aesthetically shaping the modern landscape and may comprise important landmarks.[2]

---

[1] Peacock, Rome in the Desert: A Symbol of Power; Bloxam, The Organisation, Transportation and Logistics of Hard Stone Quarrying in the Egyptian Old Kingdom: A Comparative Study; Bloxam, Storemyr and Heldal, Hard Stone Quarrying in the Egyptian Old Kingdom (3rd Millennium BC): Rethinking the Social Organisation.
[2] Stanier, Stone Quarry Landscapes.

Research of ancient quarry sites, from both a geological and archaeological perspective, is still a relatively new area of study, in Egypt, pioneered and furthered by scientists such as Engelbach[3], Röder[4], Klemm and Klemm[5], Harrell[6] and Aston et al.[7]. Most studies have focused on stone and quarry characterisation and interpretation of extraction technologies, and only recently broader surveys and excavations have been carried out. The most comprehensive studies have been undertaken in the large Roman quarry landscapes in the Eastern Desert.[8] Similar studies of Pharaonic period quarrying, particularly during the third millennium BC, have been undertaken at the quarry sites of Widan el-Faras in the Faiyum, Chephren's Quarry, southern Egypt and the Aswan West Bank quarries (see below). Such studies have added significantly to our understanding of stone production, logistics and aspects of the social context of these operations. Yet, conceptualising these sites within broader aspects of landscape studies and their recognition as major heritage sites is still in its infancy. Moreover, for the majority of lay people, such landscapes remain visually and conceptually obscure.

The failure to recognise ancient quarry landscapes as constituting major heritage sites has also made them largely invisible to national and local authorities. Hence, the majority still remain undocumented, unregistered and, with a few exceptions, legally unprotected as archaeological sites. As a consequence, these landscapes are disappearing at an alarming rate, from actions such as modern development projects and urban expansion, modern quarrying operations, looting, vandalism and tourist pressure, natural hazards and weathering.[9]

---

[3] Engelbach, The Quarries of the Western Nubian Desert. A Preliminary Report; Engelbach, The Quarries of the Western Nubian Desert and the Ancient Road to Tushka.

[4] Röder, Zur Steinbrüchgeschichte des Rosengranits von Assuan.

[5] Klemm and Klemm, Steine und Steinbrüche im Alten Ägypten.

[6] Harrell, Brown and Masoud, Survey of ancient Egyptian quarries; Harrell, Archaeological Geology in Ancient Egypt.

[7] Aston, Harrell and Shaw, Stones (Chap. 2) in Ancient Egyptian Materials and Technology

[8] Peacock and Maxfield, Survey and Excavation Mons Claudianus 1987-1993, 1, Topography & Quarries; Maxfield and Peacock, The Roman Imperial Quarries Survey and Excavation at Mons Porphyrites 1994-1998. Vol. I: Topography and Quarries.

[9] Storemyr and Heldal, Ancient stone quarries: vulnerable archaeological sites threatened by modern development.

Ancient quarries and the landscape perspective

As in modern quarry areas, quarrying in ancient periods could influence large areas of land, sometimes counting tens and even hundreds of square kilometres, reshaping the natural landscape considerably and leaving remnants of roads, settlements, workshops and other signs of human activity, directly or indirectly linked to the extraction of stone. Hence, in addition to being "archaeological sites", these areas are "industrial landscapes" that have certain features in common, and that can be better understood using this perspective. However, there are also major differences in between them; some may be closely associated to the construction of a town, representing local sources of raw material gradually being obliterated and hidden under the expanding town itself. In such cases, the quarrying represents a limited stage within the continuous development of an urban landscape. Others are preserved as "frozen" quarry landscapes, displaying one or few campaigns of exploiting prestigious stone in remote areas. Still others may have developed over thousands of years, displaying continuous extraction from prehistory to the present time. Hence, there are important differences related to the context in which the quarrying took place and its relation to other human activities; was it the need of readily available construction materials, trade or search for prestige qualities that were the driving forces?

Quarries are situated in geological resources of specific value and in order to understand the process of stone exploitation, knowledge of these resources, their geometry and quality, is essential. The geological landscape forms the background of any quarry landscape, where the distribution of the exploitable rocks and the morphology define the framework from which the human made features evolve. The meeting between quarrying technology, human organisation and geology creates unique landscapes.

Stone acquisition may be viewed from a purely technical perspective - or not. Could quarrying of stone have been initiated by or associated with features of symbolic or religious nature? Could, in fact, quarry landscapes have ritual dimensions leaving imprints not obviously understandable from a technical extraction point of view? For instance, burials in quarries, rock art and inscriptions should not necessarily be viewed isolated from the stone acquisition, indeed there might be connections related to past perceptions of the landscape and the natural resources within them, such meanings being extremely difficult to access in the present. Due to the fact that most quarry landscapes are complex and can be interpreted from different angles, the need for multi-disciplinary approaches cannot be overestimated. This complexity will be illustrated with three examples from Egypt.

Chephren's Quarry: prestige stone acquisition in the Old Kingdom

Chephren's Quarry is one of the world's oldest hard-stone quarries. It is situated in the easternmost part of the Sahara - covering nearly 100 km^2 of flat, hyper-arid desert, some 60 km west of Lake Nasser (river Nile) and the famous Abu Simbel temple in the extreme south of Egypt. In the third and fourth millennium BC, the quarry was used for extraction of stone for now world-famous sculptures and thousands of smaller funerary objects, especially vessels (Fig. 1). Engelbach[10] and Murray[11] made the first archaeological and geological investigations of Chephren's Quarry in the 1930's. More recent geoarchaeological research was undertaken by Harrell and Brown[12], and archaeological/geological survey and excavation was undertaken between 1997 and 2004 directed by Dr. Ian Shaw.[13]

Chephren's Quarry is situated within a complex of Precambrian, metamorphic igneous rocks, occurring as a "window" where younger rocks have been removed by erosion (Fig. 2). The rock type subjected to quarrying is a light bluish, greyish to white gneiss with dark bands and spots - referred to as the "Chephren Gneiss".[14] It is predominantly composed of plagioclase feldspar (light coloured) and amphibole (dark coloured). Chephren Gneiss occurs as large and small inclusions in granitic rocks, resulting in a highly irregular outcrop pattern, and causing a similarly uneven and scattered distribution of quarries. Almost all the outcrops of Chephren Gneiss have been exploited to some degree, and a total of 665 small and large quarries have been mapped (Fig. 2).

---

[10] *Ibid.*

[11] Murray, The Road to Chephren's Quarries.

[12] Harrell and Brown, Chephren's Quarry in the Nubian Desert of Egypt; Shaw and Bloxam, Survey and Excavation at the Ancient Pharaonic Gneiss Quarrying Site of Gebel el-Asr, Lower Nubia.

[13] Shaw and Bloxam, Survey and Excavation at the Ancient Pharaonic Gneiss Quarrying Site of Gebel el-Asr, Lower Nubia; Bloxam, Transportation of Quarried Hard Stone from Lower Nubia to Giza during the Egyptain Old Kingdom; Bloxam, The Organisation, Transportation and Logistics of Hard Stone Quarrying in the Egyptian Old Kingdom: A Comparative Study; Bloxam, The Organisation and Mobilisation of Old Kingdom Quarry Labour Forces at Chephren's Quarry (Gebel el-Asr) Lower Nubia; Storemyr, Bloxam, Heldal, and Salem, Survey at Chephren's Quarry, Gebel el-Asr, Lower Nubia 2002; Shaw and Heldal, Rescue work in the Khafra Quarries at Gebel el-Asr; Heldal, Storemyr, Bloxam, Shaw, and Salem, GPS and GIS Methodology in the Mapping of Chephren's Quarry, Upper Egypt: A Significant Tool for Documentation and Interpretation of the Site.

[14] Harrell and Brown, Chephren's Quarry in the Nubian Desert of Egypt.

Fig. 5-1: Objects made of Chephren Gneiss. Life-size statue of King Chephren (left) and vessel (right).

The quarrying of the Chephren Gneiss has uniformly targeted loose boulders of gneiss on the terrain surface, formed by in situ, spheroidal weathering over long periods of time. Such boulder landscapes are common in siliceous rocks in the region, and before the quarrying started the terrain must have been covered with clusters of rounded gneiss boulders. The gneiss boulders were worked with stone hammers and axes from local sources, and also fire-setting was partially applied in the rough shaping of blocks. Essentially, the quarrying process transformed the rounded boulders into heaps of waste-rock, most of them forming circular heaps around the space where the blocks were situated (Fig. 3).

Thus, as seen from above, e.g. using a high-resolution satellite image, the quarries resemble craters. In addition to the extraction sites themselves, the quarry area comprises ramps for loading blocks, small camps and shelters, wells, cairns and other features related to the logistical side of quarrying and maintenance of the labour force. Of particular value for the interpretation of the individual quarries are semi-finished products, such as vessel-"blanks" (Fig. 4) and finely worked statue blocks (Fig. 5).

Chephren Gneiss was a prestigious stone in the Old Kingdom. Firstly, the rock is of particularly good quality for carving and sculpturing, secondly, the aesthetical appearance is attractive. Consequently, Chephren Gneiss combines the hardness and durability of granite with the beauty of marble. Evidence from the consumption record suggests that the quarrying started as early as the Late Neolithic.[15] However, evidence of consumption and from the archaeological record in the quarries, implies that exploitation peaked between the third and fourth Dynasties of the Old Kingdom (ca. 2650-2465 BC), for both vessels and statue blocks. Predominantly, the quarrying seems to have been organised as

---

[15] Bloxam, The Organisation, Transportation and Logistics of Hard Stone Quarrying in the Egyptian Old Kingdom: A Comparative Study.

short-lived campaigns for specific purposes (i.e. Chephren statues), as there is no evidence of permanent settlements in the area. It remains unknown if there ever existed a more permanent presence associated with vessel-production and trade.

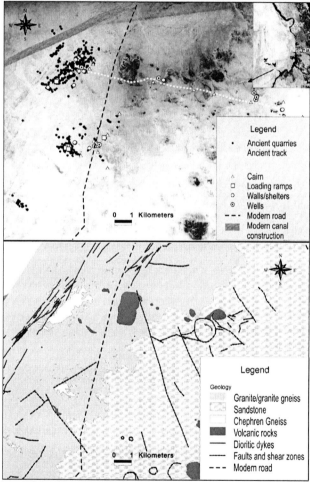

Fig. 5-2: Maps of the Chephren Quarry landscape. Top; overview of the ancient quarries and related infrastructure on satellite image. Below; geological map.

Fig. 5-3: Three examples of individual quarries at Chephren's Quarry. Very small "crater-like" extraction site (top), small extraction (middle) and part of spoil heaps and work areas in a larger quarry (below).

Fig. 5-4: Collection of vessel blanks at Chephren's Quarry. Scale = 1 m.

The uniqueness of Chephren's Quarry is related to the fact that it presents, together with Widan el-Faras (see below), the earliest evidence of prestigious stone acquisition from remote areas (outside the Nile Valley) in Antiquity, and (until the last few years) is extremely well preserved. The site is very rich in archaeological information, and only a minor part of that has been excavated. Of particular value is the evidence of settlements (or lack of such) sustaining only small groups of workers, evidence relating to the logistics/transport of stone, and there are indications that Old Kingdom quarrying took place in much more humid climatic conditions than today, periods of seasonal high rain falls following Holocene (Neolithic) "wet" phase in the Sahara.[16] As a physical landscape, the site may look "un-spectacular" at first sight, but when compiling the spatial distribution of quarries and ancient infrastructure, it reveals one of the supposedly largest industrial landscapes of Early Antiquity in the world. Unfortunately, the site is severely threatened by the Toshka land reclamation and irrigation project (under construction) and even though proper registration

---

[16] McHugh, Schaber, Breed and McCauley, Neolithic adaptation and the Holocene functioning of Tertiary palaeodrainages in Southern Egypt and Northern Sudan, 33; Pachur, and Hoelzmann, Late Quaternary palaeoecology and palaeoclimates of the Eastern Sahara, 936.

of the site has been done recently, its future as a unique quarry landscape remains unclear.

Fig. 5-5: Worked statue block, showing an asymmetric shape designed to fit the King Chephren statues.

Widan el-Faras basalt quarry: a remote source for the pyramid complexes

Widan el-Faras is located in the northern Faiyum desert, ca. 70 km southwest of Cairo. The basalt quarries are situated along the Gebel Qatrani escarpment and occur as an 8-15 metre thick layer of Cenozoic Basalt flows[17], capping a succession of soft sedimentary rocks. The basalt was used predominantly for pyramid temple construction in the fourth and fifth Dynasty (mortuary temple floors of Khufu, Userkaf, Sahura (Fig. 6) and Nyuserra[18]; but may have a history back to the Predynastic (for basalt vessels). One of the quarries was reopened in the Early Roman period (Fig. 7), probably for statuary.[19] The quarries have been known for more than a century[20], but the

---

[17] Heikal, Hassan, and el-Sheshtawi, The Cenozoic Basalt of Gebel Qatrani, Western Desert, Egypt - As and Example of Continental Tholeiitic Basalt.

[18] Mallory-Greenough, Greenough, and Owen, The Origin and Use of Basalt in Old Kingdom Funerary Temples; Hoffmeier, The Use of Basalt in Floors of Old Kingdom Pyramid Temples; Bloxam and Storemyr, Old Kingdom basalt quarrying activities at Widan el-Faras, Northern Faiyum Desert.

[19] Storemyr, Heldal, Bloxam and Harrell, New Evidence of Small-Scale Roman Basalt Quarrying in Egypt.

actual extraction areas and parts of the infrastructure were discovered by Harrell and Bown.[21] Their interpretations were brought further with detailed surveys by Bloxam and Storemyr in 2001[22] under the aegis of the Supreme Council of Antiquity (SCA). Thus, a more comprehensive picture has emerged, not only of the quarries themselves, but also of unique features related to transportation of the stone and organisation of the quarrying operations, such as roads, settlements, block storage areas and harbour facilities. The basalt blocks were taken from the quarries on the escarpment down to the plain on the southeast side immediately below, where they were collected for further overland transport to the Faiyum Depression and ancient shores of Lake Moeris (for a description of Lake Moeris, see e.g. Caton Thompson and Gardner.[23] The eleven kilometre paved road between the quarries and the ancient harbour (Figs. 8 and 9) is one of the most prominent and unique features of this quarry landscape, and is believed to be the oldest preserved paved road in the world. The use of the basalt came to a halt by the end of the fifth Dynasty, probably due to declining Nile floods, thus the basalt quarries may also be viewed as an indicator of climatic change during the Old Kingdom.

Until recently, the quarry landscape was virtually undisturbed, except for the intensive weathering of the basalt, which during 4500 years has made many of the quarry faces and quarried basalt blocks almost unrecognisable. Modern basalt quarrying has also contributed to the rapid disappearance of the ancient quarries, many are now completely destroyed. Furthermore, the rapid increase in desert tourism has put the site at risk, especially by 4WD vehicle traffic along and close to the ancient road.[24] The basalt quarries and the remaining infrastructure are situated within the Lake Qarun Nature Reserve. At the time of writing, this area has been proposed by UNESCO as an extension to the World Heritage Site of the nearby "Whale Valley", which was recently inscribed a World Heritage Site (WHS), primarily due to unique fossil locations. There are plans for integrating the basalt quarries into this extended WHS.

---

[20] Beadnell, The Topography and Geology of the Fayum Province of Egypt.

[21] Harrell and Bown, An Old Kingdom Basalt Quarry at Widan el-Faras and the Quarry Road to Lake Moeris.

[22] Bloxam and Storemyr, Old Kingdom basalt quarrying activities at Widan el-Faras, Northern Faiyum Desert; Bloxam *Ibid.*

[23] Caton-Thompson and Gardner, The Desert Fayum.

[24] Storemyr, Heldal, Bloxam, and Harrell, Widan el-Faras ancient quarry landscape, Northern Faiyum Desert, Egypt: Site description, historical significance and current destruction.

Fig. 5-6: Basalt floor, Sahura pyramid complex.

Fig. 5-7: Quarry and spoil heap located at the escarpment of Gebel Qatrani, Widan el-Faras in the background.

The uniqueness of the Widan el-Faras quarry landscape is neither related to the actual quarry traces, which are highly weathered, nor to its size. The most prominent and striking impression is given by its setting in a spectacular geological landscape[25] and that it displays the whole organisation of an Old Kingdom remote quarrying operation, topped by the transport system. Moreover, this quarry landscape represents a marker of important events in the development of technologies; the oldest paved road in the world was constructed for this exploitation, and the basalt floors in the pyramid complexes display the oldest known evidence of sawing large blocks of hard stone.[26]

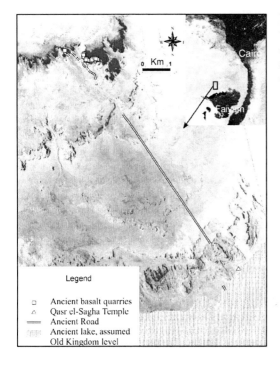

Fig. 5-8: Satellite photo of the Widan el-Faras basalt quarries (white squares) and the road to the ancient shores of Lake Moeris.

---

[25] Bown and Kraus, Geology and paleoenvironment of the Oligocene Jebel Qatrani Formation and adjacent rocks, Fayum Depression, Egypt.
[26] Moores, Evidence for Use of a Stone-Cutting Drag Saw by the Fourth Dynasty Egyptians.

Fig. 5-9: The paved, ancient road passing through a basalt block storage area.

The Aswan West Bank:
hard sandstone for utilitarian and ornamental purposes

The ancient quarries at the West Bank of the Nile at Aswan covers an area of some 50 km² between the old Aswan Dam in the south and Wadi Kubbaniya in the north. Some of the quarries, notably Gebel Tingar and Gebel Gulab (Fig. 10), are known to be a major source of prestigious objects of silicified (hard, "quartzitic") sandstone in ancient Egypt, together with Gebel el-Ahmar in Cairo.[27] However, it was also a site for production of grinding stones for food processing for a much longer period, perhaps as far back as the Late Palaeolithic.

Detailed surveys over the last few years, extending former, brief investigations[28], and conducted under the auspices of the Supreme Council of Antiquities (SCA), have revealed the large extension of the Aswan West Bank quarry landscape.[29] Studies are now underway to interpret these quarry areas in the context of the greater Aswan quarry and mining landscape, including the famous granite quarries in Aswan itself, several building stone quarries in

---

[27] Klemm, Klemm, and Steclaci, Die Pharaonischen Steinbrüche des Silifizierten Sandsteins Ägypten und die Herkunft der Memnon Kolosse.

[28] Ibid.

[29] Heldal, Bloxam, Storemyr, and Kelany, The geology and archaeology of the ancient silicified sandstone quarries at Gebel Gulab and Gebel Tingar, Aswan (Egypt); Bloxam and Storemyr, Recent Investigations in the ancient quarries of Gebel Gulab and Gebel Tingar, Aswan.

Nubian sandstone, ancient iron ore mines and additional silicified sandstone quarries on the east bank of the Nile

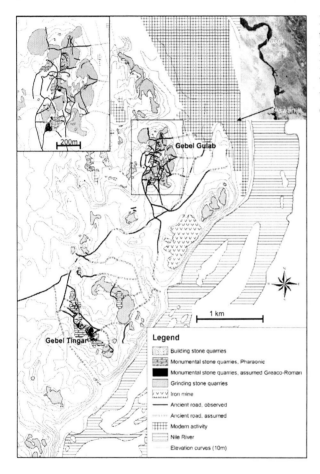

Fig. 5-10: Part of the Aswan West Bank quarry landscape. Aswan town is located in the bottom right corner of the map.

Fig. 5-11: Aswan West Bank: Topographic model showing the location of the ancient quarries on top of the hills (shaded areas), and the quarry roads (interpreted) leading down to the Nile. Seen from northeast.

The silicified sandstones are found in the Um Barmil formation of the Nubian sandstone strata[30], forming a hard, resistant layer capping the hills in the area. Generally, the quarrying has targeted the hilltops, as well as loose boulders of silicified sandstone covering the slopes (Figs. 11 and 12). The silicified sandstone is, due to extreme quartz cementation in the pores, much harder than "ordinary" sandstone, and since the pore water was "polluted" by predominantly iron and manganese, the rock appears in several attractive colours, such as pure white, purple, orange and yellow.

The Aswan West Bank quarry landscape is considerably more complex than the two other sites mentioned above. First of all, the hard sandstones have been subject to quarrying not only during many periods, but also for several different purposes. Secondly, since the site is located near the Nile, there are numerous other archaeological sites in the area, with or without any connections to the stone quarrying operations. The quarries themselves can be classified along two lines of characterisation: the desired final product (monumental, utilitarian, building stone) and the technology applied for extraction. In volume, the most important target for quarrying was production of grinding stones (Fig. 13). The

---

[30] Zaghloul, On a proposed lithostratigraphic subdivision for the Late Cretaceous in the Nile Valley; Klitzsch, Paleogeographical development and correlation of Continental strata (former Nubian Sandstone) in northeast Africa.

technical properties of the stone were particularly sought after because silicified sandstone is hard and wear-resistant and therefore suitable for this purpose. Generally, this grinding stone extraction activity has concentrated on releasing small pieces of silicified sandstone from boulders or solid bedrock by the use of stone hammers, and some places also by heating the rock face. Such quarries contain numerous small work areas, many broken or half finished pieces of grinding stones and only simple infrastructure (donkey tracks rather than ramps and roads).

The grinding stone quarrying appears to have a long history as far back as the Late Palaeolithic, indicated by the discovery of a grinding stone workshop in an 18000 year old settlement in Wadi Kubbaniya.[31] These grinding stones are of a similar shape to those found discarded throughout the quarry landscape. Since the grinding stone production continued at least into the Late Period and probably into the Graeco-Roman Period, the Aswan West Bank quarry landscapes could be one of the most long-lived stone extraction sites in the world.

Quarrying of stone for monumental purposes has mainly focused on attractive coloured varieties of silicified sandstone at Gebel Gulab and Gebel Tingar, particularly yellow (obelisks) and purple types. The monumental stone quarrying is associated with a much more elaborated infrastructure than the grinding stone quarries, and the remnants of causeways, paved roads and cleared tracks for transporting heavy blocks to the Nile remains one of the most unique and spectacular aspects of the site. Dating from the New Kingdom Period are quarries related to the extraction of obelisks (Fig. 14), including the "lost" obelisk of Seti I[32], and also quarries for other types of large objects, such as statues. Production evidence of the Pharaonic period suggests that the major extraction technologies used were a combination of fire setting and pounding with stone tools. Monumental stone was also extracted in later periods, and these quarries display wedge marks typical of the Greaco-Roman Period, indicating that splitting by wedges and working with iron tools now was the primary extraction technique.

The Aswan West Bank quarry landscape also includes several building stone quarries, especially in "softer" and more easily workable parts of the sandstone. Based on the quarry marks (wedge marks, chiselled channels around blocks) and epigraphic evidence, the majority of these quarries are interpreted to be of

---

[31] Roubet, Report on Site E-82-1: A Workshop for the Manufacture of Grinding Stones at Wadi Kubbaniya.
[32] Brand, The "Lost" Obelisks and Colossi of Seti I.

the Graeco-Roman period. However, small-scale extraction of stone for local building purposes has probably been carried out during several periods, and in fact, even at the present time, there are several artisan quarries in operation within the site. In addition to the quarries and their related infrastructure, there are numerous occurrences of petroglyphs and rock-art from different periods, some of which have a clear relationship to the quarrying. As a quarry landscape, the Aswan West Bank is a good example of a large and complex site, containing numerous quarries from different periods, transport systems and epigraphic evidence. Due to the stone quality and the proximal location of the site to the Nile, it can be viewed as a continuously evolving industrial landscape for almost 20000 years.

Fig. 5-12: Examples of silicified sandstone quarries at the Aswan West Bank. Top; monumental stone quarry (large block extraction) on a hilltop. Below; grinding stone quarries ("crater-like" features after extraction and working of boulders) on the slopes of a hill. Below right: same area seen from satellite.

Fig. 5-13: Grinding stone found in a quarry, measuring approximately 35 cm.

Fig. 5-14: Obelisk quarries at Gebel Gulab. a) Seti I quarry face, b) Seti I obelisk tip with inscriptions, c) obelisk quarry face, southern part of Gebel Gulab, d) adjacent stratified sand layer resulting from grinding and honing the silicified sandstone.

Concluding remarks

The three sites described above are in many ways different, yet what they have in common is that they are spectacular industrial landscapes of the past, which provide valuable sources of knowledge about stone acquisition in Antiquity. Studies of them have produced new ideas about quarrying methods and ancient technology, social organisation of the quarrying and raised important questions regarding stone transportation. Furthermore, they have established connections between the geological landscape and the exploitation of it.

One of the most useful exercises has been the adoption of a landscape perspective to such sites, not only regarding the physical reshaping of a natural landscape, but also raising new questions about connections between resource exploitation and other human activity. For instance, stone acquisition may relate to symbolism attached to certain stone properties, as well as the source, these perhaps having long cultural and historical antecedents. There are of course many areas of study related to ancient quarries, the ones presented in this paper represent only a fraction of their research potential, given that the majority of such sites around the Mediterranean remain unexplored, particularly from a multi-disciplinary approach.

The three case studies have yet another important aspect in common; they are all un-registered archaeological sites, they were all exceptionally well preserved a few years ago, but are now suffering acute threats from modern development. This adds a new dimension to the landscape perspective, namely the necessity of viewing the individual parts of these sites in a wider perspective. It also addresses the problem of assessing the significance of such sites: which parts of a quarry landscape is of particular value for preservation? And how much of such a landscape can be sacrificed before the landscape dimension of it is lost? The experience from Egypt is by no means unique; all over the region and also in other parts of the world, quarry landscapes are lost at a high speed, most of them not even known to the public - and the heritage authorities.

Acknowledgements

We would like to express our thanks to Zaki Hawass and the Permanent Committee of the SCA for granting us permission to undertake the survey seasons. We would also like to thank Magdy el-Ghandour, Mohi ed-Din Mustapha and Ibrahim el-Sayedi, for their generous co-operation and assistance with these surveys. Furthermore thanks to our good colleague Adel Kelany in

Aswan, who has participated in the Aswan survey, to Ashraf el Senussi who has analysed the pottery at all three sites and to Dr. Ian Shaw who directed the Chephren's Quarry surveys. The QuarryScapes project, Conservation of ancient stone quarry landscapes in the Eastern Mediterranean, is funded by the EC EC 6th Framework Programme for Research and Development (contract INCO-MED 015416). We are particularly grateful for the Commission to believe in this project. Furthermore, we thank the Leverhulme Trust, the Norwegian Ministry of foreign affairs, the Norwegian Directorate of Cultural Heritage, the Wainwright Fund and the Egypt Exploration Society for funding of Surveys.

References

Aston, B., J.A. Harrell and I.M.E. Shaw. 'Stones' (Chap. 2). In *Ancient Egyptian Materials and Technology*, edited by P.T. Nicholson and I.M.E. Shaw, 5-77. Cambridge: University of Cambridge Press, 2000.

Beadnell, H.J.L. '*The Topography and Geology of the Fayum Province of Egypt.*' Cairo: Survey Department, 1905.

Bloxam, E.G. 'Transportation of Quarried Hard Stone from Lower Nubia to Giza during the Egyptain Old Kingdom.' In *Current Research in Egyptology 2000*, edited by A. McDonald and C. Riggs, 19-27. Oxford: BAR International Series 909, 2000.

Bloxam, E.G. and P. Storemyr. 'Old Kingdom basalt quarrying activities at Widan el-Faras, Northern Faiyum Desert.' *Journal of Egyptian Archaeology* 88 (2002): 23-36.

Bloxam, E. G. 'The Organisation, Transportation and Logistics of Hard Stone Quarrying in the Egyptian Old Kingdom: A Comparative Study.' PhD. diss, Institute of Archaeology, University College London, 2003.

—. 'The Organisation and Mobilisation of Old Kingdom Quarry Labour Forces at Chephren's Quarry (Gebel el-Asr) Lower Nubia.' In *Current Research in Egyptology 2001*. Oxford: Archeopress, 2003.

Bloxam, E.G., P. Storemyr and T. Heldal. 'Hard Stone Quarrying in the Egyptian Old Kingdom (3rd Millennium BC): Rethinking the Social Organisation.' In *ASMOSIA VII: Proceedings of the Seventh International Conference on Interdisciplinary Studies on Ancient Stone,* edited by Y. Maniatis. Thassos, Greece, in press.

Bloxam, E.G and P. Storemyr. 'Recent Investigations in the ancient quarries of Gebel Gulab and Gebel Tingar, Aswan.' *Egyptian Archaeology, The Bulletin of The Egypt Exploration Society* 26 (2005): 37-40.

Bown, T.M. and M.J. Kraus. 'Geology and paleoenvironment of the Oligocene Jebel Qatrani Formation and adjacent rocks, Fayum Depression, Egypt.' *USGS Professional Paper* 1452 (1988): 1-59.

Brand, P. 'The "Lost" Obelisks and Colossi of Seti I.' *Journal of the American Research Center in Egypt* 34 (1997): 101-114.

Caton-Thompson, G. and E.W. Gardner. *The Desert Fayum* (2. vols.). London: Royal Anthropological Institute, 1934.

Engelbach, R. 'The Quarries of the Western Nubian Desert. A Preliminary Report.' *Annales du Service des Antiquitiés de l'Egypt* 33 (1933): 65-80.

—. 'The Quarries of the Western Nubian Desert and the Ancient Road to Tushka.' *Annales du Service des Antiquitiés de l'Egypt* 38 (1938): 369-390.

Harrell, J.A. and V.M. Brown. 'Chephren's Quarry in the Nubian Desert of Egypt.' *Nubica* 3, no. 1 (1994): 43-57.

Harrell, J.A. and T. Bown. 'An Old Kingdom Basalt Quarry at Widan el-Faras and the Quarry Road to Lake Moeris.' *JARCE* 32 (1995): 71-91.

Harrell, J.A., V.M. Brown and M.S. Masoud. 'Survey of ancient Egyptian quarries.' *Egyptian Geological Survey and Mining Authority, Paper* 72 (1996): 31 p.

Harrell, J.A. *Archaeological Geology in Ancient Egypt.* URL: www.eeescience.utoledo.edu/Faculty/Harrell/Egypt/AGRG_Home.html

Heikal, M.A., M.A. Hassan and Y. el-Sheshtawi. 'The Cenozoic Basalt of Gebel Qatrani, Western Desert, Egypt - As and Example of Continental Tholeiitic Basalt.' *Annals of the Geological Survey of Egypt* 13 (1983): 193-209.

Heldal, T., E.G. Bloxam, P. Storemyr and A. Kelany. 'The geology and archaeology of the ancient silicified sandstone quarries at Gebel Gulab and Gebel Tingar, Aswan (Egypt).' *Marmora* 1 (2005): 11-37.

Heldal, T., P. Storemyr, E.G. Bloxam, I. Shaw and A. Salem. 'GPS and GIS Methodology in the Mapping of Chephren's Quarry, Upper Egypt: A Significant Tool for Documentation and Interpretation of the Site.' In *ASMOSIA VII: Proceedings of the Seventh International Conference on Interdisciplinary Studies on Ancient Stone,* edited by Y. Maniatis. Thassos: Greece, in press.

Hoffmeier, J.K. 'The Use of Basalt in Floors of Old Kingdom Pyramid Temples.' *JARCE* 30 (1993): 117-123.

Klemm, D.D., R. Klemm and L. Steclaci. ‚Die Pharaonischen Steinbrüche des Silifizierten Sandsteins Ägypten und die Herkunft der Memnon Kolosse.' *Mitteilungen des Deutschen Archaologischen Instituts, Abteilung Kairo* 40 (1984): 207-220.

Klemm, R. and D.D. Klemm. *Steine und Steinbrüche im Alten Ägypten.* Berlin-Heidelberg: Springer Verlag, 1993.

Klitzsch, E. 'Paleogeographical development and correlation of Continental strata (former Nubian Sandstone) in northeast Africa.' *Journ. of African Earth Sciences* 10, no. 1-2 (1990): 199-213.

Mallory-Greenough, L.M., J.D. Greenough and J.V. Owen. 'The Origin and Use of Basalt in Old Kingdom Funerary Temples.' *Geoarchaeology* 15, no. 4 (2000): 315-330.

Maxfield, V.A. and D.P.S. Peacock. *The Roman Imperial Quarries Survey and Excavation at Mons Porphyrites 1994-1998. Vol. I: Topography and Quarries. Sixty-Seventh Memoir.* Edited by Anthony Leahy. London: Egypt Exploration Society, 2001.

McHugh W.P., G.G. Schaber, C.S. Breed and J.F. McCauley. 'Neolithic adaptation and the Holocene functioning of Tertiary palaeodrainages in Southern Egypt and Northern Sudan.' *Antiquity* 63 (1989): 320-336.

Moores, R.G. 'Evidence for Use of a Stone-Cutting Drag Saw by the Fourth Dynasty Egyptians.' *JARCE* 28 (1991): 139-148.

Murray, G. W. 'The Road to Chephren's Quarries.' *The Geographical Journal* 94, no. 2 (1939): 97-114.

Pachur, H.J. and P. Hoelzmann. 'Late Quaternary palaeoecology and palaeoclimates of the Eastern Sahara.' *Journal of African Earth Sciences* 30, no. 4 (2000): 929-939.

Peacock, D.P.S. 'Rome in the Desert: A Symbol of Power.' Inaugural Lecture, University of Southampton, 1992.

Peacock, D.P.S. and V.A. Maxfield. *'Survey and Excavation Mons Claudianus 1987-1993, 1, Topography & Quarries.* FIFAO 37, 1997.

Roubet, C. 'Report on Site E-82-1: A Workshop for the Manufacture of Grinding Stones at Wadi Kubbaniya.' In *The Prehistory of Wadi Kubbaniya. Vol. 3*, edited by A.E. Close, Assembled by F. Wendorf and R. Schild, 1989.

Röder, J. 'Zur Steinbrüchgeschichte des Rosengranits von Assuan.' *Archäeologischer Anzeiger / Deustsches Archäeologisches Institut* (1965): 467-552.

Shaw, I.M.E. and E.G. Bloxam; 'Survey and Excavation at the Ancient Pharaonic Gneiss Quarrying Site of Gebel el-Asr, Lower Nubia.' *Sudan and Nubia* Bulletin 3 (1999): 13-20.

Shaw, I.M. and T. Heldal. 'Rescue work in the Khafra Quarries at Gebel el-Asr.' *Egyptian Archaeology* 23 (2003): 14-16.

Stanier, P. *Stone Quarry Landscapes.* Stroud: Tempus, 2000.

Storemyr, P., E.G. Bloxam, T. Heldal and A. Salem. 'Survey at Chephren's Quarry, Gebel el-Asr, Lower Nubia 2002.' *Sudan and Nubia*, 6 (2002): 25-29 + Plates.

Storemyr, P., T. Heldal, E.G. Bloxam and J.A. Harrell. 'Widan el-Faras ancient quarry landscape, Northern Faiyum Desert, Egypt: Site description, historical significance and current destruction.' In *Report 2003.062, Expert Center for Conservation of Monuments and Sites.* Zürich, 2003.

Storemyr, P. and T. Heldal. 'Ancient stone quarries: vulnerable archaeological sites threatened by modern development.' In *ASMOSIA VII: Proceedings of the Seventh International Conference on Interdisciplinary Studies on Ancient Stone,* edited by Y. Maniatis, in press.

Storemyr, P., T. Heldal, E.G. Bloxam and J. Harrell. 'New Evidence of Small-Scale Roman Basalt Quarrying in Egypt: Widan El-Faras In The Northern Faiyum Desert and Tilal Sawda by El-Minya.' In *ASMOSIA VII: Proceedings of the Seventh International Conference on Interdisciplinary Studies on Ancient Stone,* edited by Y. Maniatis, in press.

Zaghloul, R.E.N. 'On a proposed lithostratigraphic subdivision for the Late Cretaceous in the Nile Valley.' In *U.A.R. 7th Arab. Petr. Congr. Proceedings,* paper 64 (B3), Kuwait, 1970.

CHAPTER SIX

ANCIENT LANDSCAPE IN ROMAN NIKOPOLIS: RECONSTRUCTION OF GEOMORPHOLOGY AND VEGETATION IN THE AREA OF THE ROMAN CITY OF NIKOPOLIS, EPIRUS, GREECE

ANNELIES L.H. STORME, LOES J.T. JANSSEN, SJOERD J. KLUIVING, SJOERD BOHNCKE AND HENK KARS

Introduction

Geoarchaeological research can be a valuable tool in the development of cultural landscapes for touristic purpose. It can provide project developers with the necessary information to present an archaeological site within its landscape in a way that is attractive for the public and at the same time both sustainable and historically correct.

The Nikopolis site in southwestern Epirus is a good example of such application of geoarchaeological research. An interdisciplinary research project has been initiated in 2004 by the Institute for Geo- and Bioarchaeology (Vrije Universiteit, Amsterdam, the Netherlands), in cooperation with the 12th Ephorate of Prehistoric and Classical Antiquities in Ioannina and supported by the Netherlands Institute in Athens. The main subject of this project is the sustainable development of the site within the modern landscape. Today many remains of the Roman but also of the Byzantine period are still visible in the field. In order to stimulate tourism in this part of Greece, the 12th Ephorate has developed a management plan for creating an archaeological-historical park on this site, which is on the tentative list of UNESCO World Heritage Sites. However, in terms of heritage management, some basic questions need to be answered first. With respect to the visible remains, an inventory has to be made of the preservation state of single monuments and the restoration measures which are needed before opening the entire area to the public. This topic is treated in a separate research project. In a second project, on which this paper reports, insight is gained into the Roman landscape in terms of geomorphology and vegetation development in the area. The ultimate aim is to evaluate the possibility of reconstructing the palaeolandscape of Roman times in the future archaeological park of Nikopolis, by developing a vegetation plan of the site based on the Roman vegetation. This could then contribute to a maintenance plan of the site. The research presented here is a first step towards obtaining that goal in the future.

The Nikopolis site

Ancient Nikopolis, 'City of Victory.' was founded by Gaius Julius Octavianus (the later emperor Augustus) to commemorate the result of the Battle of Actium in 31 BC, in which he defeated the fleet of Marcus Antonius and Cleopatra IV. That decisive battle meant the end of the Roman republican period as well as the birth of the Roman Empire and is therefore an important turning point in history. Nikopolis became an important city in the Roman Empire and regained its importance in the Greek Byzantine culture[1].

The site is situated in southwestern Epirus on the Preveza Peninsula between the Ionian Sea and the Ambracian Gulf (Fig. 1). The area has been seismically active since the Pliocene-Pleistocene. The Ambracian Gulf is a tectonically formed depression, while the Preveza Peninsula is continuously being uplifted.[2] The area studied for landscape reconstruction consists of the 'Nikopolis Isthmus.' the narrowest and lowest part of the Preveza Peninsula, just north of the ancient city (Fig. 1). It connects the more hilly southern part with the northern mainland. The eastern part of the isthmus is under water, forming the Mazoma Lagoon.

---

[1] Chrysostomou and Kefallonitou, Nikopolis, 6-10.
[2] King et al., The landscape geometry and active tectonics of northwest Greece, 137-161.

Fig. 6-1: Location of the Nikopolis site at the Preveza Peninsula, next to the Ambracian Gulf, Greece.

Methods

In order to reconstruct the palaeolandscape of the Nikopolis Isthmus, and in addition to earlier brief studies,[3] the objective was to obtain a geological record through cores covering the Nikopolis Isthmus in an evenly spread fashion. The cores were taken with a hand auger at locations connecting in straight lines in order to get readable profiles that provide the most representative view of the area. Twenty-nine cores were taken, with depths between 0.50 and 5.50 meter.[4] In the field, each core is described in detail in terms of sediment type, organic content and archaeological remains present.

From these cores, samples were taken for further analysis. From twenty sediment samples grain size distributions were determined by laser grain size analysis. The content of organic matter and carbonate in nineteen samples was measured by thermogravimetric analysis (TGA). The results of both analyses and the detailed field description were used to characterise the sediment for a stratigraphical reconstruction of the area. Ten pollen samples were palynologically analysed in order to reconstruct the vegetation during Roman and other times.

---

[3] Jing and Rapp, The coastal evolution of the Ambracian embayment and its relationship to archaeological settings, 162-173; Aalbersberg and Sykora, Preliminary investigation of the Nicopolis archaeological area and surroundings, 1-15.
[4] For more detail we refer to Janssen and Storme, Ancient landscape in Roman Nikopolis, 9-14.

Results

Sediment description

The grain size found in the cores is predominantly clay with addition of various concentrations of silt. In some cores sand and/or gravel is present as an addition or as main component, either concentrated in the top of the core or as a fine intercalated sandy/gravely layer. The colour of the sediment is mainly olive brown in lighter or darker variations. Brownish black and reddish colours were found as well. In the deeper, waterlogged parts of some cores, a grey, reduced colour occurs. The sediment is very calcareous in all cores and throughout all sedimentary layers. The humus content varies from zero to high in certain layers. Reduction and oxidation mottling was often seen in the sediments; both total reduction and total oxidation were present as well.

Some commonly found inclusions in the sediments were shells or shell fragments, root or other plant remains, iron concretions and calcium carbonate nodules (up to ca. 5 mm in diameter).

Sedimentological analyses

The grain size analysis revealed three main types of samples. On the one hand, there were rather fine grained samples and more coarse grained samples and on the other hand there was a remarkably large group of clearly bimodal samples. These show one peak with the characteristics of the 'fine grained group' and another peak with the characteristics of the 'coarse grained group'.

The resulting grain size distributions further allowed us to calculate some statistical parameters for each sample (or for each peak in case of a bimodal distribution). The most interesting parameters are the 'mean', indicating the most prevalent grain size fraction (clay, silt, sand or gravel) and the standard deviation, which is related to the degree of sorting in a sample (from very homogeneous to a mixture of grains of any size).

Our group of fine grained samples (or peaks) is characterized by grains belonging to the clay fraction (mean phi values between 6 and 8) and by poor sorting (rather high standard deviations). Our 'coarse grained group' on the other hand clearly shows a dominance of the sand fraction (mean phi values between 0.5 and 2) and a good sorting (lower standard deviations).

During the thermogravimetric analysis, samples are burned at ever increasing temperature and the loss of mass is continuously measured. The loss on ignition at certain specific temperature intervals is a measure for the amount of organic matter or carbon which was originally present in the sample.

The TGA revealed a trend of decreasing organic matter content with increasing carbonate content. Organic matter concentrations are generally higher in upslope locations, while samples from lower locations, close to the lagoon, show a higher carbonate content.

Cross sections

With the data from core descriptions and sedimentological analyses, five cross-sections were made (Fig. 2). Within the scope of this paper, we shall limit ourselves to the description of one single cross-section.[5]

Cross section 1, based on twelve boreholes and running perpendicular to the coast of the Mazoma lagoon, is considered to be representative for the whole study area. Five different lithostratigraphic units are distinguished based on the sediment characteristics (Fig. 3 and Table I). The outcrop of these units is indicated in Figure 2.

Unit A is characterised by reduced sediments consisting of slightly silty clay and shells. Unit B is found on top of unit A. It consists of medium silty clay to very silty clay, with shells and occasionally thin sandy layers. Unit C is found in the centre of the east-west elongated depression in the landscape. It consists of rather coarse material: clay or silt with considerable additions of sand and sometimes gravel. Archaeological remains and plant remains are abundantly present. The sediment is usually oxidised. Unit D is present on the hill slopes, covering the older deposits. The sediment is rather coarse, usually with significant sand and/or gravel content and hardly any shells. Unit E is present in the eastern, lagoonward part of the depression and covers the deposits of unit C. The sediment characteristics are very similar to those in unit B, but the age is younger. These five lithostratigraphic units in cross-section A extend over the whole study area.

---

[5] For results and interpretations of more cross-sections we refer to Janssen and Storme, Ancient landscape in Roman Nikopolis, 36-45.

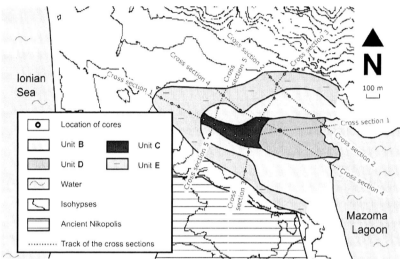

Fig. 6-2: Geological map of the study area, showing the borehole locations and cross-sections.

Fig. 6-3 (opposite): 'Cross section 1' - one of the five constructed stratigraphical cross-sections (location cf. Fig. 2).

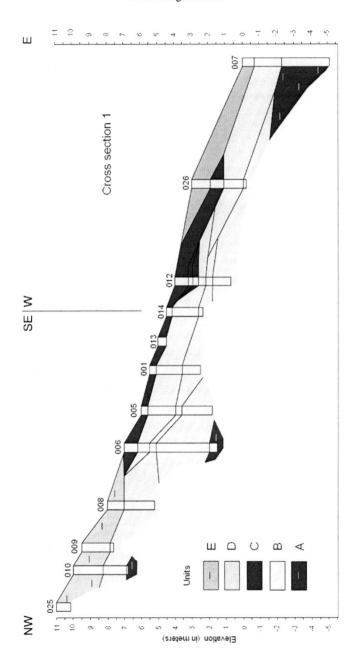

Archaeological remains

Archaeological remains have been found in most of the cores and at different levels. They mainly consist of yellowish or reddish ceramics (mostly brick) and mortar. Several pieces of charcoal and one fragment of undefined bone were found in the cores as well. Those may also be an indication of human presence, though this is not necessarily the case.

In several cores, two or more levels with archaeological remains can be distinguished, separated by an interval without such remains.

Palynological analysis

For the current project, one core (nic05-026, at the intersection of cross-sections 1 and 4, Fig. 2) was chosen for pollen analysis. The resulting pollen diagram is shown in Figure 4. Pollen preservation was not expected to be very good, due to dry conditions and consequent oxidation, as is proven by previous pollen analyses in the study area.[6] However, it turned out that some variation in the pollen spectrum is visible. Five pollen zones were distinguished based on variations in the pollen spectrum. The percentage of pollen that can be regarded as an indicator for man-made environments is represented in Figure 5.

Fig. 6-4 (opposite page): Pollen diagram for core Nic05-026.

---

[6] Aalbersberg and Sykora, Preliminary investigation of the Nicopolis archaeological area and surroundings, 8.

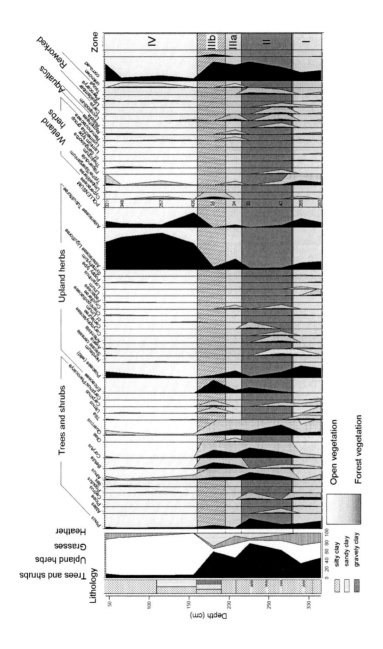

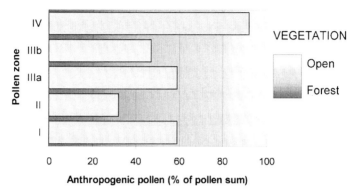

Percentage 'anthropogenic' pollen per pollen zone

Fig. 6-5: Percentage of pollen that is a possible indicator for human presence.[7]

Interpretation

Interpretation of the units within the cross-sections

The five lithostratigraphic units described in the previous section can be interpreted in terms of depositional environment and processes (Table I).

Unit A is interpreted as a deposit formed in a lagoon or embayment (it is not known whether the barrier – which is now present and which is a prerequisite for a lagoon – had already been formed). The unit is found in the deepest part of the cross-section. Considering that the relative water level used to be much higher,[8] it is presumable that the water reached this far inland during this initial period. The abundance of shells, the fine grain size and the unimodal grain size distribution in unit A point to a distal lagoon/embayment environment. The grain size of unit B is somewhat coarser, compared to unit A, and indicates a generally more proximal lagoon/embayment environment. This is supported by the bimodal grain size distribution in several samples from this unit, indicating a second coarser sediment source, most likely erosion material from the land.

In the upslope part of unit B a paleosol is recognized, which is an indication for a long-term exposure to the air, subsequent to deposition. Unit C is found in

---

[7] Included pollen types according to Behre, Anthropogenic indicators in pollen diagrams; with addition of olive pollen.

[8] Jing and Rapp, The coastal evolution of the Ambracian embayment and its relationship to archaeological settings, 162-173.

the centre of the east-west elongated depression in the landscape. It consists of rather coarse material: clay or silt with considerable additions of sand and sometimes gravel. Archaeological remains and plant remains are abundantly present. The sediment is usually oxidised. Unit C, with its elongated shape, is interpreted as the deposit gradually filling in a channel that was incised in older sediments. The deposits of unit D are interpreted as slope wash: transported downhill by gravity and water. Unit E on the other hand is deposited in the lowest parts of the landscape, during a short period of relative water level rise. It clearly takes the shape of the present-day lagoon.

In short, the water level dropped with time due to the uplift of the Preveza Peninsula and sediments were deposited in an ever-shallower environment, alternated with some short periods of relative water level rise. As uplift progressed, erosion became more important, incising a channel and washing off the hillsides.

Archaeological remains and occupation levels

In the previous section it has been stated that in some cores two or more levels with archaeological remains have been found. Given the limited amount of core locations it is almost impossible to define these levels throughout the whole study area. But if this could be done it would be a very useful tool to define occupation levels within the sediments. In the upper level of several cores, pieces of probably Roman brick were found; in addition, foundations of Roman buildings were hit on some occasions. Therefore, it is temping to interpret the upper level with archaeological remains as Roman.

However, it would be premature to say that the different levels within the cores are related to different occupational stages based on this limited amount of data. More data are needed and some dating on samples should be done to make a statement regarding human occupation phases. However, within the integration of geomorphological, palynological and archaeological results, a model will be proposed that follows the suggestion that there are two occupational stages present.

Palynological interpretation

The five pollen zones show alternating periods of open and forested vegetation (Fig. 4). In zone I, the pollen suggests rather open vegetation consisting of some trees and relatively much grass. Combined with a pollen diagram from Aalbersberg and Sykora,[9] an evolution from open towards forested vegetation can be inferred. The pollen in Zone II shows a nearly completely forested peninsula, with *Ericaceae* (heather) present in some open spots. Composites on the other hand must have been extremely rare. In zone IIIa, the pollen spectrum shows that the forest starts to retreat and is replaced by open vegetation with grasses and composites. In zone IIIb on the other hand, we witness an apparent return of forest vegetation. However, this zone coincides with the bottom of the channel fill deposit of unit C. Possibly the incision of this channel caused a hiatus in the pollen record between zone IIIa and IIIb. The source of the arboreal pollen might not be the contemporaneous vegetation, but reworked pollen from the sides of the channel. Finally in zone IV, trees have become rare in the area and most of the vegetation consists of composites, in particular *Liguliflorae*.

Integration of sedimentological, archaeological and palynological results

By combining the results and interpretations of the geomorphological, archaeological and palynological research, an integrated picture of the landscape can be created. For this purpose, core nic05-026 is taken as an example that more or less represents the situation in the study area. Three phases could be distinguished in core nic05-026 (Fig. 6) and are likely to extend over a larger part of the study area. This preliminary model is just one of the possible interpretations, which can be used as the hypothesis for future research in the area.

- Phase 1

In core nic05-026, phase one corresponds with the lower part of stratigraphic unit B and pollen zone Nic-I. At the time of this phase, the relative water level was still much higher than it is today. This implies the existence of a larger lagoon, reaching further into the isthmus. Phase one is generally characterised by an open landscape with at the end an increasing amount of trees. The pollen types indicate a rather high possibility of human interference in the vegetation, as is clear from Figure 5. Another potential indicator for human presence is the appearance of bits of charcoal, which by comparison to other cores at similar depth can probably be correlated with the lower level of archaeological remains within lagoonal sediments. Although charcoal can also have a non-anthropogenic origin, the combination with palynological results and the

---

[9] Aalbersberg and Sykora, Preliminary investigation of the Nicopolis archaeological area and surroundings, 11-12.

correlation with other remains offer a strong indication for a phase of human occupation. Not enough data are available to attribute an absolute age to this phase. However, it can be assumed that phase one is situated before the period of Roman occupation, because of its deep stratigraphic occurrence, much deeper than the layers in which the fundaments of Roman buildings are present.

- Phase 2

Phase two corresponds with the part of unit B with coarse interlayers and with pollen zone Nic-II. The stratigraphy reveals a more coastal depositional environment, which implies that the lagoon/embayment was in a state of regression and thus getting smaller. The pollen spectrum shows a forested landscape on the Preveza Peninsula during this phase. There is no indication for long-lasting human presence in the area. Permanent habitation would probably have left some archaeological remains and more pollen typical for man-made habitats would have been present in the sediments. Of course short-term passage of nomadic people (for instance pastoralists) can not be excluded.

The latter could even be confirmed by the minor occurrence of grass- and heathland within the forested landscape. Whether emigration by humans was the cause of afforestation is a question that can not be answered here with certainty, but it is a plausible explanation based on comparison with similar research from the region.[10]

- Phase 3

During phase three, deposition in lagoonal environment continued for a while and the forest declined. The start of phase three corresponds with the upper part of unit B, which is truncated by channel erosion in core nic05-026. As a result a layer of lagoonal sediments of unknown thickness has disappeared and the corresponding pollen record is absent as well. However, the pollen record in a core by Aalbersberg and Sykora,[11] outside the area of channel erosion, shows that during this phase, the landscape quickly became open.

---

[10] More details in Janssen and Storme, Ancient landscape in Roman Nikopolis, 69-70.
[11] Aalbersberg and Sykora, Preliminary investigation of the Nicopolis archaeological area and surroundings, 11-12.

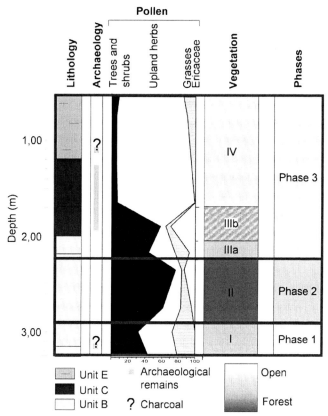

Fig. 6-6: Three phases: combination of lithostratigraphical, archaeological and palynological results.

The cause of this deforestation can not be ascertained, but the return of humans in the area is definitely a possibility. The third phase can indeed be correlated with the occurrence of archaeological remains in the upper part of core nic05-026 as well as of all other cores. These remains usually consist of ceramics and mortar. In some cases brick could be identified. The abundance of archaeological remains in the upper units is a strong indicator for permanent human occupation. The abundance of typically anthropogenic pollen confirms this interpretation. The type of archaeological material (brick, mortar) points to Roman construction style. Hence a possible interpretation would be that the Roman foundation and colonisation of the city of Nikopolis was the immediate cause of deforestation. However, this interpretation needs checking by means of an absolute dating method. A consequent result of the observed deforestation is erosion. Evidence of erosion is found in the presence of the channel, later filled up with the deposits of unit C, and in the slope wash deposits of unit D, originating from erosion on a barren hill slope. Channel incision and slope erosion were caused by increased runoff and peak discharges in the open landscape. In a forested environment, such severe erosion could never have occurred. If humans (possibly Romans) were responsible for deforestation, they indirectly caused erosion and possibly land degradation as well.

During phase three, the relative water level continued to drop, as is clear from the transition from lagoonal deposits to channel deposits. Possibly uplift of the peninsula caused a change in the gradient line of the channel and hence higher discharge caused incision. In that case uplift could be an additional explanation for the channel formation. But still, it can not be a substitute explanation, because without deforestation, incision would not have been that pronounced, as trees consolidate the soil. Uplift can only be an intensifying factor of erosion. Possible tectonic evidence of uplift must be found at least in units A and B, underlying the channel incision. Retreat of the lagoon was not gradual in one direction, but a rise and drop alternation, as can be seen from the short period of slight relative water level rise in the lagoon, responsible for deposition of unit E.

Discussion

At this point, sufficient data are available to make a first attempt at answering the research questions: "What did the landscape in the Nikopolis area look like in Roman times?" and "How feasible is it to bring back these conditions to the modern landscape, in order to create an attractive archaeological park?"

If the preceding interpretation, namely that phase three corresponds with Roman times and later, is assumed to be correct, the first question can be answered. In that case, the Roman landscape was dominated by a retreating lagoon (reaching somewhat further inland than today), open vegetation, significant hill slope and channel erosion. Man had an important effect on the landscape, first of all by cutting the former forest and subsequently by using the arable land for food production. In addition, large public buildings, private houses, fortification walls and infrastructure like roads and an aqueduct, influenced the landscape. Parts of these structures are still present as archaeological monuments, in various states of preservation.

If an archaeological park is considered, the first thought is of restoring or preserving the archaeological monuments, in order to enhance the visibility and accessibility. This topic is treated by Kootker.[12] However, if the aim is to bring back the landscape as a whole, there is more to a site than monuments alone. Of course it is impossible to influence the geomorphological processes that were responsible for the erosion and lagoon size. Vegetation on the other hand, is a promising feature for restoration: it is possible to influence anthropogenic vegetation. Crops on arable land, wild flowers in grassland and some scarce trees would make the landscape look like it did in Roman times. This would not be very different from the present-day situation. Agriculture could be stimulated, with crops such as cereals and flax.

To conclude, some remarks regarding present and future research in the area need to be made. It is of course tempting to correlate a level with archaeological remains to a certain occupation phase. Certainly with the aim to reconstruct the Roman landscape, there is the wish to determine the Roman occupation level in the deposits. However, there are quite a few restrictions to a direct correlation. Firstly, it is impossible to define the extension of a level with archaeological remains due to the limited amount and depth of cores. Moreover, erosion and redeposition cause a disturbed configuration of levels with archaeological remains. Secondly, if a distinguishable cultural level is found, it is not evident with which age it corresponds. Absolute dating methods certainly are a prerequisite for better understanding of the occupation history, but in that case it needs to be certain that the deposit is primary and not reworked. In any case, it is necessary to take into account the stratigraphy and subsequent geomorphology, in order to correctly recognize and date the distinctive levels.

Finally, two remarks regarding pollen analysis must also be made. At first, pollen preservation in the analysed core was rather bad, especially in zones II and III. Better quality pollen could be obtained if samples were gathered from a core within the lagoon, where the sediment has always been waterlogged since deposition. Secondly, a pollen type taken as an indicator for possible human influence on the landscape is never unambiguously anthropogenic. Other factors controlling the pollen spectrum could be involved, like climate. Therefore the approach to use certain pollen types to determine human occupation phases is not very accurate, but does give a valuable indication. Moreover, many other palynological studies in the region show that human occupation was the most

---

[12] Kootker, the Roman theatre in Nikopolis, Epirus, Greece.

important controlling factor for vegetation changes during the last few millennia.[13]

Acknowledgements

Dr. K. Zachos and his team of the 12th Ephorate of Prehistoric and Classical Antiquities are thanked for their cooperation in the project. Also the support by the Netherlands Institute in Athens was greatly appreciated. Finally, we are very grateful to M. Konert and M. Hagen from the laboratory of sediment analysis at the Vrije Universiteit for their help in the sample treatment.

References

Aalbersberg, Gerard and Karle Sykora, *Preliminary investigation of the Nicopolis archaeological area and surroundings, IGBA Report 2004-05*, Vrije Universiteit Amsterdam, 2004.

Behre, Karl-Ernst. *Anthropogenic indicators in pollen diagrams*. Rotterdam: A.A. Balkema, 1986.

Bottema, Sytze. *Palynological investigations in Greece with special reference to pollen as an indicator of human activity. Palaeohistoria 24*. Groningen: Barkhuis Publishing, 1982.

Chrysostomou, Pavlos and Frangiska Kefallonitou. *Nikopolis*. Athens: Ministry of Culture, Archaeological Receipts Fund, 2001.

Hempel, Ludwig. 'The "Mediterraneanization" of the climate in Mediterranean countries – a cause of the unstable ecobudget.' *GeoJournal* 14, no. 2 (1987).

Janhs, Susanne. *The Holocene history of vegetation and settlement at the coastal site of Lake Voulkaria in Acarnania, western Greece. Vegetation History and Archaeobotany* 14. Berlin/Heidelberg: Springer, 2005.

Janssen, Loes and Annelies Storme. *Ancient landscape in Roman Nikopolis. Reconstruction of geomorphology and vegetation in the area of the Roman city of Nikopolis, Epirus, Greece*. Master research project archaeometry, Vrije Universiteit, Amsterdam, 2006.

Jing, Zhichun and George Rapp. 'The coastal evolution of the Ambracian embayment and its relationship to archaeological settings.' In *Landscape*

---

[13] Some examples of other case studies in the region: Bottema, Palynological investigations in Greece with special reference to pollen as an indicator of human activity, 257-289; Hempel, The "Mediterraneanization" of the climate in Mediterranean countries, 163-173; Jahns, The Holocene history of vegetation and settlement at the coastal site of Lake Voulkaria in Acarnania, Western Greece, 55-66.

Archaeology in Southern Epirus, Greece 1, edited by J. Wiseman and K. Zachos. American School of Classical Studies at Athens, 2003.

King, Geoffrey, Derek Sturdy and John Whitney. *The landscape geometry and active tectonics of northwest Greece. Geological Society of America Bulletin* 150. Boulder, Colorado: GSA, 1993.

Kootker, Lisette. *The Roman theatre in Nikopolis, Epirus, Greece: strategies for preservation, an archaeometric approach.* Master research project archaeometry, Vrije Universiteit, Amsterdam, 2006.

Appendix

Unit	Sediment	Grain size	Environment	Process
E	Medium to very silty clay with shells	Fine	Lagoon	Lagoon sedimentation proximal to coast
D	Clayey sand, sandy clay and very silty clay	Coarse	Hill slope	Slope wash from hills due to water
C	Clayey sand, sandy clay and very silty clay	Coarse	Channel / depression in landscape	Deposition in channel due to water and slope wash
B	Medium to very silty clay with shells	Fine	Lagoon / embayment	Lagoon/embayment sedimentation proximal to coast
A	Slightly silty clay with shells	Very fine	Lagoon / embayment	Lagoon/embayment sedimentation distal from coast

Table 6-I: Characteristics and interpretation of units A-E.

CHAPTER SEVEN

MEDIEVAL SETTLEMENTS AND LANDSCAPES IN NORTHERN ITALY: METHODS, STRATEGIES AND PROBLEMS

FABIO SAGGIORE

A short introduction

Current research on medieval landscapes in Italy appears to follow two distinct trends: one is to ascertain the general aspects of territorial transformations (such as the role of cities and aristocracy, crisis of settlement systems, etc.) and the other deals with specifically local aspects of landscape and attempts to assess the processes and reasons for transformations, starting of course with more limited territorial contexts.[1]

The focus of researchers analysing landscapes – particularly in the younger generations – has shifted. It could be remarked that the questions set for research on archaeological sites a decade ago, which were often limited to the sites (Who were the settlers? What did they eat? What was their lifestyle? What did they produce? etc.), are now taken as self-evident (in terms of the strategies that are employed rather than the answers that are found) and focus is more on how sites relate to their surroundings: in a nutshell, their relationship with the environment and other sites in the area. This kind of approaches has carried more attention to the sharpening of methods: remote sensing, geophysical systems, survey practice, GIS applications.

On the other hand, during the last few years some excavations of medieval villages in Po plain have been published, such as Piadena, Sant'Agata

---

[1] On the medieval population in Italy see Wicham, Framing the Early Middle Ages, 481-495; Francovich, Changing structures of settlements; Francovich and Hodges, Villa to village; Valenti, L'insediamento altomedievale nelle campagne toscane. Also see papers in Brogiolo, Chavarria Arnau and Valenti (eds.), Dopo la fine delle ville: le campagne dal VI al IX secolo.

Bolognese, Bovolone and scholars seem to be paying greater attention to the topic of the shaping of medieval villages and landscapes.

In this paper we are going to briefly discuss three aspects of this research: 1) the approaches and strategies adopted for studying medieval landscapes in northern Italy; 2) methods and techniques used for analyses and their results; 3) some examples of recent digs and surveys.

On-site research: methods, examples and approaches

Systematic and detailed field surveys have been conducted in recent years throughout the Po plain by different research groups from the universities of Padua, Venice and Bologna.[2] The area in question here, known as the lower Po plain, is a vast cultivated zone which offers different levels of archaeological visibility of the surface data: these levels are commonly considered high or very high in the archaeological practice of these areas.[3] This implies a greater probability to recognize also small clusters of archaeological remains on surface.

Research problems in the Po plain

It appears clear that this type of landscape is particularly suited for surveys both during the site identification and analysis phases, the latter in particular conducted through quantitative and spatial surveys.[4] The practice of fieldwalking has been one of the most widespread approaches in studying classical and medieval landscapes in these areas since the 1970's and 1980's, when local and volunteer Archaeological Groups began to assist some researchers.[5] From the start these studies also integrated aerial photo interpretation and geomorphologic analyses, creating a picture of the

---

[2] Ravenna: Augenti, De Brasi, Mancassola, L'Italia senza corti?; Gelichi, Librenti and Negrelli, La transizione dall'Antichità al Medioevo nel territorio dell'antica Regio VIII; Negrelli, Il territorio tra Claterna ed Imola; Saggioro, Insediamenti, proprietà ed economie tra Adda e Adige (VIII-IX secolo). More recently also Verona.

[3] Terrenato, The visibility of sites and her interpretation of field survey results: towards an analysis of incomplete distributions.

[4] Alcock, Extracting meaning from ploughsoil assemblages; Aldenderfer, Quantitative Methods in Archaeology.

[5] Calzolari, Le ricerche di superficie in aree centro-padane; papers in Maragno (ed.), La ricerca archeologica di superficie in area padana; Nanni, La ricognizione di superficie: metodi e tecniche.

archaeological record of specific areas.[6] During this phase of research many sites were located and distribution maps were produced – mainly for the Roman era – which made possible an early understanding of the archaeological heritage of these often little known areas.

In survey practice the attention for medieval sites seems to have started only in the mid 1980's. At this time, however, surveys were not always conducted in a systematic manner and made use of a framework which, given the restricted knowledge of the materials from the 7th to 12th centuries, did not permit a good chronological classification of the records. In some cases the medieval data is considered as marginal, supplementing the picture offered by data from the Roman era and at times Late Antiquity.

The development of research has recently led some researchers to sustain that the Early Middle Age site in survey practice represents or may represent a specific problem,[7] on an equal level with other sites which present "quantitatively poor" material culture. The problem which seems to involve the period from the 7th to 10th/11th centuries may be summarised in a few points:

1) there are few elements dated for this period: pottery, soapstone as well as some other objects;[8]

2) the settlements are constructed out of wood or degradable materials;[9]

3) agricultural activity in the Po plain is intensive and highly destructive for archaeological records, in particular for Middle Age records, composed as they are of much fainter traces than those of the Roman era.[10]

---

[6] Ferri and Calzolari, Ricerche archeologiche e paleoambientali nell'area padana; Allen, Analysing the landscape.

[7] Zadora-Rio, Prospections au sol systematiques à l'echelle d'un terroir; Francovich and Valenti, Il rapporto tra superficie e sottosuolo; Librenti, Ricognizioni di superficie ed insediamento medievale nella pianura emiliano-romagnola; Saggioro, Distribuzione dei materiali e definizione del sito.

[8] Brogiolo and Gelichi, La ceramica grezza medievale nella pianura padana; Gelichi and Sbarra, La Tavola di San Gerardo (about X-XI c.); Lusuardi Siena, Negri and Villa, La ceramica altomedievale tra Lombardia e Friuli.

[9] Brogiolo (ed.), Edilizia residenziale tra V e VIII secolo.

[10] Schofield (ed.), Interpreting artefact scatters.

The characteristics of the Early Middle Age sites in the field

The question of small sites: examples on the ground, data and problems

During a project on the Verona plain a small sunken-featured building (6th-7th century) was uncovered which offers a concrete example of these problems.[11] In this structure – found on the western bank of the Tartaro river, near Nogara (Verona) – a hearth and twelve small finds were found (Fig. 1). The sunken-featured building measured 28 m². During a land survey on ploughed land this site would have a density of one find every 2 m² – in maximum visibility conditions – or assuming that the ploughing had brought to the surface only half of the finds (six finds) the site density would become one find for every 4 m². Comparing this case with other recent digs on sites from the 7th to the 11th centuries conducted in this area confirm this trend:[12] the Early Middle Age site is generally characterised by a low quantity of material and the scarce elements available for site-identification (Fig. 2). In other words, concrete difficulties exist with regard to recognising and identifying some of the Early Middle Age sites, even in areas with high visibility.

Fig. 7-1 (above): The sunken-featured building. Olmo di Nogara (VR).

---

[11] Also: Millett, The comparison of surface and stratified artefact assemblages.
[12] This only refers to the levels of use of the buildings of Nogara (Verona) and Bovolone (Verona).

SITE (VII-X c.)	find/mq	Area (mq)
Excavation		
Olmo (Nogara) - sunken featured building	0,5	27
Bovolone (building)	0,6	230
Nogara MdS (building)	0,7	100
Survey		
Trevenzuolo 1	0,5	134
Trevenzuolo 2	0,2	4000
Gazzo Coazze/Le Basse	0,6	820
Moratica UT 100	0,3	135
Moratica UT 30	0,3	140
Boaria Quarta	0,2	172
Gazzo UT 73	0,7	140

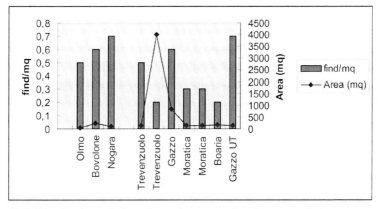

Fig. 7-2: Distributions, finds and area in surveyed and excavated sites.

Elements influencing visibility of sites

The visibility problem of some types of Early Middle Age sites seems thus connected to the material characteristics of the site and parallel to use factors of the area. The problem of low artefact numbers is also linked to the more general issue of visibility, which for archaeologists is known as 'a characteristic of the environment in which archaeological materials may be found'.[13] This factor may make it easy or difficult to recognise the distributions of finds on different

---

[13] Banning, *Archaeological Survey*.

types of lands.[14] It is a well known fact that the variation of ploughing, human intervention and the actions of natural agents may easily affect the identification of a "poor site". Repeating surveys of already identified sites in different seasons may offer further examination and greater understanding of these processes.[15]

Surveys through fieldwalking are often related to the plant covering of the area and in certain cases – like in river valley areas – even to sediments and alluvium.[16] In some cases Early Middle Age sites are covered with thick alluvium, but this problem is actually more general and affects sites from all epochs. Recognition of an Early Middle Age site in the field is related to so-called obtrusiveness. The occupation of a settlement for a brief period of time or its construction with perishable material generally produces small distributions of finds with a low artefact-density.[17] Roman era sites, on the other hand, with their greater use of stone or brick, are easier to identify.

Problems and limits of interpretation: reoccupation of sites

An additional problem for understanding an Early Middle Age site is the interpretation given to the reoccupation of Roman era settlements.[18] These situations are connected to general population phenomena and may be very complicated to interpret based solely on surface data. Surveys lead us to understand that the area of a Roman era site was often also occupied in a subsequent phase, in the Early Middle Ages, but the nature of the occupation or its characteristics may be difficult to understand. We can give an example from these areas: cases like Pontevico near Brescia are most likely impossible to read on the surface. In this particular instance an extensively excavated Roman settlement was abandoned after a fire in the 2nd century AD. It was rebuilt with wood structures during the 4th and 5th centuries, with an additional reoccupation

---

[14] Leonardi, Assunzione e analisi dei dati territoriali in funzione della valutazione della diacronia e delle modalità del popolamento; Cambi, Quando i campi hanno pochi significati da estrarre.

[15] Francovich and Patterson, Extracting meaning from ploughsoil assemblages.

[16] For example see: Marchetti, Cambiamenti idrogeologici nella Pianura Padana centrale a nord del fiume Po. On the pedology of the Po Plain: Cremaschi, Paleosols and vetusols in the central Po plains (Northern Italy). Also see: Peretto, Idrografia e ambiente del Polesine in età medioevale in rapporto alle attuali conoscenze archeologiche.

[17] De Guio, "Archeologia della complessità" e calcolatori; De Guio, Archeologia della complessità e "pattern recognition" di superficie.

[18] Papers in Brogiolo (ed.), La fine delle ville romane; Gelichi and Librenti, L'edilizia in legno altomedievale nell'Italia del nord.

phase in the 6th century.[19] The sequence of this site shows that the evolution of a settlement may not be linear and stable, neither in the structural characteristics of the building, nor in settlement function. In the wider frame of northern Italian archaeology the repercussions of this recognition are all the greater, given that researchers have so far only tried in a few circumstances to perform a more detailed analysis of the distributions of medieval material to obtain more detailed images of these complex sites. Some recent experiences have shown that a more complex approach to the study of tilled areas, with application of quantitative/spatial methods, may provide new elements that allow for a better understanding of multi-layered sites. One example is given by Nicola Mancassola in the Decimano Project, near Ravenna, in the analysis of UT 527 – San Zaccaria – a large Roman villa reoccupied in the Early Middle Ages.[20] This study, similar to other sites examined in recent years, was conducted using extensive fieldwalking and through the application of 2x2 meter grids, supported by test coring.[21] The result is a distribution map, broken down by chronological phases and produced through a spatial analysis which provides help in interpreting the site (from the Roman to medieval period).

Intra-site analysis: geophysical systems, remote sensing, GIS applications

Another similar case was proposed a few years ago by the Verona plain Project.[22] A vast distribution of medieval finds (datable from the 9th to the 13th century), related to the presence of a castle, was studied through an analysis of square grids, test pits and aerial photography. The analysis by grid – conducted during a survey with high visibility – was based on the spatial density of finds (pottery, soapstone, sherds of bricks and miscellanea). It was then observed that the concentrations of finds obtained from this analysis generally overlapped with chromatic anomalies, due to damage of the buried stratigraphy by ploughing. The repetition of site surveying in five different visibility situations also made it possible to uncover the variability of the find distributions and consequently shed light on the difficulties of their interpretation (Fig. 3).

---

[19] Mancassola and Saggioro, Insediamento rurale e campagne tra tarda antichità e altomedioevo.

[20] Augenti, De Brasi and Mancassola.

[21] On the test in Tuscany: Francovich and Valenti, Il rapporto tra superficie e sottosuolo – dal survey allo scavo.

[22] Saggioro, Distribuzione dei materiali e definizione del sito.

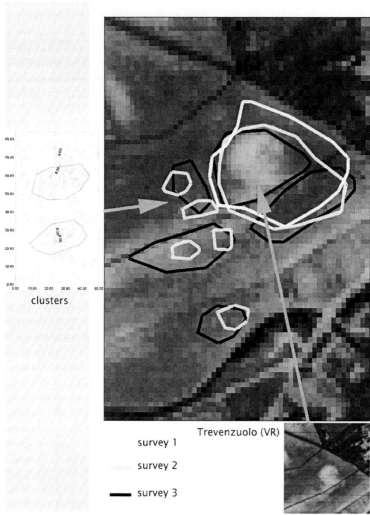

clusters

survey 1

survey 2

survey 3

Trevenzuolo (VR)

Fig. 7-3: Different distribution recorded in Trevenzuolo (Vr).

In some recently examined areas of the Po plain it has been noted that the finds of these sites are located a short distance from currently inhabited towns. In other cases the areas of many settlements from the medieval period are still occupied by towns and consequently studies are hindered by the scarce and limited windows of visibility present. To compensate for this problem some studies have been carried out with geophysical systems to integrate this different type of data. For example: around the Romanesque church of S. Maria di Gazzo, an Early Middle Age monastery, a GPR[23] was used to cover some sample areas. These data were then supplemented with those from the survey, aerial photos, written sources and historical cartography.

Along with these instruments in some studies, starting as early as the 1980's, some researchers have used aerial photography, mainly employed to identify larger sites – such as castles or villages (Fig. 4) – or in some cases used in the analysis of old agricultural property divisions.[24]

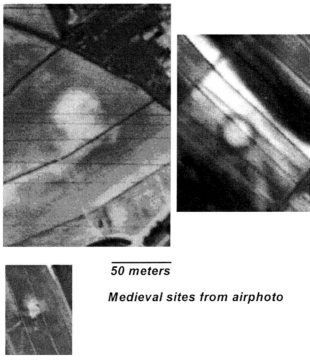

50 meters

Medieval sites from airphoto

Fig. 7-4: Medieval settlements in aerial photographs.

---

[23] Ground Penetrating Radar Sir 3000. Papers in Pasquinucci and Trement (eds.), Non-Destructive Techniques Applied to Landscape Archaeology.
[24] Campana and Forte (eds.), Remote sensing in archaeology; Musson, Palmer and Campana, In volo nel passato.

The example of the lower Verona plain (8th – 13th century)

These problems set out higher have been faced in some projects of territorial surveying that have tried to integrate approaches and methods described above. One of the projects in recent years that has dealt with some of these issues, involves the lower Verona plain (Fig. 5).

The study area is part of the Po plain, crossed by two rivers: the Tione and the Tartaro.[25] Other small bodies of water once traversed this area.

The southern area

Research has made it possible to distinguish two subregions. The first is located near the course of the Po river, consisting of a depressed area to the north of the river. The terrace of the Po river is higher than the surrounding plain and creates a vast area with drainage problems. During the medieval period this region was covered in woods and swamps, documented in written sources as early as the 9th century. Currently it is assumed that these uncultivated areas were formed between the Late Antiquity and Early Middle Ages.[26] The studies underlined how the Early Middle Age settlements are positioned around this depressed area, which in the medieval period was filled by a small lake.

In a nearby area – Valli Grandi Veronesi – scholars have shown that population crises and abandonment of parts of the area were followed by episodes of flooding. Radiocarbon dating for these alluviums suggest that this occurred between the end of the 6th century AD and the beginning of the 8th. The abandonment of settlements in these parts of the plain seems to have followed one of two trends. On the one hand, some areas witness abandonment of certain categories of sites (farms or single houses, while large farms and rural villas seem to survive), while other areas show a more generalised abandonment of sites.

It is certainly difficult to estimate the population level of the Late Antiquity, but it seems possible to suggest that occupation numbers decreased profoundly between the 2nd and 3rd centuries – even if only in some specific areas – and a

---

[25] For similar approaches: Trement, The integration of historical, archaeological and paleoenvironmental data at the regional scale. For the medieval period: Castagnetti, Aziende agrarie, contratti e patti colonici (secoli IX-XII); Varanini (ed.), Governo ed uso delle acque nella Bassa Veronese.

[26] For these areas: Saggioro, Late Antiquity Villas in plain of Verona: studies about trasformations of rural settlements.

second time between the 5th and 7th centuries. In this sense flooding and abandonment were not necessarily closely related, even if it is clear that these transformations affected the environment over an extended period of time.

After these phases of abandonment, the differences between territories (southern and northern area) – that were produced and matured between the Late Antiquity and Early Middle Ages – probably increased in the 9th-11th centuries.

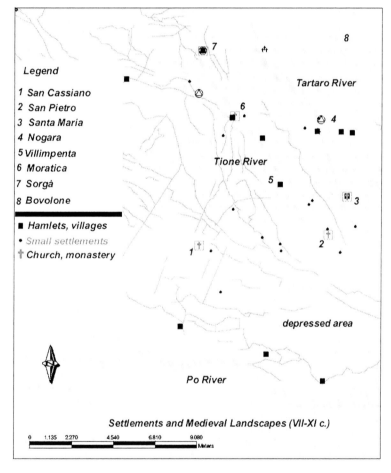

Fig. 7-5: Area under study between Mantova and Verona.

Three monasteries (S. Maria di Gazzo, San Cassiano and San Pietro in Valle) and some small settlements developed in the medieval period in the southernmost sector of the plain. It were these monasteries, some dependent on urban religious communities, which managed the exploitation of the uncultivated areas. From the 11th century onwards, the urban monasteries of Verona were major owners of these lands, together with the ruling dynasty, and played a fundamental role in the development of the property by exploiting and reclaiming the woods and swamped areas.[27]

The northern area

The northern areas of the plain witnessed a different trend.[28] Here, from the 8th to 13th centuries the main settlements were located near the rivers. The population of these areas was composed of villages and farms often connected to royal or monastery lands.[29] These settlements seem often clustered in limited areas, contained within an area rarely greater than 5-6 km².[30] One example of this is provided by Bovolone (Fig. 6),[31] a concentrated settlement excavated in the last ten years and located in the central plain. The first occupation of the area seems to date to the 9th century, consisting of a modest group of wood structures. The settlement developed in the 10th and 11th centuries, including the presence of a castle in the southernmost sector of the settlement.[32] The settlement also witnessed a demographic increase during this time. Small farms and other buildings of a minor entity were gathered in the village around the castle.

---

[27] Castagnetti, Aziende agrarie, contratti e patti colonici (secoli IX-XII); Varanini, Un esempio di ristrutturazione agraria nella "bassa" veronese; Varanini, Le campagne veronesi del '400 fra tradizione e innovazione.
[28] To compare with a larger zone: Saggioro, Insediamenti, proprietà ed economie tra Adda e Adige (VIII-IX secolo).
[29] Castagnetti, Aziende agrarie, contratti e patti colonici (secoli IX-XII).
[30] Saggioro, Modelli di popolamento nella pianura veronese (VIII-X secolo).
[31] F. Saggioro, Di Anastasio, Malaguti, Manicardi and Salzani, Insediamento ed evoluzione di un castello della Pianura Padana.
[32] About castles in these areas: Saggioro, Alla ricerca dei castelli in legno della Bassa Pianura veronese.

Fig. 7-6: Bovolone (VR).

Shaping medieval landscapes and settlements: Nogara Project

Other Early Middle Age villages have been recently studied in the Po Valley. Archaeologists currently date their first phases during the 9th century (aside from the Villa Poma settlement currently being studied which seems to have been continuous from the Late Roman period to the 13th century); the sites in question are: Piadena (CR),[33] S. Agata (BO),[34] and Bovolone (VR),[35] Villa Poma and Nogara.

Study of this latter site, located in the lower Verona plain, within the aforesaid project, offers further opportunity for in-depth study. The Nogara (Fig. 7)[36] site can be dated between the 9th century and 13th century. The main

---

[33] Brogiolo and Mancassola (eds.), Scavi al castello di Piadena (CR).
[34] Gelichi and Librenti, Un villaggio fortificato dei secoli centrali del medioevo nei pressi di S. Agata Bolognese (BO).
[35] Saggioro, Di Anastasio, Malaguti, Manicardi and Salzani, Insediamento ed evoluzione di un castello della Pianura Padana.
[36] Saggioro, Mancassola, Salzani, Malaguti, Possenti and Asolati, Alcuni dati e considerazioni sull'insediamento d'età medievale nel Veronese. Il caso di Nogara – secoli IX-XIII.

excavation is located in the western area of the current town, near the old valley of the Tartaro river, but the site extends over the entire territory and even the area of the castle, 400 m away. The first occupation of the area seems to be connected with the reclamation of swamp area and subsequent construction of buildings.

Fig. 7-7: Building in Nogara excavation (9th – 11th century) (VR).

One structure has been excavated so far, dated between the mid 9th century and 11th century, but it is assumed that other buildings are present in nearby sectors, as suggested by the most recent excavations (campaign 2006) and surveys.

The building was erected on wood structures which are believed to have been used to stabilise the swampy area. A large hearth has been excavated in the southern sector of the house with various phases of use. During the 10th century phases the structure was probably enclosed by a fence. After being abandoned the area was used for different artisan activities, most likely connected with the nearby shore and perhaps connected with a docking for small boats.

Deciphering medieval landscapes:
interdisciplinarity and future prospects

To sum up, the analysis of the medieval landscape seems to meet two problems in these territories. On the one hand it seems necessary to integrate a wide range of tools and methods in order to face the complexity of medieval sites: GIS applications, remote sensing, geophysical methods, geoarchaeological analysis, field surveys and, obviously, excavations. This kind of approach – for example – is now carried out in Tuscany by the Siena University.[37] Research of this kind has over the past years also demonstrated the importance of studying the landscape in diachronic perspective, in order to evaluate the *longue durée* of phenomena and processes.[38] Obviously, these tools and methods should be adapted to each specific territory, attempting to measure local trends and general aspects of population.

On the other hand, we can also note the growing awareness regarding the necessity of researching the relationships between sites in a territorial context, in order to evaluate economic and social structures, transformations and paleoenvironmental characteristics, in manner shown in the Pianura Veronese and the Nogara Project. Scholars are starting to note that the study of resources, which determine broad sectors of medieval economy (agriculture, animal rearing, etc.), requires more strongly than ever the integration of research carried out on the various sites through different disciplines (such as also paleobotanical analysis or archaeozoological analysis) and the understanding of relationships between these sites.

References

Alcock, S.E. 'Extracting meaning from ploughsoil assemblages: assessments of the past, strategies for the future.' In *Extracting meaning from ploughsoil assemblages,* edited by Riccardo Francovich and Helen Patterson, 1-14. The Archaeology of Mediterranean Landscapes 5, Oxford: Oxford Books.
Aldenderfer, M. 'Quantitative Methods in Archaeolgy: a review of recent trends and Developments.' *Journal of Archeological Research* 6, no. 2 (1998): 91-120.

---

[37] Francovich and Hodges, *Villa to village*; Valenti, *L'insediamento altomedievale nelle campagne toscane.*
[38] Francovich, *Changing structures of settlments*; Francovich and Hodges, *Villa to village.*

Allen, M.J. 'Analysing the landscape: a geographical approach to archaeological problems.' In *Interpreting artefact scatters. Contribution to ploughzone archaeology*, A. J. Schofield, 39-58. Oxford, 1991.

Augenti, A., G. De Brasi and N. Mancassola. 'L'Italia senza corti? L'insedimento rurale in Romagna tra VI e IX secolo.' In *Dopo la fine delle ville: le campagne dal VI al IX secolo*, edited by G. P. Brogiolo, A. Chavarria Arnau and M. Valenti, 17-52. Mantova, 2005.

Banning, E.B. *Archaeological Survey*. New York, 2002.

Barker G. and J. Lloyd. *Roman landscapes. Archaeological survey in the Mediterranean Region*. London, 1991.

Bintliff, J. and A.M. Snadograss, 'Off-site pottery distributions: a regional and inter-regional perspective.' *Current Anthropology* 29 (1998): 506-513.

—. 'Appearance and reality: understanding the buried landscape trough new techniques in field survey.' In *Archeologia del Paesaggio I*, edited by Manuela Bernardi, 89-140. Firenze, 1992.

—. 'The concepts of "site" and "off-site" archaeology in surface artefact survey.' In *Non-Destructive Techniques Applied to Landscape Archaeology*, edited by Marinella Pasquinucci and Frederic Trement, 200-215. Oxford: Oxford Books, 2000.

Brogiolo, G.P. (ed.). *Edilizia residenziale tra V e VIII secolo, "IV Seminario sul Tardo Antico e l'Altomedioevo in Italia Centrosettentrionale"*. Mantova, 1994

—. (ed.). *La fine delle ville romane: trasformazioni nelle campagne tra tarda antichità e alto medioevo*. I Convegno Archeologico del Garda. 14 ottobre 1995, Mantova, 1996.

Brogiolo, G.P. and S. Gelichi. 'La ceramica grezza medievale nella pianura padana, in La ceramica medievale nel Mediterraneo occidentale,' In *Atti del III Congresso Internazionale, Siena-Faenza 1984*, 294-316. Firenze, 1986.

Brogiolo, G.P. and N. Mancassola (eds.). 'Scavi al castello di Piadena (CR),' In *Campagne medievali. Strutture materiali, economia e società nell'insediamento rurale dell'Italia Settentrionale (VIII-X secolo)*, edited by S. Gelichi, 119-120. Mantova, 2005.

Brogiolo, G.P., A. Chavarria Arnau, M. Valenti (ed.). *Dopo la fine delle ville: le campagne dal VI al IX secolo*. Mantova, 2005.

Calzolari. M. 'Le ricerche di superficie in aree centro-padane: Mantovano, Veronese e Bassa Modenese,' In *La ricerca archeologica di superficie in area padana,Atti del Workshop- Villadose – 1 ottobre 1994*, edited by Enrico Maragno, 85-140. Padova, 1996.

—. 'Il territorio di San Benedetto di Polirone: idrografia e topografia nell'alto Medioevo,' In *Storia di San Benedetto Polirone. Le origini (961-1125)*, edited by P. Golinelli, 1-33. Bologna, 1998.

Cambi. F. 'Quando i campi hanno pochi significati da estrarre: visibilità archeologica, storia istituzionale, multi-stage work.' In *Extracting meaning from ploughsoil assemblages*, edited by Riccardo Francovich, Helen Patterson, 72-76. Oxford: Oxford Books, 2000.

Cambi, F. and N. Terrenato. *Introduzione all'archeologia dei paesaggi*. Roma: La Nuova Italia Scientifica, 1994.

Campana, S. and M. Forte (eds.). *Remote sensing in archaeology, Quaderni del Dipartimento di Archeologia e Storia delle Arti Sezione archeologica – Università di Siena*. Firenze, 2001.

Carrara, Vittorio. *Proprietà e giurisdizioni di San Silvestro di Nonantola a Nogara (Vr) secoli X-XIII*. Bologna, 1992.

Castagnetti, A. 'Aziende agrarie, contratti e patti colonici (secoli IX-XII).' In *Uomini e civiltà agraria in territorio veronese I*, edited by G. Borelli. Verona, 1982.

—. *L'organizzazione del territorio rurale nel medioevo. Circoscrizioni ecclesiastiche e civili nella "Langobardia" e nella "Romania"* (2nd editon). Bologna, 1982.

Cremaschi, M. *Paleosols and vetusols in the central Po plains (northern Italy)*. Milano: Unicopli, 1987.

De Guio, A. 'Archeologia della complessità" e calcolatori: un percorso di sopravvivenza fra teorie del caos, "attrattori strani", frattali e … frattaglie del postmoderno.' In *Archeologia del Paesaggio I*, edited by Manuela Bernardi, 305-390. Firenze, 1992.

—. 'Archeologia della complessità e "pattern recognition" di superficie.' In *La ricerca archeologica di superficie in area padana, "Atti del Workshop-Villadose – 1 ottobre 1994"*, edited by Enrico Maragno, 275-318. Padova, 1996.

Ferri, R. and M.Calzolari. *Ricerche archeologiche e paleoambientali nell'area padana: il contributo delle foto aeree*. Modena, 1989.

Francovich, R. 'Changing structures of settelments.' In *Italy in the Early middle ages*, edited by C. La Rocca, 144-167. Oxford, 2002.

Francovich, R. and H. Patterson (eds.). *Extracting meaning from ploughsoil assemblages,* Oxford: Oxford Books, 2000.

Francovich, R. and M. Valenti. 'Il rapporto tra superficie e sottosuolo – dal survey allo scavo: insediamento e circolazione della ceramica tra V e XI secolo nella Toscana centro – meridionale.' In *Extracting meaning from ploughsoil assemblages*, edited by R. Francovich and H. Patterson, 213-226. Oxford: Oxford Books, 2000.

Francovich, R. and R. Hodges. *Villa to village. The Transformation of the Roman Countryside in Italy, c. 400-1000*. London, 2003.

Gelichi, S. and M. Librenti. 'L'edilizia in legno altomedievale nell'Italia del nord: alcune osservazioni.' In *I Congresso Nazionale di Archeologia Medievale*, edited by S. Gelichi, 215-220. Pisa, 1997.

Gelichi, S. and M. Librenti. 'Un villaggio fortificato dei secoli centrali del medioevo nei pressi di S. Agata Bolognese (BO).' In *Campagne medievali. Strutture materiali, economia e società nell'insediamento rurale dell'Italia Settentrionale (VIII-X secolo)*, edited by S. Gelichi, 101-117. Mantova, 2005.

Gelichi, S. and F. Sbarra. 'La Tavola di San Gerardo. Ceramica tra X e XI secolo nel Nord Italia: importazioni e produzioni locali.' *Rivista di Archeologia* (2004), 119-146.

Gelichi, S., M. Librenti and C. Negrelli. 'La transizione dall'Antichità al Medioevo nel territorio dell'antica Regio VIII.' In *Dopo la fine delle ville: le campagne dal VI al IX secolo*, edited by G.P. Brogiolo, A. Chavarria Arnau and M. Valenti, 53-80. Mantova, 2005.

Hamerow, H. *Early Medieval Settlements. The Archaeology of Rural Communties in North-West Europe (400-900).* New York: Oxford University Press, 2002.

Kvamme, K.L. 'Recent Directions and Developments in Geographical Information Systems.' *Journal of Archaeological Research* 7, no. 2 (1999): 153-202.

Leonardi, G. 'Assunzione e analisi dei dati territoriali in funzione della valutazione della diacronia e delle modalità del popolamento.' In *Archeologia del Paesaggio I*, edited by M. Bernardi, 25-66; Firenze, 1992.

Librenti, M. 'Ricognizioni di superficie ed insediamento medievale nella pianura emiliano-romagnola. Alcune considerazioni.' In *II Congresso Nazionale di Archeologia Medievale (Brescia 2000)*, edited by G. P. Brogiolo, 170-174. Firenze, 2000.

Lusuardi Siena, S., A. Negri and L. Villa. 'La ceramica altomedievale tra Lombardia e Friuli. Bilancio delle conoscenze e prospettive di ricerca (VIII-XI sec.).' In *La ceramica altomedievale in Italia, Atti del V Congresso di Archeologia Medievale – Roma*, edited by S. Patitucci Uggeri, 59-102. Firenze, *s.d.*

Mancassola, N. and F. Saggioro. 'Insediamento rurale e campagne tra tarda antichità e altomedioevo.' *Antiquité Tardive* 9 (2001): 307-330.

Maragno, E. (ed.). *La ricerca archeologica di superficie in area padana, "Atti del Workshop- Villadose – 1 ottobre 1994"*. Padova, 1996.

Marchetti, M. 'Cambiamenti idrogeologici nella Pianura Padana centrale a nord del fiume Po: i casi di "underfit streams" dei fiumi Mincio, Oglio e Adda.' *Geografia Fisica e Dinamica Quaternaria* 13 (1990): 53-62.

Mattingly, D. 'Methods of collection, recording and quantification.' In *Extracting meaning from ploughsoil assemblages*, edited by R. Francovich and H. Patterson, 5-15. Oxford: Oxford Books, 2000.

Millett, M. 'The comparison of surface and stratified artefact assemblages.' In *Non-Destructive Techniques Applied to Landscape Archaeology*, edited by Marinella Pasquinucci, Frederic Trement, 216-222. Oxford: Oxford Books, 2000.

Musson, C., R. Palmer and S. Campana. *In volo nel passato. Aerofotografia e cartografia archeologica*. Firenze, 2005.

Nanni, A. 'La ricognizione di superficie: metodi e tecniche.' In *La ricerca archeologica di superficie in area padana, "Atti del Workshop- Villadose – 1 ottobre 1994"*, edited by E. Maragno, 375-382. Padova, 1996.

Negrelli, C. 'Il territorio tra Claterna ed Imola: dati archeologici e valutazioni storiche dalla tarda antichità all'alto medioevo.' In *San Pietro prima del Castello. Gli scavi nell'area dell'ex cinema teatro "Bios" a Castel San Pietro Terme (Bo)*, edited by J. Ortalli, 267-300. Firenze, 2003.

Pasquinucci, M. and F. Trement (eds.). *Non-Destructive Techniques Applied to Landscape Archaeology*. Oxford: Oxford Books, 2000.

Peretto, R. 'Idrografia e ambiente del Polesine in età medioevale in rapporto alle attuali conoscenze archeologiche.' In *Uomini terra e acque. Politica e cultura idraulica nel Polesine tra Quattrocento e Seicento*, edited by F. Cazzola and A. Olivieri, 49-54. Padova, 1990.

Saggioro, F. 'Distribuzione dei materiali e definizione del sito": processi di conoscenza e d'interpretazione dei dati di superficie altomedievali in area padana.' In *III Congresso Nazionale SAMI*, edited by R. Fiorillo, P. Peduto, 533-538. Salerno, 2003.

—. 'Late Antiquity Villas in plain of Verona: studies about trasformations of rural settlements.' In *Late Antiquity Archaeology 2 "Recent Research on the Late Antiquity Countryside"*, edited by William Bowden, Luke Lavan and Carlos Machado, 505-534. Leiden: BRILL Academic Publishers, 2004.

—. 'Alla ricerca dei castelli in legno della Bassa Pianura veronese.' In *Archeologia dei castelli medievali. Dal censimento alla valorizzazione*, edited by G.P. Brogiolo and E. Possenti Mantova 53-64. 2005.

—. 'Modelli di popolamento nella pianura veronese (VIII-X secolo).' In *Campagne Medievali,* edited by S. Gelichi, 80-101. Mantova, 2005.

—. 'Insediamenti, proprietà ed economie tra Adda e Adige (VIII-IX secolo).' In *Dopo la Fine delle Ville*, edited by G.P. Brogiolo, A. Chavarria Arnau and M. Valenti, 80-107. Mantova, 2005.

Saggioro, F., N. Mancassola, L. Salzani, C. Malaguti, E. Possenti and M. Asolati. 'Alcuni dati e considerazioni sull'insediamento d'età medievale nel

Veronese. Il caso di Nogara – secoli IX-XIII.' *Archeologia Medievale* 28 (2001): 465-495.

Saggioro, F., G. Di Anastasio, C. Malaguti, A. Manicardi and L. Salzani. 'Insediamento ed evoluzione di un castello della Pianura Padana (Bovolone VR (1995-2002), Località Crosare e Via Pascoli.' *Archeologia Medievale* 32 (2005): 169-186.

Schofield, A.J. (ed.). *Interpreting artefact scatters. Contribution to ploughzone archaeology.* Oxford, 1991.

Schofield, A.J. 'Artefacts distributions as activity areas: examples from southeast Hamphire.' In *Interpreting artefact scatters. Contribution to ploughzone archaeology,* Edited by J. Schofield, 117-128. Oxford, 1991.

Terrenato, N. 'The visibility of sites and her interpretation of field survey results: towards an analysis of incomplete distributions.' In *Extracting meaning from ploughsoil assemblages,* edited by R. Francovich and H. Patterson, 60-71. Oxford: Oxford Books, 2000.

Trement, F. 'The integration of historical, archaeological and paleoenvironmental data at the regional scale: the Etang de Berre, southern France.' In *Environmental reconstruction in Mediterranean Landscape Archaeology,* edited by P. Leveau, F. Trement, K. Walsh and G. Barker, 193- 206. Oxford: Oxford Books, 2000.

Valenti, M. *L'insediamento altomedievale nelle campagne toscane. Paesaggi, popolamento e villaggi tra VI e X secolo.* Firenze: Biblioteca del Dipartimento di Arch. e Storia delle Arti – Sezione Archeologica Università di Siena, 2004.

Varanini, G.M. 'Un esempio di ristrutturazione agraria nella "bassa" veronese: il monastero di S. Maria in Organo e le terre di Roncanova.' *Studi Storici Veronesi Luigi Simeoni* (1980-1981): 30-31, pp. 1-104.

—. 'Le campagne veronesi del '400 fra tradizione e innovazione.' In *Uomini e civiltà agraria in territorio veronese I,* edited by G. Borelli, 187-262. Verona, 1982.

—. (ed.). *Governo ed uso delle acque nella Bassa Veronese. Contributi e ricerche (XIII-XX sec.).* Verona: Centro Studi per la storia della Bassa veronese, 1984.

Wickham, C. *Framing the Early Middle Ages.* Oxford, 2005.

Zadora-Rio, E. 'Prospections au sol systematiques à l'echelle d'un terroir. Problèmes d'interpretation du materiel de surface.' In *Structures de l'habitat et occupation du sol dans les pays méditerranéens. Les Méthods et l'apport de l'archeologie extensive,* edited by G. Noyé, 375-385. Rome-Madrid : École Francaise de Rome – Casa de Velazquez, 1988.

CHAPTER EIGHT

ENVIRONMENT AND SETTLEMENT ANALYSIS: INVESTIGATING THE BRONZE AND IRON AGE LATIUM VETUS PHYSICAL AND POLITICAL LANDSCAPE

FRANCESCA FULMINANTE

Introduction[1]

From the 1970s onward, different research projects (excavations, surveys, *repertoires*) have greatly increased our knowledge of Bronze Age and Early Iron Age settlement distribution in the territory of Rome and the surrounding region *(Latium vetus)*. In the last twenty years different scholars have proposed several syntheses of *Latium vetus* settlement patterns both at a local and at a regional scale.[2] One of the main issues and the background theme for these studies was the keenly-debated question of settlement evolution from Bronze Age villages to the cities of the Archaic period.

---

[1] This paper present some preliminary analysis conducted within my PhD research at Cambridge University.

[2] Bietti Sestieri, Siti e territori nell'età dei metalli, 227-249; Bietti Sestieri, Preistoria e Protostoria nel territorio di Roma, 30-69; Bietti Sestieri, La media età del Bronzo nel territorio di Roma, 439-454; di Gennaro, F., Forme di insediamento fra Tevere e Fiora dal Bronzo Finale al principio dell'età del Ferro, Firenze; di Gennaro, Il popolamento dell'Etruria meridionale e le caratteristiche degli insediamenti tra l'età del Bronzo e l'età del Ferro, 59-82; di Gennaro, Italia Centrale e Meridionale, 234-245; di Gennaro, F., 2000, '"Paesaggi di Potere"', 95-119; Angle et al. Un progetto di simulazione sulla distribuzione degli insediamenti pre- e protostorici nel Latium Vetus, 125-136; Angle, et al.Casale Nuovo e la tarda età del Bronzo nel Lazio meridionale, 265-294; Angle, Gianni and Guidi, Nuovi dati sul Lazio centro- meridionale, 716-719; Gianni, Il Farro, il Cervo ed il villaggio mobile, 99-161; Guidi, Il Lazio e la Sabina tra la tarda età del Bronzo e l'età del Ferro, 85-94; Pacciarelli, Topografia dell'insediamento dell'età del Bronzo Recente nel Lazio, 161-170; Pacciarelli, Dal villaggio alla citta'.

My ongoing research aims to contribute to this debate with a landscape approach focused on the territory of Rome and its surrounding region (Fig. 1), from the Bronze Age to the Archaic period (Fig. 2). The territory of the city (micro-scale) will be analysed in the wider context of its regional setting (macro-scale), using GIS tools to investigate the collected data. This paper presents some preliminary analysis conducted at the regional level. The first part of the paper focuses on the relationship between settlement patterns and the environment. Site distribution will be examined in relationship to some environmental variables (geology, elevation, slope, landform and distance from modern rivers) in order to find general patterns in the settlement strategies of Bronze Age and Iron Age *Latium vetus*.[3] The second part focuses on some locational models, aimed at defining settlement hierarchy and potential regional political patterns.

Both environmental and spatial analysis have in the past undergone strong criticism: the former as being positivistic and deterministic, the latter as based on a "maximising economy" considered anachronistic in pre-capitalist societies. In addition there are many critical issues which have to be taken into account when performing settlement pattern analysis. Firstly, there is no demonstrated link between patterns detected in the archaeological evidence and real cause-effect relationships. Secondly, there may exist correlations between variables: for example, two apparently related variables may actually be jointly driven by a third not considered variable. In fact, the environment and human behaviour interact dynamically and here, too, it is difficult to detect real cause-effect relationships. Finally, there may exist any number of biases in data acquisition such as, for instance: correlating primary and secondary data; combining systematic data acquisition with occasional and non systematic information; the taking into account of depositional and post-depositional factors; or the awareness of different research design and sampling strategies.

Nevertheless, quantitative analysis and abstract models can still be employed, given a certain degree of critical awareness, as useful frameworks in the analysis and interpretation of archaeological data, as the following hopes to demonstrate.

---

[3] Locational information has been extracted using the following GIS applications: ArcGIS 9, ArcView 3.2 and different ArcView extensions produced by Jenness (Jenness, Surface Tools (surf_tools-avx) extension for ArcView 3.x, v.1.6.; Jenness, Topographic Position Index (tpi_jen.avx) extension for ArcView 3.x.

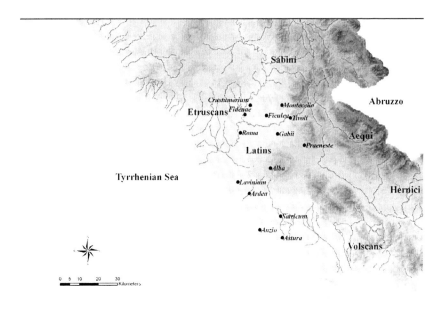

Fig. 8-1: The geographical context: *Latium vetus.*

Physical landscape:
settlement patterns and environmental variables

Geology

The association between sites and geology has been examined applying the model of *site catchment analysis*. Buffers of 2 km for Bronze Age sites and 5 km for Iron Age sites (in this time carriage transport is more common) were applied. The percentage of each geological Type in the buffers has been summarised in percentages.

The analysis showed that in all the periods three main soil type groups seem to be preferred: a) alluvial and colluvial soils (Type B); b) sand deposits (Type D2); c) volcanic and tuff soils (Type Q) (Fig. 3). Alluvial-colluvial and sand are important agricultural soils; sand deposits, in particular, can be important shallow groundwater *reservoirs* (aquifer). Volcanic and tuff porous soils are excellent for the production of wine and oil, especially combined with the mild mediterranean climate of this area. In addition porous soils are good water-holding terrains; they retain water during the dry season, enabling farmers to obtain up to three crops per year. Not surprisingly, settlements are constantly associated with the best and most productive agricultural soils. If geological variables are considered singularly it is possible to notice that volcanic and tuff soils (Type Q) show a general increase from the Bronze Age to the Iron Age, while alluvial and colluvial soils (Type B) decrease (Table I): it would be interesting to investigate if this change could be connected with any parallel variation in the type of agricultural production.[4] Tuff (Type S1 and S2) is also quite common within the *catchment area* of Bronze Age and Iron Age settlements. In particular it has to be noted that most plateaux and small hills in this area are of volcanic origin and originated from the eruptions of the Alban Hills (the most recent one dating to 3500 years ago)[5]. Not surprisingly the combination of lithoid tuff and stratified tuff soils constitute the greater part of the lithological composition of soils within the settlement area (Fig. 4). Obviously, in this case, habitation exigencies are dominant over agrarian purposes.

Following pages:

Fig. 8-2: Absolute chronology in central Italy from the Bronze Age to the Republican Period (Bronze Age and Iron Age absolute chronology has been based on recent proposals by Pacciarelli 2001 and Nijboer 2005).

Fig. 8-3: Lithology within a catchment area of 2 km for Bronze Age sites and 5 km for Early Iron Age sites.

Fig. 8-4: *Latium vetus*: lithology within the settlement area.

---

[4] I recently learned about an interesting work on archaeological land evaluation. A reconstruction of the suitability of ancient landscapes for various land uses in Italy focused on the first millennium BC, a PhD Thesis by Ester van Joole presented at Groningen University in 2003, but it has not been possible to take into account her dissertation in this preliminary interpretation of my data.

[5] Heiken, Funiciello, and de Rita , The Seven Hills of Rome.

Central Italy

Relative and Absolute Chronology

Period	Phase	Latium	Veio	Tarquinia	Absolute Chronology
MBA	MBA 1-2	Grotta Nuova-Protoappennine	Grotta Nuova	Grotta Nuova	1700/1650-1400
	MBA 3	Appennine	Appennine	Appennine	1400-1325/1300
RBA	RBA	Subappennine	Subappennine	Subappennine	1325/1300-1175/1150
FBA	FBA 1-2	Protovillanovan	Protovillanovan	Protovillanovan	1175/1150-1025/1000
	FBA 3	I	Protovillanovan	Protovillanovan	1025/1000-950/925
EIA1	EIA1E	IIA	IA	IA	950/925-900/875
	EIA1L	IIB	IB-IC	IB	900/875-850/825
EIA2	EIA2E	IIIA	IIA-IIB	II	850/825-775
	EIA2L	IIIB	IIC	II	775-730/725
OA	EOA	IVA1	IIIA	IIIA	730/725-670/660
	MOA	IVA2	IIIB	IIIB	670/660-640/630
	LOA	IVB	IV	IV	640/630-580
AP	AP	AP	AP	AP	580-509
ERP	ERP	ERP	ERP	ERP	509-400
MRP	MRP	MRP	MRP	MRP	400-200
LRP	LRP	LRP	LRP	LRP	200-14 A.D.

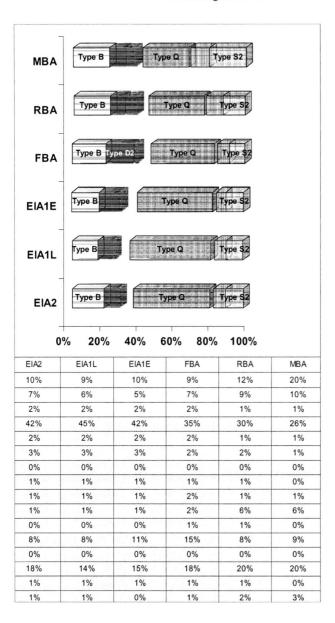

EIA2	EIA1L	EIA1E	FBA	RBA	MBA
10%	9%	10%	9%	12%	20%
7%	6%	5%	7%	9%	10%
2%	2%	2%	2%	1%	1%
42%	45%	42%	35%	30%	26%
2%	2%	2%	2%	1%	1%
3%	3%	3%	2%	2%	1%
0%	0%	0%	0%	0%	0%
1%	1%	1%	1%	1%	0%
1%	1%	1%	2%	1%	1%
1%	1%	1%	2%	6%	6%
0%	0%	0%	1%	1%	0%
8%	8%	11%	15%	8%	9%
0%	0%	0%	0%	0%	0%
18%	14%	15%	18%	20%	20%
1%	1%	1%	1%	1%	0%
1%	1%	0%	1%	2%	3%

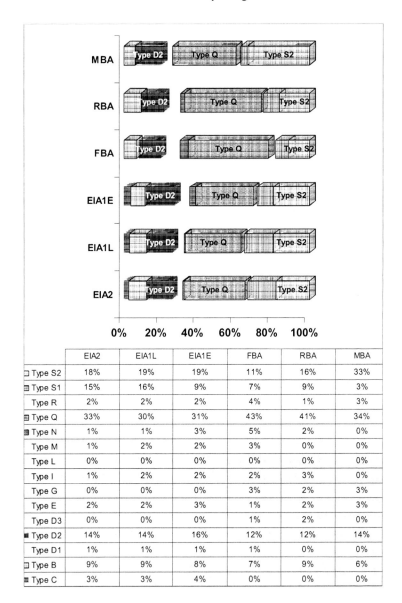

	EIA2	EIA1L	EIA1E	FBA	RBA	MBA
❑ Type S2	18%	19%	19%	11%	16%	33%
⊞ Type S1	15%	16%	9%	7%	9%	3%
Type R	2%	2%	2%	4%	1%	3%
⊞ Type Q	33%	30%	31%	43%	41%	34%
▨ Type N	1%	1%	3%	5%	2%	0%
Type M	1%	2%	2%	3%	0%	0%
Type L	0%	0%	0%	0%	0%	0%
Type I	1%	2%	2%	2%	3%	0%
Type G	0%	0%	0%	3%	2%	3%
Type E	2%	2%	3%	1%	2%	3%
Type D3	0%	0%	0%	1%	2%	0%
■ Type D2	14%	14%	16%	12%	12%	14%
Type D1	1%	1%	1%	1%	0%	0%
❑ Type B	9%	9%	8%	7%	9%	6%
≣ Type C	3%	3%	4%	0%	0%	0%

Elevation and slope

Different analyses have been performed on elevation and slope both for site location and settlement *catchment areas.*

Site elevations were extracted from a DEM (20 m resolution) using the Surface Tools extension for ArcView 3.x produced by Jenness,[6] after which the mean and the standard deviation of these values were calculated. The analysis showed a general increasing trend in the mean elevation of sites from the Middle Bronze Age until the end of the Bronze Age and the beginning of the Early Iron Age, followed by a more stable trend during the Early Iron Age (Fig. 5). The analysis of the association between site locations and elevation showed that Bronze Age settlements are fairly evenly distributed between plain and hilltop locations. The latter then increased constantly from the Recent Bronze Age onward and became dominant over plain location during the Early Iron Age (Table III).

Slope analysis showed that flat and lower slope locations decreased significantly from the Middle Bronze Age to the Final Bronze Age and reached very low values during the Iron Age. On the contrary, ridges and upper slope locations increased constantly from the Middle Bronze Age to the end of the Early Iron Age (Table IV). Slope (%) within a *catchment area* of 2 km for Bronze Age sites and of 5 km for Early Iron Age sites has been calculated as well. Four different classes of slope have been considered and the variation between each phase and the previous has been calculated. The results (Fig. 6) show that the occupation of areas with steeper slopes increases from the Middle Bronze Age to the Early Iron Age. This could indicate an improvement in agriculture techniques and/or a demographic increment with occupation of less accessible land.

---

[6] Jenness, Surface Tools (surf_tools-avx) extension for ArcView 3.x, v.1.6.

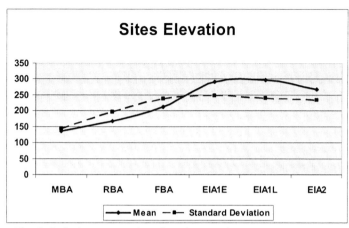

Fig. 8-5: *Latium vetus*: sites elevation trend.

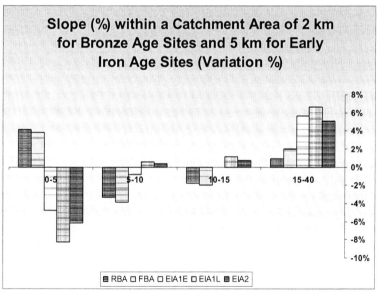

Fig. 8-6: *Latium vetus*: slope (%) within a *catchment* area of 2 km for Bronze Age sites and 5 km for Early Iron Age sites (variation %).

Distance from modern rivers

The *catchment model* has also been applied for the analysis of hydrographical data. A cost surface based on walking time distance to the rivers has been calculated using parameters provided in an unpublished study of Machovina and applied by Rajala in her PhD Thesis.[7] Soils have been classified according to their walking distance from rivers into three categories: 1.5 hours, three hours and more than three hours.

Then, as with the other analyses, *catchment areas* were defined around each settlement and the areal percentage of different classes was calculated. The analysis showed that from the Bronze Age to the Early Iron Age proximity of land to water resources seems to be less important in the choice of settlement location (Fig. 7). A possible explanation is that either other factors became progressively more important or water supply technique became more advanced.

In order to investigate the importance of natural water communications, their relationship to settlement location has been further investigated. Rivers have been classified either as associated with alluvial deposits (B1) or not associated with alluvial deposits (B2). It is assumed that rivers associated with alluvial deposit are more consistent and may have been more important in the past for middle and long distance communication.[8] Linear distances from rivers have been calculated and classified according to three classes (0-250 m, 250-1000 m and more than 1000 m) after which site density for each class was calculated. The analysis showed that settlement distance from small rivers (B2) seems to be quite constant, while larger rivers (B1) seem to be more important for Bronze Age sites than Early Iron Age sites (Fig. 8). This may imply that fluvial communication may have been less important and other ways of communication (roads for instance) may have acquired a greater importance in the Early Iron Age.

---

[7] Machovina, Modeling Pedestrian Mobility Across a natural landscape using Geographical Information Systems; Rajala, Human Landscapes in Tyrrhenian Italy.
[8] Bietti Sestieri et al. Preistoria e Protostoria nel territorio di Roma, 30-69; Gianni, Il Farro, il Cervo ed il villaggio mobile, 99-161.

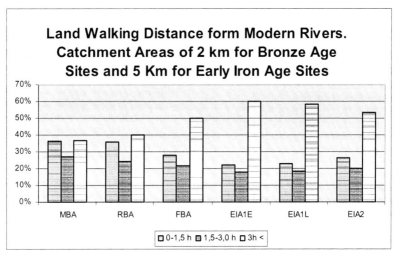

Fig. 8-7: Land walking distance from modern rivers. Catchment areas of 2 km for Bronze Age sites and 5 km for Early Iron Age sites.

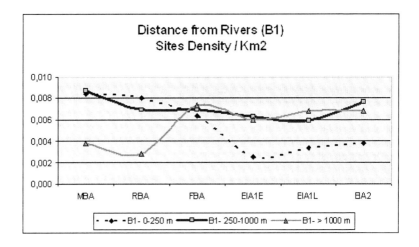

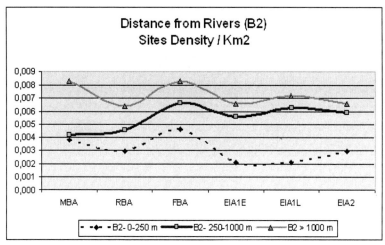

Fig. 8-8: B1 (previous page) and B2: linear distance from modern rivers: sites density/km².

Conclusions

Previous studies noticed no significant correlation between sites and geological formation.[9] This preliminary analysis of data seemed to indicate a simple, but quite logic, correlation between sites and good agricultural soils.[10] Lithoid tuff, combined with *tufiti* and stratified tuff, likewise represents a high percentage, which indicates a particular importance of stable defended settlements.

Elevation, slope and landform analysis confirmed a well known and established site location trend, on which there is a general agreement among scholars: from the Middle Bronze Age to the end of the Early Iron Age flat and

---

[9] For the territory of Rome see: Bietti Sestieri et al. Preistoria e Protostoria nel territorio di Roma, 30-69; For Latium vetus see: Angle, Gianni and Guidi, Nuovi dati sul Lazio centro- meridionale, 716-719, who noted a prevalent association of Middle Bronze Age 1-2 sites with sandy soils.

[10] A constant association between sites and alluvial soils was also noted in the Recent and the Final Bronze Age, by Bietti et al. Preistoria e Protostoria nel territorio di Roma, 30-69 and by Angle, et al. Casale Nuovo e la tarda età del Bronzo nel Lazio meridionale, 265-294.

lower slope locations in open plain positions are progressively abandoned; conversely, upper slope and ridge positions on top of small hills and large steep tuff-plateaus are chosen as location of stable, naturally defended, settlements.[11]

The analysis of distance from modern rivers showed a strict relationship between rivers and settlement location during the Bronze Age. Bietti Sestieri and other scholars related this phenomenon to the increase in aridity which occurred in the sub-boreal climatic period.[12] Recently, Rajala suggested for the Nepi area that river valleys represented a more important means of communication and a natural resource of greater economic value in this period than in the Early Iron Age, when the road system network became more important in regional communication.[13] Bietti Sestieri noted a decreasing importance of the local river valleys (B2) and an increasing importance of the long-distance network (B1) from the Bronze Age to the Early Iron Age in the Roman area, but at the regional scale the trend seems to be the opposite (Fig. 8).[14]

Political Landscape: looking for hierarchical and territorial settlement patterns (spatial efficiency model, rank-size rule and Voronoi diagrams)

Introduction: locational models

It was in the seventies that scholars, such as Clarke, became conscious that there was 'archaeological information in the spatial *relationship* between things as well as in *things* themselves'[15] and so the *spatial* or *locational* approach prospered within archaeology under the influence of the 'New Geography'

---

[11] Synthesis in Peroni, Formazione e sviluppi dei centri protourbani medio-tirrenici, 26-30 with references; see also Pacciarelli, Dal villaggio alla citta'; for Latium vetus in particular see note 1 and for Etruria see di Gennaro, Forme di insediamento fra Tevere e Fiora dal Bronzo Finale al principio dell'età del Ferro, Firenze;   Il popolamento dell'Etruria meridionale e le caratteristiche degli insediamenti tra l'età del Bronzo e l'età del Ferro, 59-82; di Gennaro, Italia Centrale e Meridionale, 234-245, di Gennaro, "Paesaggi di Potere", 95-119.

[12] Bietti Sestieri et al. Preistoria e Protostoria nel territorio di Roma, 30-69 in particular 68 ; Angle, et al. Casale Nuovo e la tarda età del Bronzo nel Lazio meridionale, 265-294, in particular 271.

[13] Rajala, GIS in the analysis of the settlement patterns in central Italy, 310-313.

[14] Bietti Sestieri, Siti e territori nell'età dei metalli, 227-249.

[15] Clarke, Spatial information in Archaeology, 1-33 in particular 5.

school.[16] In recent years, locational models have been revitalised by their incorporation in GIS, but there are still some theoretical concerns regarding their application.

The first and most serious concern is that *locational models* were elaborated for the study of modern societies based on a 'maximising economy' and therefore should not be applied to pre-capitalistic societies. Quoting Renfrew,[17] Haselgrove replied to this criticism that 'in spatial terms, the transfer of goods by distribution does not differ from market exchange'.[18] Then there are issues such as representativeness of known sites (which could have been altered by post-depositional factors) or settlement size definition, but these kinds of problems are related to the nature of archaeological data itself.

To conclude, being aware of the inevitable biases of archaeological evidence and the unavoidable distance between abstract models and reality, *locational* and *spatial* models can still be considered useful in the interpretation of archaeological data. In this section the rank-size model and some others spatial analysis will be applied in order to address the problem of proto-urban formation in *Latium vetus*, which is still not fully understood. First, I will analyse Bronze and Iron Age settlement hierarchy in this region applying a locational model proposed by Steponaitis in the late 1970s. Then I will compare the results of this analysis with an updated application of the rank-size model.[19] Finally, I will use Voronoi polygons in order to try to define the political territories of *Latium vetus* settlements and their development from the Middle Bronze Age to the end of the Early Iron Age.

Spatial efficiency model

In the late 1970s, Steponaitis was one of the researchers who questioned whether the central place model could be applied to the study of pre-capitalistic societies and developed a new locational model, in order to analyse settlement hierarchies in pre-state societies and complex chiefdoms.[20]

---

[16] Haggett, Analysis in Human Geography; Hodder and Orton, Spatial Analysis in Archaeology.

[17] Renfrew, Trade as Action at a Distance: Questions of Integration and Communication, 3-59.

[18] Haselgrove, Central Places in British Iron Age Studies: a Review and Some Problems, 3-13 in particular 7.

[19] Compare Guidi, An application of the Rank-Size rule to proto-historic settlement in the middle Thyrrenian area, 217-242.

[20] Steponaitis, Location Theory and Complex Chiefdoms: A Mississippian Example, 417-454.

I will apply this model with the intention of comparing its results with those of other settlement analyses, such as the rank-size model and multiplicatively Voronoi diagrams (following paragraphs).

Steponaitis' model is based on some assumptions regarding the locational constraints of chiefly centres. Any community is a closed environment with a certain finite amount of energy. The costs of maintaining the central institutions of complex chiefdoms (nobility, craftsmen and others non-producers' maintenance, public and religious architecture, sumptuary goods etc.) are supported by the surplus production and *corvee labour* of the commoners. The 'effort' invested by commoners in surplus production and *corvee labour* could only be maximised by minimising the 'effort' spent in movement of goods and people to and from the chiefly centres. As a consequence it has been demonstrated that minimising this cost can best be achieved by an efficient location of the chiefly centres.

A mathematical explanation of the model does not form part of the present paper (for this I refer the reader to Steponaitis), but its principles and the basic procedures and software applications I used to achieve my results will be mentioned here briefly. According to Steponaitis' model, the ideal geographical position of a chiefly centre is calculated both in relation to local and second-order settlement location and takes into account the chiefly centre's population size. But, as Steponaitis stressed, with a high degree of political centralization, the position of the lower-order centres is more important than the distribution of local settlements and the capital would be ideally located "at the centre of gravity of the minors centres" (CGMC). Then, according to Steponaitis, the spatial efficiency of a chiefly centre location can be calculated as the sum of the squared distances of the subordinate centres from the capital, divided by the sum of their squared distances from the CGMC. This formula is based on the assumption (grounded on empirical studies) that the "cost" of effort involved in movement over a certain distance is proportional to the distance squared.[21] When the centre is ideally located the spatial efficiency index is 1.0; as the capital position diverges from the ideal location the value of the index decreases. In order to know which centres pertain to each district I used both plain and multiplicative weighted Voronoi diagrams, which will be briefly presented later in this paper.[22]

---

[21] *Ibid.* 430.
[22] Again, ArcView 3.2 has been used to perform the analysis and, in particular, the Weighted Mean of Points (v. 1.2c) extension (Jenness 2004) has been adopted to calculate the CGMC.

As expected, Fig. 9 shows an increasing trend of the index of spatial efficiency during the Iron Age. This trend seems to be coherent with the presence of a process of proto-urban and urban formation towards centralisation and settlement hierarchy in *Latium vetus* in this period. However, the analysis revealed an unexpected decreasing trend from the Middle Bronze Age to the Final Bronze Age. It would have been more reasonable a continuous increasing trend through all the periods. The following explanations are possible:

- The model can be used for Iron Age settlements, but cannot be applied to Bronze Age ones, because actually no proper hierarchy of chiefly and lower order centres has as yet been identified in Bronze Age *Latium vetus* (as in Etruria).

- The model is correct for Bronze Age settlements, but does not fit Early Iron Age settlements; for this period other models, such as central place theory, may be more appropriate or other constraints, such as political choices, may have influenced site location.

- The trend could be trusted for both periods and could be explained in terms of decline and regeneration of a complex society, using a pattern proposed by Morris for Greece.[23] Nevertheless this model seems less suitable for central Italy where a linear increasing trend has always been recognised in settlement development from the Bronze Age to the Early Iron Age.

On the one hand it is quite likely that the Bronze Age sample is lacking to a greater extent, because Early Iron Age settlements are generally more visible than older ones. On the other hand, an explanation limited to data biases, probably, is too simple and further investigation is necessary.

---

[23] Morris, The Collapse and Regeneration of Complex Societies in Greece. 1500-500 BC.

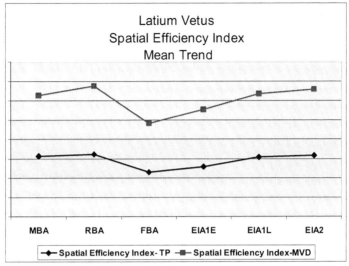

Fig. 8-9: Bronze Age and Early Iron Age *Latium vetus* districts: spatial efficiency index trend.

Rank-size model

The development of proto-urban centres towards urbanisation in the transition between the end of the Bronze Age and the Early Iron Age is also confirmed by the application of the rank-size model.[24]

The rank-size rule, advanced by Zipf in the 1940s,[25] notes the relationship between the rank of cities and their population. The formula is Pn = P1/n where Pn is the population of towns ranked n, P1 is the population of the largest town and n is the rank of the town. The formula states that the population of a town ranked n is equal to the population of the largest town divided by n. For example, if the largest town has a certain population, the second largest town will have a population of one-half that number, the third largest will have a population of one-third and so on.

---

[24] Compare Guidi, A., An application of the Rank-Size rule to proto-historic settlement in the middle Thyrrenian area, 217-242, here updated for Etruria and Latium vetus and Cardosa, Gli assetti territoriali protovillanoviano e villanoviano alla luce dei modelli dell'archeologia spaziale, 261-268, for Etruria.

[25] Zipf, Human Behaviour and the Principle of Least Effort.

If the common logarithms of rank and size (generally used in archaeological applications) are plotted against one another, the result is a straight line with a slope of -1. The rank-size model was developed and applied by Johnston to the Susiana plain – Iran – in the fourth millennium B.C.[26] This classic, 'ideal' distribution is called *log-normal* and is typical of a state-system with a high level of integration between settlements. Two deviations from the log-normal are possible: *primate* or *concave* distributions, where the largest settlement is unexpectedly 'small' (typical of imperial or colonial systems) and *convex* distributions, where the largest settlement is unexpectedly 'large' (typical of systems with a low level of integration) (Fig. 10).

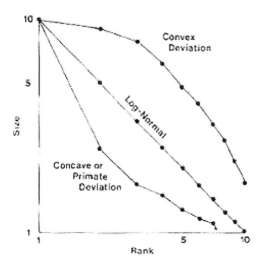

Fig. 8-10: The rank-size rule with types of deviations from the log-normal distribution (From Johnston 1981, Fig.2).

[26] Johnson, Rank-size convexity and system integration: a view from archaeology, 234-247.

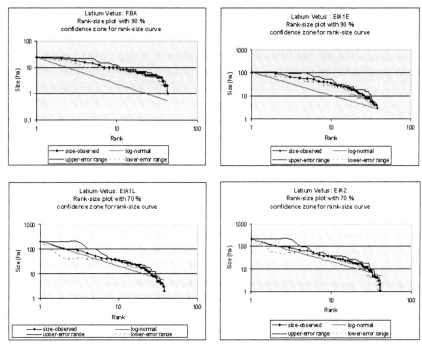

Fig. 8-11: The rank-size model applied to Final Bronze Age and Early Iron Age *Latium vetus*.

The graph (Fig. 11) shows a tendency from a convex distribution (end of the Final Bronze Age and beginning of the Early Iron Age 10th – 9th centuries BC.) towards a log-normal distribution (end of the Early Iron Age 1 and Early Iron Age 2 – second half of the 9th and 8th century BC) which suggests an increasing system integration with the development of a state-level society, according to the model proposed by Johnson for the Susiana plain.[27]

Voronoi diagrams

In order to define the development of *Latium vetus* territorial patterns from the Middle Bronze Age to the end of the Iron Age, I have used multiplicative

---

[27] *Ibid.*; Johnson, Monitoring complex system integration and boundary phenomena with settlement size data, 144-188; Johnson, Aspects of Regional Analysis in Archaeology, 479-508.

weighted Voronoi diagrams which allow us to define areas of territorial dominance and to detect dynamic changes thought time.[28]

Multiplicatively weighted Voronoi diagrams (MWVD) are an evolution of planar multiplicatively Voronoi diagrams (or Thiessen polygons), which take into account not only distance but also settlement sizes.[29] This model is quite similar to the X-Tent proposed by Renfrew and Level applied by Stoddart and recently again by Stoddart, Redhouse and Ducke, within a GIS analysis which take into account different variables in the calculation of the cost-surface.[30] The difference between the MWVD and the X-Tent is the presence of a constant added to the X-Tent, which could be quite problematic because it is not always clear which value has to be used according to which parameters.

In this paper I have applied multiplicatively weighted Voronoi diagrams to define the development of *Latium vetus* territorial patterns from the Middle Bronze Age to the end of the Early Iron Age. Multiplicative weighted Voronoi diagrams shape files were obtained using the program MWVD_Shape 1.0,[31] and then transferred into ArcView 3.2. From the model application some general patterns seemed to emerge:

- In the Middle Bronze Age, about eight bigger districts divide between themselves, more or less equally, the regional territory, vying for influence with some smaller, medium-size, districts in the Alban Hill area and in the northern part of the region (Fig. 12);
- In the Recent Bronze Age a new pattern seems to emerge: on the one hand the coastal territory is divided equally between different settlements from the mouth of the Tiber to the southern part of the region; on the other hand, the rest of the territory is dominated by a sort of tripartite division of territorial influence between three major poles (Rome, Gabii, the Alban Hills) (Fig. 12);

---

[28] Lan, Polygon Characterisation With the Multiplicatively Weighted Voronoi Diagrams, 223-239, in particular 236.

[29] *Ibid.*

[30] Renfrew and Level, Exploring Dominance: Predicting Polities from Centers, 145-167; Stoddart, The Political Landscape of Etruria, 40-51; Stoddart and Redhouse, Complexity and Landscape: a case study from Etruria; Ducke, Seminar presented within the Summer School Quantitative Methods and Data Analysis in Archaeology.

[31] Lan, Polygon Characterisation With the Multiplicatively Weighted Voronoi Diagrams, 223-239. Another application, which builds Multiplicative Weighted Voronoi Diagrams is the Gambini program, for this see Rajala, From a Settlement to an Early State?, 706-712.

- In the Final Bronze Age, the same pattern as in the Recent Bronze Age seems to be present, but with an increased number of medium and small-sized subordinate centres (Fig. 13);
- In the first part of the Early Iron Age 1 territories of big proto-urban centres start to delineate: on the coast there are Lavinium and Ardea with the smaller Anzio in the south and *Satricum* further inland; the central area of the Alban Hills has Alba and Velletri as major centres; Praeneste dominates on the west, at the foot of the Prenestine Mountains (Appenine), while in the north three major centres are dominant (Rome, Gabii and *Crustumerium*); other first rank centres of less importance (Fidenae, Ficulea, Montecelio and Tibur) control smaller territories. It is remarkable that Rome's influence has extended to all the territory on the south bank of the Tiber including Ficana and probably Castel di Decima (Fig. 13);
- In a later phase of Early Iron Age 1 and in Early Iron Age 2 the centre situated at Rome consolidates and extends its power in the region; its influence is absolutely dominant on all other centres of *Latium vetus* (Fig. 14).

To sum up, the application of multiplicative weighted Voronoi diagrams showed that three major areas of influence existed around Rome, Gabii and the Alban Hill at least from the Recent Bronze Age if not earlier. From the beginning of the Early Iron Age big proto-urban centres started to develop on the plateaux later occupied by archaic cities; at this time the area of the Alban Hill is dominated by the presence of Alba and Gabii seems to be more influential than Rome (if the latter is considered as constituted by two separated settlements). Only from a later stage of the Early Iron Age does Rome, which is now unified into one big proto-urban settlement, become the dominant centre at the regional level.

Following pages:

Fig. 8-12: Latium vetus sites' districts, MBA and RBA (multiplicative weighted Voronoi diagrams; in MWVD the dominant centre is always left without a 'polygon').

Fig. 8-13: Latium vetus sites' districts, FBA and EIA1E (multiplicative weighted Voronoi diagrams; in MWVD the dominant centre is always left without a 'polygon').

Fig. 8-14: Latium vetus sites' districts, EIA1L and EIA2 (multiplicative weighted Voronoi diagrams; in MWVD the dominant centre is always left without a 'polygon').

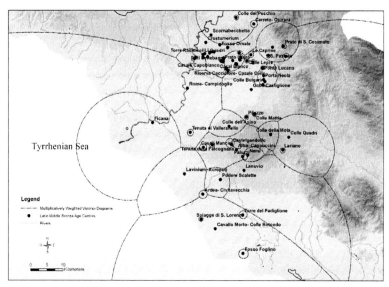

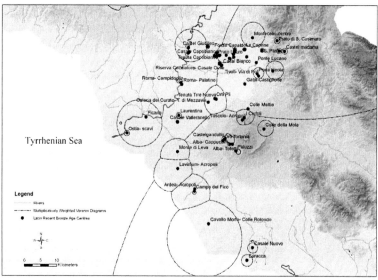

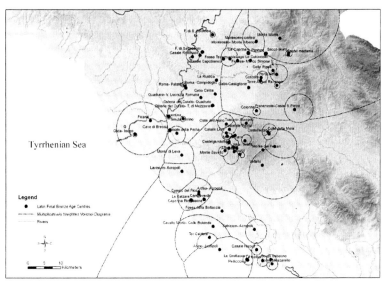

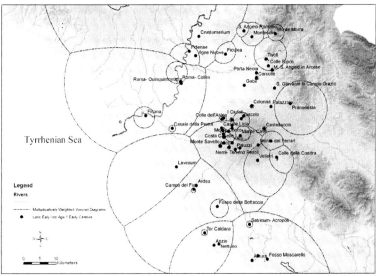

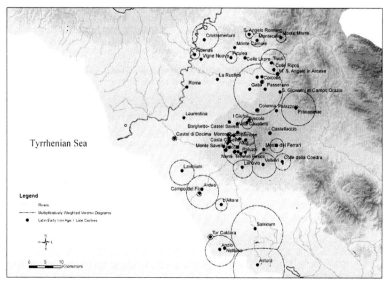

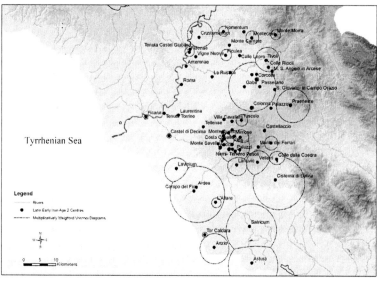

Conclusions

The analysis of environmental variables related to site distribution showed that it is possible to detect general patterns in the archaeological record, even thought it is difficult to relate these patterns to general historical trends (which are complex and connected to numerous interrelated variables) by a direct cause-effect relationship and further investigation is necessary.

The application of some locational models, presented above, seems to confirm that the cities of the Archaic period are the product of a long and local process of Bronze Age and Iron Age pre-and proto-urban formation rather than a phenomenon imported from the Eastern Mediterranean trough Greek colonisation.[32] The analytical methods applied in this study have already been used by different scholars, in some cases also in the area under study. But until now they had not been used systematically, at the regional scale and in a longer term diachronic perspective.

In this paper I have tried to integrate archaeological data with environmental analysis and theoretical models in a wider historical perspective. The process has made one realise how difficult it is to integrate such different layers of information in one, unified, coherent view. In addition, other post-processual approaches (phenomenological, ideational and symbolic/religious landscape) might also have been considered to be of potential value within this type of research.[33]

Still, as the case presented here shows, GIS tools, notwithstanding their limitations, can greatly contribute to realising this multi-layered perspective. In the future they could help to integrate more effectively different approaches (environmental, historical, phenomenological etc.), which still generally are employed separated in current landscape research.

Acknowledgements

I would like to thank the funding bodies who have allowed me staying in Cambridge and complete my research project (Università di Roma "La Sapienza", AHRC, IFUW, Dan David Prize). I would like to mention also

---

[32] See Peroni, Formazione e sviluppi dei centri protourbani medio-tirrenici: 26-30, Pacciarelli, Dal villaggio alla citta'; Peroni, Formazione e sviluppi dei centri protourbani medio-tirrenici, 26-30 and recently Fulminante, Landscape of Power in Early Iron Age Latium vetus.

[33] As demonstrated by Wilkinson, Archaeological Landscapes of the Near East.

Italian national and local administrations who have provided me with digital data necessary to perform the analyses (*Provincia di Roma, Regione Lazio* and *Ministero dell'Ambiente,*). Dr. Simon Stoddart has supervised my research with professionalism and 'Scottish' friendship. Dr. F. di Gennaro, prof. A. Guidi, dr. G. Cifani, L. Ceccarelli and C. Alexander have kindly read this paper and provided useful advises. Any responsibility for mistakes, misunderstandings or omission is my own.

References

Angle, M. et al. 'Un progetto di simulazione sulla distribuzione degli insediamenti pre- e protostorici nel Latium Vetus.' *Quaderni dei Dialoghi di Archeologia* 4 (1988): 125-136.

—., et al. 'Casale Nuovo e la tarda età del Bronzo nel Lazio meridionale.' In La Sardegna nel Mediterraneo tra il Bronzo Medio e il Bronzo Recente (XVI-XIII a.C.). Atti del III Convegno di studi "un millennio di relazioni fra la Sardegna e i paesi del Mediterraneo", Selargius-Cagliari 19-22 Novembre 1987, 265-294. Cagliari: Edizioni della Torre, 1992.

Angle, M., Gianni, A., Guidi, A. 'Nuovi dati sul Lazio centro- meridionale.' In *L'età del Bronzo in italia nei secoli dal XVI al XIV a.C.. Viareggio 26-30 Ottobre 1989, (= Rassegna di Archeologia, 10)*, edited by D. Cocchi Genick, 716-719. Firenze: All'Insegna del Giglio, 1991-1992.

Bietti Sestieri, A.M. 'Siti e territori nell'età dei metalli. Elementi per l'inferenza archeologica sulle componenti politiche dell'organizzazione territoriale.' In *Dottrina e metodologia della ricerca preistorica. Atti della XXVII riunione scientifica, Ferrara, 17-20 Novembre 1987*, 227-249. Ferrara, 1989.

—., et al. 'Preistoria e Protostoria nel territorio di Roma. Modelli di insediamento e vie di comunicazione.' *Archeologia Laziale* 7.2 (1986): 30-69.

—., et al. 'La media età del Bronzo nel territorio di Roma.' In *L'età del bronzo in Italia nei secoli dal XVI al XIV a.C.. Viareggio 26-30 Ottobre 1989 (= Rassegna di Archeologia, 10)*, edited by D. Cocchi Genick, 439-454. Firenze: All'Insegna del Giglio, 1991-1992.

Cardosa, M. 'Gli assetti territoriali protovillanoviano e villanoviano alla luce dei modelli dell'archeologia spaziale.' In Preistoria e Protostoria in Etruria. Atti del Primo Incontro di Studi. Saturnia (Manciano)-Farnese 17-19 maggio 1991. La cultura di Rinaldone. Ricerche e Scavi., edited by N. Negroni Catacchi, 261-268. Milano: Eureka Graph Lab, 1993.

Clarke, D.L. 'Spatial information in Archaeology.' In *Spatial Archaeology*, edited by D.L. Clarke, 1-33. London- New York- San Francisco : Academic Press, 1977.

di Gennaro, F. Forme di insediamento fra Tevere e Fiora dal Bronzo Finale al principio dell'età del Ferro, Firenze. Firenze: All'Insegna del Giglio, 1986.

—. 'Il popolamento dell'Etruria meridionale e le caratteristiche degli insediamenti tra l'età del Bronzo e l'età del Ferro.' In *Etruria meridionale. Conoscenza, conservazione e fruizione (Atti del Convegno, Viterbo, 1985)*, edited by G. Colonna, C. Bettini and R.A. Staccioli, 59-82. Roma: Ed. Quasar, 1988.

—. 'Italia Centrale e Meridionale.' In *L'antica età del Bronzo. Atti del Congresso di Viareggio, 9-12 Gennaio 1995*, edited by D. Cocchi Genick, 234-245. Firenze: Octavo Franco Contini Editore, 1996.

—. '"Paesaggi di Potere": l'Etruria meridionale in età protostorica.' In *Paesaggi di potere. Problemi e prospettive, Atti del Seminario Udine 16-17 maggio 1996*, edited by A. De Guio G. Camassa and F. Veronese, 95-119. Roma: Quasar, 2000.

Ducke, B. Seminar presented within the Summer School Quantitative Methods and Data Analysis in Archaeology, Campiglia Marittima, 10th-17th September 2006, *s.l.*, 2006.

Fulminante, F. *Landscape of Power in Early Iron Age Latium Vetus: defining proto-urban developments in Middle Tyrrhenian Italy*. Paper presented at paper presented at TRAC Conference (Theoretical Roman Archaeology Conference), Department of Classics, University of Cambridge, 24th - 25th March, 2006, Cambridge, England, 2006.

Gianni, A. 'Il Farro, il Cervo ed il villaggio mobile: Economia di sussistenza, insediamento, territorio, tra III e II millennio a.C. nel Lazio meridionale e nella Campania settentrionale.' *Scienze dell'Antichità. Storia, Archeologia, Antropologia* 5 (1991): 99-161.

Guidi, A. 'An application of the Rank-Size rule to proto-historic settlement in the middle Thyrrenian area.' In *Papers in Italian Archaeology, 4, 3. Pattern in proto-history*, edited by Malone C. and S. Stoddart, 217-242. Oxford: BAR international series, 1985.

—. 'Il Lazio e la Sabina tra la tarda età del Bronzo e l'età del Ferro.' In *Paesaggi di potere. Problemi e prospettive, Atti del Seminario Udine 16-17 maggio 1996*, edited by A. De Guio G. Camassa and F. Veronese, 85-94. Roma: Quasar, 2000.

Haggett, P. *Analysis in Human Geography*. London: Edward Arnold, 1965.

Haselgrove, C. 'Central Places in British Iron Age Studies: a Review and Some Problems.' In *Central Places, Archaeology and History*, edited by E. Grant, 3-13. Sheffield: Sheffield University Print Union, 1986.

Heiken, G., R. Funiciello and D. de Rita. *The Seven Hills of Rome. A geological Tour of the Ethernal City*. Princeton- Oxford: Princeton University Press, 2005.

Hodder, I. and C. Orton, C. (eds.). *Spatial Analysis in Archaeology*. Cambridge: Cambridge University Press, 1976.

Jenness, J. *Surface Tools (surf_tools-avx) extension for ArcView 3.x, v.1.6. Jenness Enterprises*, 2005. URL: www.jennessent.com/arcview/surface_tools.htm.

—. *Topographic Position Index (tpi_jen.avx) extension for ArcView 3.x. Jenness Enterprises*, 2005. URL: www.jennessent.com/arcview/tpi.htm.

Johnson, G.A. 'Aspects of Regional Analysis in Archaeology.' *Annual Review of Anthropology* 6 (1977): 479-508.

—. 'Rank-size convexity and system integration: a view from archaeology.' *Economic geography* 56 (1980): 234-247.

Johnson, J.A. 'Monitoring complex system integration and boundary phenomena with settlement size data.' In *Archaeological approaches to the study of complexity*, edited by S.E. vander Leeuw, 144-188. Amsterdam: Universiteit van Amsterdam, 1981.

Lan, M. 'Polygon Characterisation With the Multiplicatively Weighted Voronoi Diagrams.' *The Professional Geographer* 56, no. 2 (2004): 223-239.

Machovina, B.J. Modeling Pedestrian Mobility Across a natural landscape using Geographical Information System, Master Dissertation, Ohio: Ohio State University, 1996.

Morris, I. 'The Collapse and Regeneration of Complex Societies in Greece. 1500-500 B.C. (Version 1.0, December).' In *Princeton/Stanford working Papers in Classics*, 2005. URL: *www.princeton.edu/~pswpc/*.

Pacciarelli, M. 'Topografia dell'insediamento dell'età del Bronzo Recente nel Lazio.' *Archeologia Laziale* 2 (= Quaderni del centro di studio per l'archeologia etrusco- italica, 3) (1979): 161-170.

—. Dal villaggio alla citta'. La svolta proto-urbana del 1000 a.C. nell'Italia tirrenica. Firenze: All'Insegna del Giglio, 2001.

Peroni, R. 'Formazione e sviluppi dei centri protourbani medio-tirrenici.' In *Roma, Romolo, Remo e la fondazione della città (exhibition catalogue)*, edited by R. Cappelli and A. Carandini, 26-30. Milano: Electa, 2000.

Rajala, U. 'Gis in the analysis of the settlement patterns in central Italy. The possibilities and problems in studying south-east Etruria.' In *Classical Archaeology towards the Third Millenium. Reflections and Perspectives. Proceedings of the XVth International Congress of Classical Archaeology, Amsterdam, July 12-17*, edited by R.F. Docter, and E.M. Moormann, 310-313. Amsterdam: Allan Pearson Museum, 1999.

—. Human Landscapes in Tyrrhenian Italy. GIS in the study of urbanisation, settlement patterns and land use in south Etruria and western Latium. Unpublished PhD Dissertation, University of Cambridge, Cambridge, 2002.

—. 'From a Settlement to an Early State? The Role of Nepi in the Local and Regional Settlement Patterns of the Faliscan Area and inner Etruria during the Iron Age.' In *Papers in Italian Archaeology VI. Communities and Settlements from the Neolithic to the Early Medieval Period. Proceedings of the 6th Conference of italian Archaeology held at the University of Groningen, Groningen Institute of Archaeology, The Netherlands, April 15-17, 2003*, edited by P. Attema, A. Nijboer and A. Zifferero, 706-712. Oxford: Hadrian Book, 2005.

Renfrew, C. 'Trade as Action at a Distance: Questions of Integration and Communication.' In *Ancient civilization and trade*, edited by C.C. Lamberg-Karlovsky and J. Sabloff, 3-59. Albunquerque: University of New Mexico Press, 1975.

Renfrew, C., Level, E.V. 'Exploring Dominance: Predicting Polities from Centers.' In *Transformations. Mathematical Approaches to culture Change*, edited by Cooke K.C. and C. Renfrew, 145-167. New York-San Francisco-London, 1979.

Steponaitis, V.S. 'Location Theory and Complex Chiefdoms: A Mississippian Example.' In *Mississippian Settlement Patterns*, edited by B.D. Smith, 417-454. New York-San Francisco-London: Harcourt Brace Jovanovich Publisher, 1978.

Stoddart, S. 'The Political Landscape of Etruria.' *The Accordia Research Paper* 1 (1990): 40-51.

Stoddart, S. and D. Redhouse. Complexity and Landscape: a case study from Etruria. Paper presented at Defining Social Complexity. Approaches to power and interaction in the archaeological record, 11-13 March. Cambridge, 2005.

Wilkinson, T.J. *Archaeological Landscapes of the Near East*. Tucson: The University of Arizona Press, 2003.

Zipf, G.K. Human Behaviour and the Principle of Least Effort. An Introduction to Human Ecology. New York: Hafner, 1949.

Appendix

Table 8-I: *Latium vetus*: lithology within a catchment area of 2 km for Bronze Age sites and 5 km for Early Iron Age sites: single variables.

Class Type	Class description
classe A	Anthropic soils
classe B	Alluvial and colluvial soils
Classe C	Travertine
classe D1	Gravel deposits
classe D2	Sand deposits
classe D3	Coastal, lake and dune sands
classe E	Clay deposits
classe G	Calcarenitic, organic, clay-limestone and marls
classe L	Marls, calcareous-marls, dolomic limestone
classe I	Scaglia cinerea formations
classe M	Majolica, marleous and selciferous limestone
classe N	Cavernous limestone
classe Q	Volcanic scoria, lapilli and pozzolana
classe R	Volcanic *lava*
classe S1	Lithoid tuff
classe S2	Stratified tuff, *tufiti* and *tuff* soils

Table 8-II (top): Legend to Figs. 3 and 4 and Table I.
Table 8-III (bottom): *Latium vetus*: sites-elevation association.

Latium Vetus: sites- elevation association plain= 0-75 m; hill= 75-800 m; mountain= 800- m

data						
Elevation	MBA	RBA	FBA	EIA1E	EIA1L	EIA2
0-75	33	30	34	17	17	21
75-800	32	24	37	46	41	43
800-			3	3	3	3
Total	65	54	74	66	61	67

%						
Elevation	MBA	RBA	FBA	EIA1E	EIA1L	EIA2
0-75	51%	56%	46%	26%	28%	31%
75-800	49%	44%	50%	70%	67%	64%
800-			4%	5%	5%	4%

chi-square test probability value					
MBA	RBA	FBA	EIA1E	EIA1L	EIA2
0,849	0,485	0,917	0,053	0,016	0,045

Latiu Vetus: sites- slope association 6 slope classes					

	data					
Slope	MBA	RBA	FBA	EIA1E	EIA1L	EIA2
Ridge	15	19	36	34	36	40
Upper Slope	9	7	13	11	15	16
Middle Slope	17	7	5	6	6	7
Flat Slope	16	14	12	4	3	3
Lower Slope	5	5	5	1	1	1
Valley	3	2	2			
total	65	54	73	56	61	67

	%					
Slope	MBA	RBA	FBA	EIA1E	EIA1L	EIA2
Ridge	23%	35%	49%	61%	59%	60%
Upper Slope	14%	13%	18%	20%	25%	24%
Middle Slope	26%	13%	7%	11%	10%	10%
Flat Slope	25%	26%	16%	7%	5%	4%
Lower Slope	8%	9%	7%	2%	2%	1%
Valley	5%	4%	3%	0%	0%	0%

Chi- square test probability value					
MBA	RBA	FBA	EIA1E	EIA1L	EIA2
0,000	0,000	0,000	0,000	0,000	0,000

Table 8-IV: *Latium vetus*, sites-slope association.

CHAPTER NINE

BY THE RIVERS DARK:
HALHALLA[KI], CITY OF SOLDIERS
AND PRIESTESSES, OR: HOW CUNEIFORM
DOCUMENTS CAN CONTRIBUTE TO THE STUDY
AND RECONSTRUCTION OF PAST LANDSCAPES[1]

KATRIEN DE GRAEF

> By the rivers dark, where it all
> goes on. By the rivers dark, in
> Babylon.
> —L. Cohen

Introduction

Contrary to most of the papers given during this colloquium, in which the use of field and aerial survey techniques in the study of past landscapes are discussed, we start our inquiry from a completely other point of view, namely that of the cuneiform tablets from Mesopotamia. What do these texts say? Which information do they contain? What can they contribute to the reconstruction of the past landscape?

To answer these questions, we shall focus on one particular case, namely that of the city of Halhalla. This city is mentioned in forty-three tablets presumably originating from Sippar[2] all dating from the Old Babylonian period,

---

[1] This article presents research results of the "Interuniversity Pole of Attraction Programme V/14, Belgian State, Federal Office for Scientific, Technical and Cultural Affairs".
[2] An earlier, very extensive study on the Old Babylonian city of Halhalla not centering on its location, can be found in Stol, Die altbabylonische Stadt Halhalla.

roughly the first half of the second millennium BCE[3], By "Sippar" we mean one of the two cities named Sippar, located respectively at Abu Habbah and Tell ed-Dēr, whose appellations changed according to periods and contexts.[4] In the Old Babylonian period, present Abu Habbah was called Sippar-Jahrārum and Tell ed-Dēr was called Sippar-Amnānum. Both Sippars were located on the course of the Euphrates in this period.[5] In many cases though, our tablets only mention "Sippar" without specifying whether Jahrārum or Amnānum is meant. For the Old Babylonian scribae it must have been quite obvious which city they meant. Unfortunately, this is not always the case for us... consequently we use "Sippar", meaning one of the two cities.

Thank heavens, it seems that there is only one city called Halhalla. However, the location of Halhalla is as yet unkown. In what follows, we shall examine to what extent the Old Babylonian tablets can shed further light to the location of Halhalla in particular, and can contribute to the reconstruction of the Mesopotamian landscape in the Old Babylonian period in general.

Most of the texts in our corpus mention the sale, lease or inheritance of immobilia – mostly fields and houses – in Halhalla and its area. In writing down these transactions, detailed information on the location of the field or house in question is given, such as the neighbours, the *ugārum* or irrigation district in which it is situated and sometimes a river, canal or *namkarum* (large irrigation canal) situated nearby. This means that for some fields and houses, it is possible to draw a detailed map of the immediate neighbourhood and to bring to life the microcosm of a particular small area. Unfortunately, it is not always very easy to find any coherence in this patchwork of small indications due to the many black spots still existing on the map.

As for Halhalla, there is hope: the proximity of Halhalla to three important watercourses – the Euphrates, the Tigris and the King's Canal – makes it possible to narrow down the region of its location. Recent studies by Gasche, Cole and Tanret have proposed new courses of these three watercourses which

---

[3] All dates referred to in this article follow the Short Chronology as stated in Gasche, Armstrong, Cole and Gurzadyan, Dating the Fall of Babylon. The difference with the so-called "Middle Chronology" is -96 years for the reigns of the Old Babylonian kings.

[4] Cf. Charpin, Sippar: deux villes jumelles, Dekiere, Some Remarks on Sippar-Amnānum = Sippar rabûm, Woestenburg, Sippar rabûm and Woestenburg and Jagersma, The Continuing Story of *Sippar-Amnānum = Sippar-rabûm*.

[5] Cf. Cole and Gasche, Second- and First Millennium BC Rivers in Northern Babylonia, p. 24 and p. 45, Map 5.

allow to go further in the localization of the town and relate this significantly to the landscape.

The corpus: archival and archaeological problems

Before making an excursion to the Old Babylonian city of Halhalla, we should have a look at our corpus of tablets.

Forty-one Old Babylonian texts mention the toponym Halhalla.[6] Most of them are said to have been found in Sippar, but since all of them – apart from one tablet belonging to the archive of Ur-Utu, chief dirge singer of Annunītum, excavated in the '70s by De Meyer and Gasche in Tell ed-Dēr, ancient Sippar-Amnānum[7] – originate from illicit excavations, we have no external indication of their origin. Fortunately, most of them have textual indications that point to Sippar: an oath sworn by the city of Sippar[8], or the involvement of individuals known to be from Sippar as witnesses or parties.[9]

In any case, since the city of Halhalla is not yet located, neither by archaeologists nor by looters, the tablets cannot have been kept in Halhalla itself. This does not mean that they could not have been written in this city, it only means that they were kept by their last owners, in Sippar. Some of them were certainly written in Sippar, others might have been written in Halhalla but transported and stored in Sippar.

---

[6] *CT* 6, 20a (Si 29), *CT* 6, 21c (s.d.), *CT* 6, 33a (Si 8), *CT* 8, 6b = *MHET* II 378 (Si 3), *CT* 8, 20a (Sm), *CT* 8, 39b = *MHET* II 112 (Sm), *CT* 45, 34 (Si 15), *CT* 47, 29 (Ha 7), *CT* 47, 56 (Si 4), *CT* 47, 62 (Si 9), *CT* 47, 64 (Si 16), *CT* 47, 65 (Si 25), *CT* 47, 68 (s.d.), *CT* 47, 70 (Ae p), *CT* 47, 78 (s.d.), *CT* 48, 19 (Ha 27 ?), *BDHP* 40 (Sm), *MHET* II, 63 (s.d.), *MHET* II, 131 (Ha), *MHET* II, 135 (Ha), *MHET* II, 248 (Ha 32), *MHET* II, 255 (Ha 34), *MHET* II, 333 (Ha), *MHET* II, 413 (Si 8), *MHET* II, 417 (Si 10), *MHET* II, 426 (Si 14), *MHET* II, 430 (Si 15), *MHET* II, 607 (s.d.), *MHET* II, 615 (s.d.), *MHET* II, 616 (s.d.), *MHET* II, 627 (s.d.), *MHET* II, 630 (s.d.), *MHET* II, 748 (s.d.), *MHET* II, 843 (Za), Van Lerberghe, *On Storage in Old-Babylonian Sippar*, p. 40 (BM 81128 [s.d.]), BM 22546 (Aṣ 10), BM 22636 (Si 30), BM 22661 (s.d.), BM 22697 (AS 8), BM 80529 (s.d.) and Di 1633 (Aṣ 2).

[7] Di 1633 (Aṣ 2).

[8] E.g. *CT* 47, 29: (20) mu ^dutu ^dAMAR.UTU *Ha-am-mu-ra-bi* (21) *ù* uru ud.kib.nun^{ki} *it-mu-ú* (They swore an oath by Šamaš, Marduk, Hammurabi and the city of Sippar).

[9] E.g. the first witness in the sale document *CT* 47, 56, which is Annum-pī-Aja, a well-known *sanga* of Šamaš from Sippar, cf. Harris, Ancient Sippar, p. 155 sq.

Three of the tablets mentioning Halhalla are actually tags which were attached to wicker baskets in antiquity.[10] We know these wicker baskets were used to transport as well as to stock tablets. The first tag is published and reads "basket with tablets from Halhalla and Meriqat".[11] The two others are not yet published, but are described in the British Museum catalogue as follows: "basket with tablets concerning the fields in Halhalla" and "basket with tablets about *kaparru*-sheperds, some of them sealed by king Hammurabi, others by the town of Halhalla". It goes without saying that the wicker baskets bearing these tags – certainly the first two – belonged to the archive of an individual, probably an inhabitant of Old Babylonian Sippar. These persons or families kept the documents stating their property in the area of Halhalla – and Meriqat as stated in the first tag; these might have been neighbouring regions – in a separate basket. Unfortunately we have no clue as to which tablets were kept in these baskets, due to the fact that the tags as well as the tablets have come to us separately as the result of illicit excavations. Consequently, we will never be able to reconstruct the archival context of these tablets which would provide us no doubt with much information that is now irretrievably lost. Here, we can only but stress again the great importance of the archival and archaeological context in interpreting and understanding cuneiform tablets.

Apart from the 41 texts mentioning Halhalla, we can add other texts to our corpus, namely those texts mentioning a geographical feature, for instance an irrigation district, which can be located in Halhalla with certainty.[12] This increases our corpus of texts considerably and provides us with extra information on the region.[13]

---

[10] Van Lerberghe, On Storage in Old-Babylonian Sippar, p. 40 (BM 81128 [s.d.]), BM 22546 (Aṣ 10) and BM 22661 (s.d.).

[11] Ibid., p. 40: (1) gi.pisan (2) dub-*pa-at hal-hal-la* (3) *ù me-ri-ga-at* "Reed basket: Tablets of Halhalla and Merigat".

[12] We know for example from *MHET* II 417 (Si 10) that the irrigation district *Gaminānum* is located in Halhalla (*MHET* II 417: (1) 0.0.3 iku a.šà šà 0.1.0 iku (2) *i-na* a.gàr *ga-mi-na-num ša hal-hal-la*^{ki} "a field of 1.08 ha, part of a field of 2.16 ha, located in the irrigation district *Gaminānum* situated in Halhalla"), which means that all other texts mentioning fields located in the irrigation district *Gaminānum* (*MHET* II 850 [Ha 14?], *CT* 2, 41 [Ha 38] and *BDHP* 3 [Ad 5?]) concern fields located in Halhalla. Also other elements, such as the appearance of the mayor (*rabiānum*) of Halhalla – mostly as first witness – in a text, can link the fields, watercourses and/or irrigation districts mentioned in this text with Halhalla.

[13] An enumeration of geographical features which can be located in Halhalla with certainty and the texts mentioning these would lead us to far for the purpose of this article. A complete list of texts mentioning geographical features which can be located in

Geographical elements

Apart from the corpus of Old Babylonian administrative documents, two other sources providing us with information on the location of Halhalla should be mentioned: 1) A watercourse called Halhalla is known to us from Sumerian mythology[14]. In later lexical lists, this watercourse is equated with the Tigris[15], which stresses the importance and proximity of the Tigris for and to the city of Halhalla. 2) A letter from Mari states that Halhalla is located *šaplānum* Sippar[16]. In his article on the city of Halhalla, Stol translates *šaplānum* here as "below, beneath" – Halhalla being located in his opinion below Sippar, but *šaplānum* can also be interpreted as "downstream", which we think is the right interpretation in this context. Halhalla is not located *below* Sippar, which is way to far from the Tigris, but downstream the Euphrates, which leads – following the recent reconstruction of the course of the Euphrates in the second millennium BC proposed by Cole and Gasche[17] – indeed to the Tigris.

It goes without saying that commenting the whole of our corpus – more than 150 tablets – would lead us too far for this paper. Therefore, we shall discuss here the tablets mentioning the key points in locating Halhalla. These key points are the three watercourses Euphrates, Tigris and King's Canal. For every one of

---

Halhalla with certainty will be given in our forthcoming study on the Old Babylonian city of Halhalla.

[14] In Sumerian mythology texts íd hal-hal-la is translated as "rolling river" (often in plural), cf. "How Grain Came to Sumer" l. 17: íd hal-hal a ki-ta DU.DU X AM? X X X ("... the rolling river, where the water wells up from earth"), "Lugalbanda in the Mountain Cave", l. 266: íd hal-hal-la ama hur-sag-gá-ke$_4$ a nam-til-la im-tùm ("The rolling rivers, mothers of the hills, brought life-saving water"), l. 306: a íd hal-hal-la-ka i-im-na$_8$-na$_8$-dè ("It was drinking the water of the rolling rivers") and l. 318: a íd hal-hal-la-ka i-im-na$_8$-na$_8$-ne ("They were drinking the water of the rolling rivers"), "Lugalbanda and the Anzud Bird", l. 99: íd hal-hal-la nun nam tar-re-bi-me-en ("I am the prince who decides the destiny of rolling rivers"), "Šulgi and Ninlil's Barge (Šulgi R)", l. 49: [íd] hal-hal-la [i]-kur$_9$-ru X a mul-mul-la? [X X] X X X [X] ("... enters the rolling river; ... on the shining water"), and "A šir-namšub to Utu (Utu F)", l. 30: íd hal-hal-la a-ki-ta sù-ud-bi-[šè kur-šè] ("to the distant source of the rolling rivers, to the mountains"). All transliterations and translations are taken from the ETCSL. Cf. also Stol, Die altbabylonische Stadt Halhalla, p. 418 n. 12 with further references.

[15] Cf. Ibid., p. 418 n. 12 with references.

[16] *ARMT* 26/1, 100-bis: (5) *i-na a-lim ha-al-ha-la*^{ki} *ša-ap-⌈la⌉-nu-um* ⌈zimbir⌉^{ki} *[e-pu-uš]* "in the city of Halhalla, downstream of Sippar [he did]".

[17] Cf. Cole and Gasche, Second- and First-Millennium BC Rivers in Northern Babylonia, p. 24-25 and p. 49 Map 8.

these three elements, we shall give one or more examples showing how our texts describe the location of a field or house in relation to these watercourses and consequently what conclusion can be drawn from these texts regarding to the location of Halhalla.

The Euphrates

Several texts mention the Euphrates in connection with Halhalla.[18] Two of them are discussed as an example:

A. *MHET* II, 426[19] is a contract stating the exchange of three fields in the area of Halhalla, all situated along the Euphrates, dated from the 14th year of reign of Samsu-iluna. Sîn-aham-iddinam gives a field located between the western bank of the Euphrates and the Great Dike – which is located next to the *atappum* or small irrigation canal called after Ikūn-pī-Sîn, adjacent to the West Road on the one side, and to the *atappum* called after Ikūn-pī-Sîn and a field owned by Sîn-aham-iddinam on the other, to Ikūn-pī-Sîn. In exchange, he receives from Ikūn-pī-Sîn two fields of the same size. One located between the

---

[18] For a complete list of texts linking the Euphrates with Halhalla or geographical features located in Halhalla, see our forthcoming study on Halhalla.

[19] (1) ⌈0.0.2⌉ iku 10 sar a.šà ⌈ú⌉.[sal ^id ud.kib.nun^ki] (2) *i-ta* e gu.la *ša i-ta a-⌈tap⌉-[pu]-⌈um⌉* (3) *i-ku-un-pí-sin* dumu *sin-ta-⌈ia⌉-ar* (4) *ù i-ta* ^id ud. ⌈kib⌉.nun (5) sag.bi.1.kam *ia-ru-⌈x⌉-ú* (6) sag.bi.2.kam *a-tap-pu-um* (7) *ša ⌈i⌉-ku-un-pí-sin* dumu ^d EN.ZU⌉-*ta-ia-⌈ar⌉* (8) *ù a.šà sin-šeš-i-din-nam* ⌈dumu⌉ *tu-za-lum* (9) a.šà ^d EN.ZU-šeš-*i-din-nam* dumu *tu-za-lum* (10) *pu-ha-ti-šu* (11) 0.0.1 iku 6 sar a.šà ú. ⌈sal⌉ ^id ud.⌈kib⌉.nun^ki (12) ^d utu.sú.a (13) *i-ta* e gu.la (14) *ù i-ta* ^id ud.kib.⌈nun⌉^ki (15) ⌈sag⌉.bi.1.kam ⌈*nam*⌉-*kar a-⌈tá⌉-nu-um* (16) ⌈sag⌉.bi.2.kam a.šà ⌈*a*⌉-*hu-um-li-ši-ir* (17) ⌈dumu⌉ *ip-qú-ša* (18) [0.0.1] iku ⌈ù? 4⌉ sar a.šà (19) ú.sal ^id ud.kib.nun^ki (20) ^d utu.sú.a (21) *i-ta* e *ša i-ku-un-pí-sin* dumu *sin-ta-⌈ia⌉-[ar]* (22) *ù i-ta* ^id ud.kib.nun^ki (23) sag.bi.1.kam *nam-kar a-tá-nu-um* (24) sag.bi.2.kam a.šà *be-la-[nu]* dumu *ta-ri-bu-um* (25) šu.nígin 0.0.2 iku 10 sar a.šà (26) a.šà *i-ku-un-pí-sin* dumu *sin-ta-⌈ia⌉-[ar]*.

"7560 m² field on the bank of the Euphrates, located next to the Great Dike, which is next to the small irrigation canal of Ikūn-pī-Sîn, son of Sîn-tajjar, and next to the Euphrates; on the one side lies the West Road, on the other the small irrigation canal of Ikūn-pī-Sîn, son of Sîn-tajjar and the field of Sîn-aham-iddinam, son of Tuzālum; field of Sîn-aham-iddinam, son of Tuzālum, his exchange property (for) 3816 m² field on the bank of the Euphrates, at the West side, located next to the Great Dike and the Euphrates; on the one side lies the irrigation canal Atānum, on the other the field of Ahum-lišir, son of Ipquša (and) 3744 m² field at the bank of the Euphrates, at the West side, located next to the dike of Ikūn-pī-Sîn, son of Sîn-tajjar and the Euphrates; on the one side lies the irrigation canal Atānum, on the other the field of Bēlanu, son of Taribum; a total (surface) of 7560 m² field; field of Ikūn-pī-Sîn, son of Sîn-tajjar".

This text is also discussed in Tanret, Le Namkarum, pp. 86-90.

western bank of the Euphrates and the Great Dike, adjacent to the *namkarum* (large irrigation canal) Atānum and a field owned by Ahum-lišir, the other located between the western bank of the Euphrates and the dike called after Ikūn-pī-Sîn, adjacent to the Euphrates and the *namkarum* Atānum. It goes without saying that all three fields are neighbouring. The purpose of the exchange is no doubt the concentration of the land by both landowners.

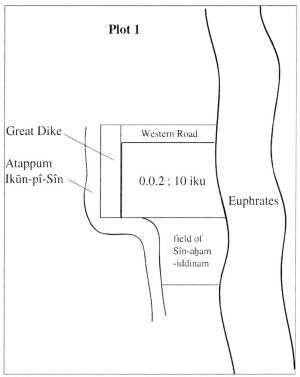

Fig. 9-1a: Relationship between Halhalla and the Euphrates

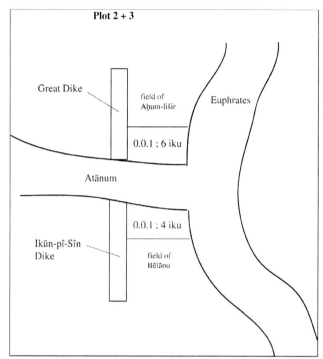

Fig. 9-1b: Relationship between Halhalla and the Euphrates

B. *CT* 47, 56[20] records the sale of a field from Naramtāni, *nadītu*-priestess of Šamaš, to Amat-Šamaš, also *nadītu*-priestess of Šamaš, in the 4th year of Samsu-iluna. The field is situated in the irrigation district Abi in the city of Halhalla, along the bank of the Euphrates and opposite the steppe, adjacent to a field owned by Tarībum on the one side and a field owned by Rīm-Sîn on the other.

---

[20] (1) 0.0.4 iku a.šà a.gàr ⌈a-bi⌉ (2) *i-na* ᵘʳᵘ*hal-hal-la*ᵏⁱ (3) *i-ta* a.šà *ta-ri-bu-um* dumu *ṭà-*⌈*ab*⌉*-ṣíl-lí* (4) *ù i-ta* a.šà *ri-im-*ᵈEN.ZU (5) sag.bi ⁱᵈud.kib.nunᵏⁱ (6) sag.bi.2.kam *pa-ni* edin (7) ki *na-ra-am-ta-ni* lukur ᵈutu (8) dumu.munus *ri-iš-*ᵈutu (9) ¹géme-ᵈutu dumu.munus dingir-*šu-i-bi-šu* (10) *i-na* har kù.babbar-*ša* in.ši.in.šám (11) šám.til.la.bi.šè (12) 1/2 ma.na 1 gín 20 še kù.babbar (13) in.na.an.lá.
"1.44 ha field of the irrigation district Abi, located in the city of Halhalla, next to the field of Tarībum, son of Tāb-ṣilli, and the field of Rīm-Sîn; on the one side lies the Euphrates, on the other the front side of the steppe; from Naramtāni, *nadītu*-priestess of Šamaš, daughter of Rēš-Šamaš, Amat-Šamaš, daughter of Ilšu-ibbišu (she) bought (it) with her ring money; as its total price, 259.3 gr. of silver she paid".

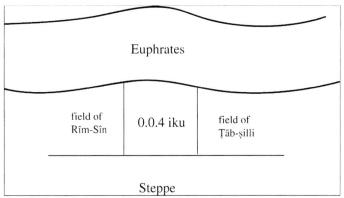

Fig. 9-2: Relationship between Halhalla and the Euphrates

From these and other texts, we can conclude that Halhalla was located not far from the Euphrates. Halhalla itself was not located along the banks of the Euphrates, but several fields belonging to its territory were. Especially since the irrigation district Abi, located along the Euphrates, is said to be situated *in* the city of Halhalla – which probably means this irrigation district started within or at the border of the city itself – the city must have been located not far from the bank of the Euphrates.

The Tigris

One text, *CT* 47, 58[21], the testamentary disposition of Aja-kuzub-mātum, a *nadītu*-priestess of Šamaš, daughter of Ṣilli-Akšak, dated in the 7th year of reign of Samsu-iluna, mentions the Tigris. This Aja-kuzub-mātum leaves to Nīši-

---

[21] (1) ibila ^da-a-ku-zu-ub-ma-tum lukur ^dutu (2) dumu.munus ṣíl-lí-úh^{ki} (3) ^Ini-ši-i-ni-šu lukur ^dutu dumu.munus ^dutu-na-ṣir (4) re-di-it wa-ar-ka-ti-ša (5) 0.1.5 1/2 iku a.šà i-na a.gàr qá-ab-li-im (6) i-ta a.šà wa-tar-^di-ku-nu-um (7) ù i-ta sa-bi-bu-um dumu ha-ia-ab-ni-dingir (8) 0.2.0 iku a.šà i-na ká uru^{ki} (9) ^{íd}idigna i-ka-al ù i-na-ad-di-ma
"Testamentary disposition of Aja-kuzub-mātum, *nadītu*-priestess of Šamaš, daughter of Ṣilli-Akšak. Nīši-inīšu, *nadītu*-priestess of Šamaš, daughter of Šamaš -nāṣir, is her legitimate heir: 4.14 ha field in the irrigation district Qablûm, located next to the field of Watar-Ikūnum and (the field of) Sabibum, son of Hajabni-el; 4.32 ha field in (the irrigation district) Bāb ālim, the Tigris eats and throws."
Although the city of Halhalla is not mentioned on this particular tablet, we know for sure that both irrigation districts mentioned on this tablet – *Qablûm* and *Bāb ālim* – are to be located in the vicinity and/or area of Halhalla, cf. Stol, Die altbabylonische Stadt Halhalla, p. 419 and pp. 429-431.

inīšu, a *nadītu*-priestess of Šamaš adopted by her, two fields in the area of Halhalla. Of one field, situated in the irrigation district *Bāb ālim*, it is said that the Tigris "eats and throws". This indicates a process of erosion which allows us to conclude that this field was situated on the bank of the Tigris, more specifically in a bend/meander of this watercourse.

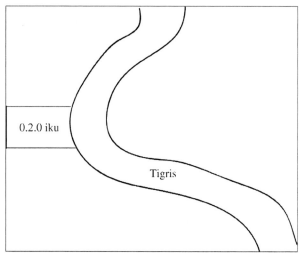

Fig. 9-3: Relationship between Halhalla and the Tigris

We know for sure that the irrigation district *Bāb ālim* is situated in the area of Halhalla, and since *Bāb ālim* means "gate of the city", the district must have been located rather close to the city itself. This means Halhalla was located not far from the bank of the Tigris.

How can we bring these facts into conformity with the reality on the field? A city being located near the Euphrates *and* the Tigris is impossible with the present-day courses of both rivers, which at their closest point, near Baghdad, are situated ca. 50 km apart from one another.

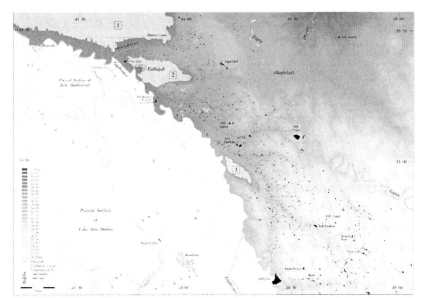

Fig. 9-4: Sites and levee systems in Mesopotamia (from Cole and Gasche, p. 43, Map 3)

Recently, Cole and Gasche[22] stated that in the Old Babylonian period the Euphrates came very close to the Tigris and both probably even joined. This hypothesis is based largely on a cuneiform text published by Feigin in which a single field bordering both on the Euphrates *and* on the Tigris in the hinterland of Puš is given to the *nadītu*-priestess Bēltāni during the reign of Samsu-iluna.[23] The fact that Halhalla must have been situated near the Euphrates and the Tigris confirms the hypothesis of Cole and Gasche. Indeed, the location of Halhalla is to be found in that area where the Euphrates and Tigris came very close to one another in the Old Babylonian period, namely in the general region of the later Seleucia.

---

[22] Cf. Cole and Gasche, Second- and First-Millennium BC Rivers in Northern Babylonia, p. 24-25 and p. 49 Map 8.

[23] *YOS* 12, 469 (Si 25): (4) ⌈sag.bi⌉.1.kam [id]idigna (5) sag.bi.[2.kam id]ud.kib.nun^ki "One the one side lies the Tigris, on the other the Euphrates". For this passage, also cf. Cole and Gasche, Second- and First-Millennium BC Rivers in Northern Babylonia, p. 17, n. 71.

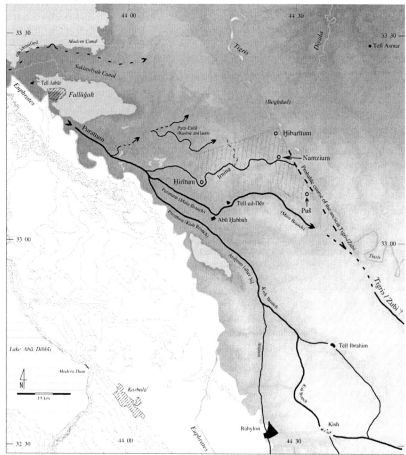

Fig. 9-5: Old Babylonian hydrology (from Cole and Gasche 1998, p. 45, Map 5)

The King's Canal

Besides the Euphrates and the Tigris, another important watercourse is mentioned in connection with Halhalla in various texts[24], namely the King's Canal. Some examples:

---

[24] For a complete list of texts linking the King's Canal with Halhalla or geographical features located in Halhalla, see our forthcoming study on Halhalla.

A. *MHET* II/5, 615[25], an undated tablet, mentions a field located in the irrigation district of Halhalla, situated along the bank of the King's Canal and between the fields owned respectively by Akšaja, son of Sîn-remēni, and by Erra-nada, son of Nakārum. We do not know if this field is bought, leased or given, since the rest of the tablet is broken.

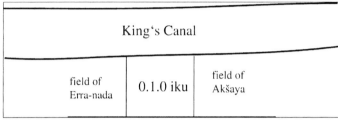

Fig. 9-6: Relative placement of the King's Canal

B. *MHET* II/1, 108[26] is the sale document of a field sold by Šamaš-ili, son of Watar-Ikūnim to Erišti-Aja, a *nadītu*-priestess of Šamaš during the reign of Sîn-muballiṭ. This field is situated in the irrigation district *Bāb ālim* – of which we have just come to know that it is situated in the area of Halhalla – between the fields owned respectively by Ibnātum, son of Wardīja, and by Taridum, son of Būr-Sîn, adjacent to the dike of the King's Canal and a field owned by Sîn-rimēni, son of Ikūn-pīša.

---

[25] (1) 0.1.0 iku a.šà *i-na* a.gàr *hal-hal-la*ki (2) *i-na* é *i-me-er-*[x] (3) *i-ta* a.šà úhki-*ia* dumu *sin-ri-me-ni* (4) *ù i-ta* a.šà ìr.ra-*na-da* (5) dumu *na-ka-ru-um* (6) sag.bi.1.kam idlugal
"2.16 ha field located in the irrigation district Halhalla, located in the house of Imer-x (?), next to the field of Akšaja, son of Sîn-remēni and the field of Erra-nada, son of Nakārum; on the one side lies the King's Canal".
[26] (1) 0.0.3 iku a.šà *i-na* ká *a-li-im* (2) *i-ta* a.šà *ib-*[*na*]-*tum* dumu ìr-*i-ia* (3) *ù i-ta* a.šà *ta-ri-du-um* dumu *bur-sin* (4) sag.bi.1.kam.ma e idšar-ri (5) sag.bi.2.kam.ma a.šà dEN.ZU-*ri-me-ni* (6) dumu *i-ku-un-pi-ša* (7) ki dutu-dingir dumu *wa-tar-i-ku-ni-im* (8) l*e-ri-iš-ti-*d*a-a* lukur dutu (9) dumu.munus *u-bar-*dutu (10) *i-na* har-*ša* in.ši-in.šám
"1.08 ha field in (the irrigation district) Bāb ālim, next to the field of Ibnātum, son of Wardīja and the field of Taridum, son of Būr-Sîn; on the one side lies the dike of the King's Canal, on the other the field of Sîn-remēni, son of Ikūn-pīša; from Šamaš-ilum, son of Watar-Ikūnum, Erišti-Aja, *nadītu*-priestess of Šamaš, daughter of Ubar-Šamaš (she) bought (it) with her ring money".

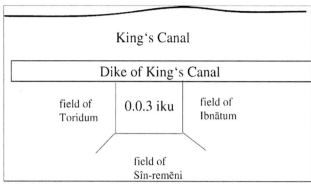

Fig. 9-7: Relative placement of the King's Canal

From these and other texts, we can conclude that Halhalla was also located near the King's Canal. The irrigation district called after the city – which no doubt must have been located close to or even in or at the border of the city – is situated along the banks of the King's Canal. Another irrigation district nearby Halhalla, namely *Bāb ālim* "gate of the city" is also situated on its banks. Yet, we know that *Bāb ālim* is also situated along the banks of the Tigris. From other texts, we know that the King's Canal branches off from the Euphrates. Taking into account that in the northern part of the Mesopotamian floodplain the altitude of the Tigris was lower than that of the Euphrates, it seems probable that the King's Canal flowed from the Euphrates onwards and joined the Tigris somewhere in the Halhalla area, above the point where the Euphrates may have joined the Tigris.

The same King's Canal, íd lugal in Sumerian and *nār šarrim* in Akkadian, also appears in later sources like the Talmud[27], where it is referred to as *nahar malka*. Even in present-day Irak, a canal called *nahr malka* still exists in that area.[28] The canal which is now called *nahr malka* corresponds to the watercourse which was called Euphrates in the Old Babylonian period.[29] Since we have proposed that the Old Babylonian King's Canal was a northern branch

[27] Cf. the Talmud tractates *Shabbath* 37b, 43a, 108a, *Beitzah* 29a, *Gittin* 73a, *Baba Metzia* 81b, *Eiruvin* 6b, *Yoma* 10a, *Yemavoth* 17a, *Kethuboth* 40a, *Kiddishin* 49b, 70b, 71b and *Sanhedrin* 64a. For the geography of Babylonia in Talmudic sources in general, cf. Obermeyer, Die Landschaft Babylonien im Zeitalter des Talmuds und des Gaonats and Oppenheimer, Babylonia Judaica in the Talmudic Period.

[28] Cf. Paschoud, La Naarmalcha: à propos du tracé d'un canal en Mésopotamie moyenne.

[29] Cf. Cole and Gasche, Second- and First-Millennium BC Rivers in Northern Babylonia, p. 51 Map 9.

of the Euphrates following a similar course in the direction of the Tigris, we must conclude that there must have been a name shift. Just like the name Euphrates shifted to the watercourse previously known as Arahtum, the name *nār šarrim* shifted from a side branch to the whole branch of the former part of the Euphrates which ran in the direction of the Tigris.

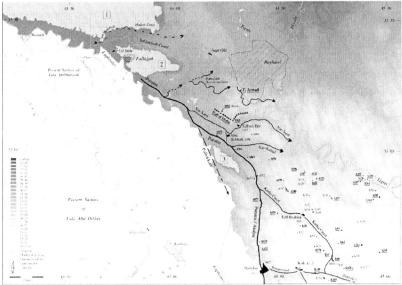

Fig. 9-8: Old Babylonian hydrology (from Cole and Gasche 1998, p. 51 Map 9)

In conclusion, we can locate Halhalla in the triangular region between the Euphrates, the Tigris and the King's Canal, more specifically in that area where the Euphrates and the King's Canal come very close or even join the Tigris.

Other elements: presence of soldiers and priestesses

Apart from the many geographical elements, our texts also provide us with other interesting information on the nature of life in this city and which may provide some additional suggestions as to its location.

Soldiers

Many texts point to a strong military presence in and around the city of Halhalla. This is remarkable since this seems not to be the case in other Old

Babylonian cities. A good example is *CT* 6, 20a[30], a sales document from the 29th year of reign of Samsu-iluna. Here, Amat-Mamu, a *nadītu*-priestess, daughter of Akšaja, buys a field and a house, both located in Halhalla, from Ibbatum, son of Mār-erṣētim. The field is located in the irrigation district Taptiātum, which is located in the city of Halhalla, between two fields owned by soldiers, adjacent to an area consisting of 3 iku fields and a field owned by Ikūn-pī-Sîn. The area of 3 iku (*ca.*1.08 ha) fields no doubt points to an area of *ṣibtum*-fields: land-holdings assigned by the state to soldiers as subsistence allotments in return for labour performed.[31] The house is located in the city of Halhalla, between the house of the daughter of Buṣum and the house of the soldiers, adjacent to an unnamed street on the one side, and Baṣum Street on the other.

Taking into account the location of Halhalla, the large presence of soldiers in and around the city should not surprise us. Like Šarrum-Laba and Hirītum in the north, alongside the Irnina, Halhalla is located in what we could call the northeastern border area of the Babylonian kingdom in this particular period, a border at least in part determined by the landscape of this time.[32] Indeed, from the Diyala region, in the hinterland of the Tigris, several enemies threatened the Old Babylonian empire: the city of Ešnunna and the Elamites in the beginning and the Kassites at the end of the period.[33] It seems thus very plausible that Halhalla was a garrison town. This hypothesis is actually confirmed by a newly

---

[30] (1) 0.1.0 iku a.šà a.gàr *tap-ti-a-tum* (2) *i-na hal-hal-la*[ki] (3) *i-ta* a.šà aga.uš.meš (4) *ù i-ta* a.šà aga.uš.meš-*ma* (5) sag.bi.1.kam.ma a.šà.hi.a 0.0.3 iku.ta.a (6) sag.bi.2.kam.ma a.šà *i-ku-un-pí-*[d]EN.ZU (7) dumu [d]EN.ZU-*ta-ia-ar* (8) *ša* ki SIG-*i-lí-šu* ugula dam.gàr *iš-ša-mu* (9) kù.bi 1/3 ma.na (10) 3 sar é.dù.a *i-na hal-hal-la*[ki] (11) da é dumu.munus *bu-ṣú-um* (12) *ù* da é aga.uš (13) sag.bi.1.kam sila (14) egir.bi sila *ba-ṣum* (15) kù.bi 10 gín (16) ki *ib-ba-tum* dumu dumu-ki (17) [ʾ]*a-ma-at-*[d]*ma-mu* lukur [d]utu (18) dumu.munus *ak-ša-ia* (19) *i-na* har kù.babbar.bi in.ši.in.šám

"2.16 ha field in the irrigation district Taptiātum, located in Halhalla, next to the field(s) of the soldiers and the field(s) of the soldiers; on the one side lie the fields measuring 1.08 ha per field, on the other side lies the field of Ikūn-pī-Sîn, son of Sîn-tajjar, which was bought from Ipiq-ilīšu, overseer of the merchants for the price of 166.6 gr. of silver; 108 m[2] of house located in Halhalla, next to the house of the daughter of Buṣum and the house of the soldiers, on the front side lies the street, on the rear side lies Baṣum Street, its price is 83 gr. of silver; from Ibbatum, son of Mār-erṣētim, Amat-Mamu, *nadītu*-priestess of Šamaš, daughter of Akšaja (she) bought (it) with her ring money".

[31] Cf. most recently De Graef, An Account of the Redistribution of Land to Soldiers in Late Old Babylonian Sippar-Amnānum with references.

[32] Cf. De Graef, Two ilšu-ibni's, two ugula gidru's. Šarrum-Laba[ki], a military settlement at the Irnina, pp. 76-77.

[33] Cf. Kuhrt, The Ancient Near East, pp. 76-80 and 332-333.

discovered text from the British Museum mentioning Halhalla in relation to "the enemy".[34]

Priestesses

It turns out that many of the landowners in Halhalla were *nadītu*-priestesses. In our view, there is no specific "religious" reason for this. We know of two cults in Halhalla: that of the god Ikūnum[35] and of the goddess Urkītum[36], but there is no particular relation between these cults and the *nadītu*-priestesses who were on the contrary dedicated to the sungod Šamaš. In our view, there are only economic reasons. Only daughters of the high elite in Sippar became *nadītu*-priestesses of Šamaš[37]. They could not marry nor have children so that the property given to them by their father would stay undivided within the family: every generation had its *nadītu*-priestess who inherited the family property as a whole and passed it on to the following generation. Why would they have owned land relatively far from Sippar? We can be sure that fields in the area of Halhalla were of great quality and well watered thanks to the vicinity of three great watercourses. For that reason it must have been a choice property for the upper class in the Old Babylonian society.

Conclusion

In this paper, we tried to give an idea on how cuneiform tablets can contribute in the reconstruction of the past landscape. In contracts such as sales, leases etc., the Old Babylonian scribes named elements of the contemporary landscape. When a field or house was sold, the city or greater area and irrigation district in which it was situated as well as the neighbours of the field or house in

---

[34] BM 80529 (s.d.), Rev. 6' and 14'. For the publication of this tablet, cf. our forthcoming study on the Old Babylonian city of Halhalla.

[35] Cf. for example Sîn-šaduni, sanga of Ikūnum in *CT* 47, 29: seal and *CT* 47, 62: 5-6, and the personal names Watar-Ikūnum in *CT* 47, 78: 7 and Ikūnum-gāmil in *MHET* II/3, 417: 3; cf. also Stol, Die altbabylonische Stadt Halhalla, pp. 437-438.

[36] BM 22697 (A-S 8) mentions ^d*ur-ki-tim ša hal-hal-la*^ki "Urkītum of Halhalla", cf. Stol, Die altbabylonische Stadt Halhalla, p. 438.

[37] On *nadītu's* in the Old Babylonian period in general, cf. Harris, The nadītu Laws of the Code of Hammu-rapi in Praxis, Biographical Notes on the nadītu Women of Sippar, The Organisation and Administration of the Cloister in Ancient Babylonia, The nadītu Women, Notes on the Babylonian Cloister and Hearth and Ancient Sippar, pp. 305-312 et passim, Renger, Untersuchungen zum Priestertum in der altbabylonischen Zeit, Janssen, Samsu-iluna and the Hungry Nadītums, Jeyes, The Naditu Women of Sippar and Stol Women in Mesopotamia and Titel altbabylonischer Klosterfrauen.

question were described in detail as a means of identifying the property in question. These neighbours could be fields or houses owned by other individuals or groups, such as soldiers, but could also be watercourses, irrigation canals, streets, temples or other geographical features, such as the steppe.

With these accurate descriptions, we are now able to draw detailed maps of the immediate neighbourhood of the field or house and to locate the field or house more generally when larger elements such as watercourses are mentioned. It is of course by integrating them in the larger whole of remote sensing, geomorphological and archaeological research that they can be fully exploited, as is shown by the case of Halhalla.

Abbreviations and Bibliography

Primary Sources

ARMT 26/1 = Durand, Jean-Marie. *Archives épistolaires de Mari I/1*. Paris: Editions Recherche sur les Civilisations, 1988.

BDHP = Waterman, Leroy. *Business Documents of the Hammurapi Period from the British Museum*, London: Luzac, 1916.

CT 6 = Pinches, Theophilus G. *Cuneiform Texts from Babylonian Tablets in the British Museum – part 6*, London: British Museum, 1898.

CT 8 = Pinches, Theophilus G. *Cuneiform Texts from Babylonian Tablets in the British Museum – part 8*, London: British Museum, 1899.

CT 45 = Pinches, Theophilus G. *Cuneiform Texts from Babylonian Tablets in the British Museum – part 45: Old-Babylonian Business Documents*, London: British Museum, 1963.

CT 47 = Figulla, Hugo N. *Cuneiform Texts from Babylonian Tablets in the British Museum – part 47: Old-Babylonian Nadītu Records*, London: British Museum, 1967.

ETCSL = The Electronic Text Corpus of Sumerian Literature (URL: etcsl.orinst.ox.ac.uk).

MHET = Dekiere, Luc. *Old Babylonian Real Estate Documents from Sippar in the British Museum*, Part 1: *Pré-Hammurabi Documents*, Part 2: *Documents from the Reign of Hammurabi*, Part 3: *Documents from the Reign of Samsu-Iluna*, Part 4: *Post-Samsu-Iluna Documents*, Part 5: *Documents without Date or with Date lost*, Part 6: *Documents from the Series 1902-10-11 (from Zabium to Ammi-ṣaduqa)* (= *Mesopotamian History and Environment Series* III: *Texts* II, 1-6), Ghent: University of Ghent, 1994-97.

YOS 12 = Feigin, Samuel I. *Legal and Administrative Texts of the Reign of Samsuiluna*, New Haven: Yale University Press, 1979.

Secondary Sources

Charpin, Dominique. "Sippar: deux villes jumelles." In *Revue d'assyriologie et d'archéologie orientale* 82, 13-32. Paris: Leroux, 1988.

Cole, Steven W. and Hermann Gasche. 1998: "Second- and First-Millennium BC Rivers in Northern Babylonia." In *Changing Watercourses in Babylonia. Towards a Reconstruction of the Ancient Environment in Lower Mesopotamia* (= *Mesopotamian History and Environment Series* II: *Memoirs* 5), edited by Hermann Gasche and Michel Tanret, 1-64. Ghent-Chicago: University of Ghent-Oriental Institute of the University of Chicago, 1998.

De Graef, Katrien. "An Account of the Redistribution of Land to Soldiers in Late Old Babylonian Sippar-Amnānum." In *Journal of the Economic and Social History of the Orient* 45, 141-178. Leiden: Brill, 2002.

De Graef, Katrien. "Two Ilšu-ibni's, two ugula gidru's. Šarrum-Laba[ki], a military settlement at the Irnina." In *Aula Orientalis* 20, 61-98. Sadabell (Barcelona): AUSA, 2002.

Dekiere, Luc. "Some Remarks on Sippar-Amnānum = Sippar-rabûm." In *Nouvelles Assyriologiques Brèves et Utilitaires*, 18. Paris: Société pour l'étude du Proche-Orient ancien, 1991.

Gasche, Hermann, Armstrong, James A., Cole, Steven W. and Gurzadyan, Vaje G. *Dating the Fall of Babylon. A Reappraisal of Second-Millennium Chronology* (= *Mesopotamian History and Environment Series* II: *Memoirs* 4), Ghent–Chicago: University of Ghent-Oriental Institute of the University of Chicago, 1998.

Gasche, Hermann and Michel Tanret, eds. *Changing Watercourses in Babylonia. Towards a Reconstruction of the Ancient Environment in Lower Mesopotamia* (= *Mesopotamian History and Environment Series* II: *Memoirs* 5), Ghent-Chicago: University of Ghent-Oriental Institute of the University of Chicago, 1998.

Gasche, Hermann, Tanret, Michel, Cole, Steven W. and Kris Verhoeven. "Fleuves du temps et de la vie. Permanence et instabilité de réseau fluviatile babylonien entre 2500 et 1500 avant notre ère." In *Annales HSS* 57, 531-544. Paris: Editions de l'école des hautes études en sciences sociales, 2002.

Harris, Rivkah. "The *nadītu* Laws of the Code of Hammu-rapi in Praxis." In *Orientalia* 30, 163-169. Rome: Pontifical Biblical Institute, 1961.

—. "Biographical Notes on the *nadītu* Women of Sippar." In *Journal of Cuneiform Studies* 16, 1-12. New Haven: American Schools of Oriental Research, 1962.

—. "The Organization and Administration of the Cloister in Ancient Babylonia." In *Journal of the Economic and Social History of the Orient* 6, 121-157. Leiden: Brill, 1963.

—. "The *nadītu* Women." In *Studies Presented to A. Leo Oppenheim*, edited by Robert D. Biggs, 106-135. Chicago: Oriental Institute of the University of Chicago, 1964.

—. "Notes on the Babylonian Cloister and Hearth." In *Orientalia* 38, 133-145. Rome: Pontifical Biblical Institute, 1969.

—. *Ancient Sippar. A Demographic Study of an Old-Babylonian City* (= *Publications de l'Institut historique et archéologique néerlandais de Stamboul* 36). Istanbul: Nederlands Historisch-Archeologisch Instituut te Istanbul, 1975.

Janssen, Caroline. "Samsu-iluna and the Hungry Nadītums." In *Northern Akkad Project Reports* 5, 3-39. Ghent: University of Ghent, 1991.

Jeyes, Ulla. "The Naditu Women of Sippar." In *Images of Women in Antiquity*, edited by Averil Cameron and Amélie Kuhrt, 260-272. London: Croom Helm, 1993.

Kuhrt, Amélie. *The Ancient Near East c. 3000-330 BC*. London-New York: Routledge, 1995.

Obermeyer, Jacob. *Die Landschaft Babylonien im Zeitalter des Talmuds und des Gaonats*. Frankfurt-am-Main: I. Kauffmann, 1929.

Oppenheimer, Aharon. *Babylonia Judaica in the Talmudic Period (= TAVO Beih. B Nr. 47)*. Wiesbaden: Reichert, 1983.

Paschoud, François. "La Naarmalcha: à propos du tracé d'un canal en Mésopotamie moyenne." In *Syria* 55, 345-359. Paris: Paul Geuthner, 1978.

Renger, Johannes. "Untersuchungen zum Priestertum in der Altbabylonischen Zeit, 1. Teil." In *Zeitschrift für Assyriologie* 58, 110-188. Berlin: de Gruyter, 1967.

Stol, Marten. "Women in Mesopotamia." In *Journal of the Economic and Social History of the Orient* 38, 125-143. Leiden: Brill, 1995.

—. "Die altbabylonische Stadt Halhalla." In *Dubsar anta-men. Festschrift für W. H. Ph. Römer*, edited by Manfried Dietrich and Oswald Loretz, 415-445. Münster: Ugarit-Verlag, 1998.

—. "Titel altbabylonischer Klosterfrauen." In *Assyriologica et Semitica. Festschrift für Joachim Oelsner (= Alter Orient und Altes Testament 252)*, edited by Joachim Marzahn, Hans Neumann and Andreas Fuchs, 457-466. Münster: Ugarit-Verlag, 2000.

Tanret, Michel. "Le Namkarum. Une étude de cas dans les textes et sur la carte." In *Changing Watercourses in Babylonia. Towards a Reconstruction of the Ancient Environment in Lower Mesopotamia (= Mesopotamian History and Environment Series* II: *Memoirs* 5), edited by Hermann Gasche

and Michel Tanret, 65-132. Ghent-Chicago: University of Ghent-Oriental
    Institute of the University of Chicago, 1998.

Van Lerberghe, Karel. "On Storage in Old-Babylonian Sippar." In *Orientalia
    Lovaniensia Periodica* 24, 29-40. Leuven: Peeters, 1993.

Woestenburg, Els. "Sippar *rabûm*." In *Nouvelles Assyriologiques Brèves et
    Utilitaires*, 82. Paris: Société pour l'étude du Proche-Orient ancien, 1991.

Woestenburg Els and Bram Jagersma. "The Continuing Story of Sippar-
    Amnānum = Sippar-râbum." In *Nouvelles Assyriologiques Brèves et
    Utilitaires*, 28. Paris: Société pour l'étude du Proche-Orient ancien, 1992.

CONCLUDING REMARKS

BART OOGHE

The study of landscapes of the past has long exceeded standard disciplinary boundaries. As the preceding papers have amply shown, landscapes can be approached from a multitude of perspectives which we might in traditional terms label as a.o. archaeological, geological, biological, cultural or historical. Their study can be perceived as one focused on the physical remains of human occupation, on the complex relationships between man and environment and their cultural, political or societal interactions, or on the recreation of vegetation patterns of the past. Landscapes can be approached from methodological angles regarding the collection of archaeological data and their semi-automated interpretation, dealing with the place of the historical in an archaeological context, with the practical and economic function of heritage archaeology, or they can take on a more epistemic dimension in the uncovering of paradigms that might bias our ways of thinking about landscape change. Landscapes can be seen as occupation patterns, as vegetation and hydrology, as GIS-produced abstractions, as viewed from satellites or through a geological core.

Choosing one's path amid such myriad approaches, with corresponding questions to be asked and specific means of obtaining answers, is by no means a straightforward task. As a result, the past decades have seen interdisciplinarity (the term now becoming replaced by 'multidisciplinarity') evolve from a buzz-word to a taken-for-granted in the study of landscapes of the past, as in so many other research areas. It is deemed an impossibility to approach this diverse field of enquiry from any one angle without incorporating disciplines which are essentially beyond our own particular chosen specialisations, and rightly so.

Yet such multidisciplinarity is not always as straightforward as the academic field might hope or pretend. For example, despite all overwhelming new research using GIS to its best advantage there are still those who would hope for it to be a near-magical tool which, at the flip of a switch, will provide the questions to all answers. Boundaries between approaches deemed respectively archaeological and historical have yet to be overcome in certain sub-fields of either discipline. And it is often not easy for non-specialists to truly grasp the complexities of landscape formation processes when we have no geologist close at hand.

As we ourselves became only too aware of when organising Broadening Horizons, past landscape study itself has the distinct tendency to polarize into respectively 'geoarchaeology', centred primarily around archaeologists and geologists/geographers, and 'the others', a.o. the natural sciences (archaeobotany, archaezoology etc.), historical geographies, sedimentology etc. Crossing these boundaries is not always an easy task. In a field where cooperation is a necessity, the ever increasing overspecialisation within each of the individual disciplines in other words carries with it the risk of estrangement between these various researchers, as preconceptions on their nature may drive a wegde between those who might greatly benefit from closer contacts.

That being said, there is no need to end this volume on such a bleak note, especially given the wide range of productive interdisciplinary cooperation that is now being carried out all over the world. What I would simply argue is that, in the end, we must always remain aware of that lingering danger of one or another approach slowly slipping out of reach. Interdisciplinarity should remain a continuous effort on behalf of all those concerned, to be actively strived for rather than taken for granted. Acknowledging the methods and questions presented by fields other than our own allows us to continuously improve our own research and arms us against possibly unproductive paradigms, without however loosing sight of the specific nature or our own, chosen discipline(s).

It was this conviction which led to the creation of this book, so consciously not a specialised geo-archaeological, GIS or historical geographical publication but rather a more all-inclusive format. Beyond the disciplinary specialisation needed to perform any in-depth study lies a need to understand, even if only on a basic level, (some of the) other possible approaches to these research topics. It is up to us to keep such interdisciplinary ties going strong and to continue our researches in a field of disciplinary and methodological open-mindedness, replete of overly stringent presuppositions and aware that on our own we can at best tackle only singular aspects of an extremely rich and varied object of study. The papers collected here fully show the richness of such diversified yet cooperative approaches.

In the end we can only benefit from looking at the question of landscape from as many angles as possible, integrating both familiar and perhaps at first seemingly strange materials and methods into our study and discussing at leasure across those preset boundaries of what our own specialistation should and should not entail. Keeping our eyes and our minds open can do nothing but broaden our personal and professional horizons and extend our gaze accross the multi-facetted past that so intrigues us.

LIST OF CONTRIBUTORS

Ziad al-Saad, Faculty of Archaeology and Anthropology, Yarmouk University, Jordan

Rupert Bäumler, Institute of Geography, Friedrich-Alexander University Erlangen-Nürnberg, Germany

Elizabeth G. Bloxam, Institute of Archaeology, University College London, United Kingdom

Sjoerd Bohncke, Institute for Earth Sciences, Vrije Universiteit Amsterdam, The Netherlands

Katrien De Graef, Department of Languages and Cultures of the Near East and North-Africa, Ghent University, Belgium

Katleen Deckers, Ältere Urgeschichte und Quartärökologie, Univerity of Tübingen, Germany

Francesca Fulminante, Department of Archaeology, Cambridge University, United Kingdom

Tom Heldal, Geological Survey of Norway, Norway

Vasiliki Ivrou, Department of Archaeology, University of Glasgow, United Kingdom

Loes J.T. Janssen, Institute for Geo- and Bioarchaeology, Vrije Universiteit Amsterdam, The Netherlands

Henk Kars, Institute for Geo- and Bioarchaeology, Vrije Universiteit Amsterdam, The Netherlands

Sjoerd J. Kluiving, Institute for Geo- and Bioarchaeology, Vrije Universiteit Amsterdam, The Netherlands

Bernhard Lucke, Chair of Environmental Planning, Brandenburg University of Technology Cottbus, Germany

Bjoern H. Menze, Interdisciplinary Centre for Scientific Computing (IWR), University of Heidelberg, Germany

Sabine Muhl, Institüt für Altertumswissenschaften (IAW), University of Heidelberg, Germany

Bart Ooghe, Department of Near Eastern Studies, Ghent University, Belgium

Fabio Saggiore, Padua University, Italy

Michael Schmidt, Chair of Environmental Planning, Brandenburg University of Technology Cottbus, Germany

Andrew G. Sherratt (†), Department of Archaeology, University of Sheffield, Great Britain

Per Storemyr, Geological Survey of Norway, Norway

Annelies Storme, Institute for Geo- and Bioarchaeology, Vrije Universiteit Amsterdam, The Netherlands

Dimitri Vandenberghe, Ghent Luminiscence Laboratory, Laboratory of Mineralogy and Petrology, Geological Insitute (S8), Ghent University, Belgium

Geert Verhoeven, Department of Archaeology and Ancient History of Europe, Ghent University, Belgium

Tony Wilkinson, Professor in the Department of Archaeology, Durham University, UK

INDEX